EVERYBODY HAS SOMEBODY IN HEAVEN

ESSENTIAL JEWISH TALES OF THE SPIRIT

Avram Davidson

Edited by Jack Dann and
Grania Davidson Davis

DEVORA PUBLISHING

Design: Tiffen Studios (T.C. Peterseil)

Jacket Illustration: Avi Katz

ISBN: 1-930143-10-9

Printed in Israel

To the *Wunderebbes* Chaim, Shlomo, and Niwa-san

To the great Jewish fantasy writers of the past:
Isaac Singer, Isaac Asimov, Judith Merril

And to our grandchildren in the future –
We pass on this heritage

ACKNOWLEDGMENTS

The Golem (The Magazine of Fantasy and Science Fiction, March, 1955)
Dan Cohen (Jewish Life, Oct. 1947)
The Land of Sinim (Jewish Life, June, 1948)
The Countenance of the Priest (Jewish Life, Oct. 1948)
Nephilim (Jewish Life, June 1947)
Who Knoweth Five? (Jewish Life, Oct. 1949)
Rediscovery (Jewish Life, Summer, 1950)
The Fisherman...A Tashlich Legend (Jewish Life, Oct. 1950)
Of Making Many Books (Jewish Life, June, 1954)
Yochanan ben Zakkai (Jewish Life, Dec. 1947)
Six Sketches of Israel or The Various Jews of Israel (Commentary, Dec. 1950)
In Israel's Green Pastures (Commentary, June, 1952)
The Waters of Eden (Jewish Life, Feb. 1949)
Caphtor and Other Places (Commentary, Aug. 1952)
The Tomb of Jethro (Commentary, Nov. 1952)
On the Horizon – A Citizen of France (Commentary, Jan. 1953)
A Song of Degrees (Jewish Life, June, 1955)
The Ascalon Light (Commentary, Jan. 1957)
Goslin Day (Orbit 6, 1970)
Dr. Morris Goldpepper Returns (Galaxy, Dec. 1962)
Who is Ethel Schnurr (Jewish Life, June, 1970)
Shemiras Shabbos (Jewish Life, Feb. 1948)
The Crown Jewels of Jerusalem – From the World Fantasy Award
   Winning collection: *Enquiries of Dr. Eszterhazy* (F&SF, Aug. 1975)
The Metaphysical Force (Century 3, Oct. 1995)

CONTENTS

CONTENTS (continued)

CONTENTS (continued)

Stand-alone chapters from an unfinished novel:

A BIOGRAPHY OF AVRAM DAVIDSON

JACK DANN has written or edited over fifty books, including the groundbreaking Jewish anthologies *Wandering Stars* and *More Wandering Stars*. He is the author of the international bestseller *The Memory Cathedral*, which is currently published in over ten languages and was #1 on *the age* Bestseller list. The *San Francisco Chronicle* called *The Memory Cathedral* "A grand accomplishment," and the *Australian Book Review* thought it was "as much a pleasure to the senses as it is to the intellect".

Dann's work has been compared to Jorge Luis Borges, Roald Dahl, Lewis Carroll, Castaneda, J. G. Ballard, and Mark Twain. He is a recipient of the *Nebula Award*, the *World Fantasy Award*, the *Australian Aurealis Award* (twice), the *Ditmar Award*, and the *Premios Gilgames de Narrativa Fantastica Award*. He has also been honoured by the Mark Twain Society (Esteemed Knight). His latest novel *the silent* has been compared to Mark Twain's *Huckleberry Finn*.

Jack Dann lives in Melbourne, Australia and "commutes" back and forth to Los Angeles and New York.

An Angry Celebration
by Jack Dann

This introduction should be easy, easy as falling off logs, slipping on bananas, baking cakes (which, upon reflection, isn't so easy)...or breaking wind in the sitting room in front of all the aunts and uncles after Tante Bess has made you eat a second helping of her oh-so-delicious gassy, gassy chicken soup *mit lokshen*.[1]

And *you*, Mr. Jack Dann, big shot co-editor of this volume, should be taking this very seriously and making certain that the readers (blessed are they) who have spent their good money to purchase this book are properly introduced to Avram Davidson's brilliant stories and essays and poetry contained herein.

After all...all the hard work has already been done. Your co-editor Grania Davis has written her own introduction (and most of the story notes) and thanked everyone for helping make this event (yes, it *is* an event) possible. Eileen Gunn has written a wonderful, in-depth biography of Avram's variegated and fascinating life; and Peter Beagle, Richard A. Lupoff, Carol Carr, Barry Malzberg, and Lisa Goldstein, all noted authors, have contributed to an Avram Davidson symposium of thoughts and reminiscences, which will give you a real sense of the man.

So in this very best of all possible worlds, I should be perfectly content to write a nice little introduction, maybe something a little cheeky, a little wry, a little effervescent, and let you, gentle reader, get on to Avram's superlative infusion of Jewishness and literature.

But that ain't going to happen just yet. (Of course, you can skip all my *tummling*[2] and get on to the next, much nicer, introduction.)

So why, you might ask, is this introduction about to get not nice? Because I'm angry, right down to my very bones and *kishkas*[3]. Avram Davidson was a brilliant, idiosyncratic, lyrical polymath of a writer who most definitely paid every penny's worth of his dues. He lived on the financial knife-edge for a lifetime…and he remained true to the dreams of youth. He daydreamed his experiences into fiction of the very highest level. He was productive, prolific even, although he did keep us all agitated by starting trilogies that promised to change the shape of the genre and then going on to something else that he found more interesting. Avram spent a lifetime being angry and idealistic. Why? Because the world wasn't what it should be, could be, or might be. And that, for my money, is what writers are *supposed* to do!

In the face of a world going *Tilt*, in the face of greed, corruption, and, *feh!*, enough bad writing – enough mass market, interchangeable fat fantasies and denatured novels – to fill one of the terrible and dead kabalistic universes in its entirety, Avram Davidson stayed angry and wrote for the ages.

And you know what it got him? *Bubkes*![4] Avram died almost penniless. He lived his last years in a shabby, two room knockdown cottage in Bremerton, Washington, where he was robbed twice. Forgotten. Left behind by a culture that doesn't value brilliance and eccentricity, and genius. And I'm just warming up here.

Why am I angry? Because Avram got screwed. And he got screwed because he was cranky and wouldn't – or couldn't – play the game. Because he wouldn't write fat fantasies with all the interesting bits taken out.

Ah, yes, cranky Avram. He didn't suffer fools gladly, and he could be irritable, to put it mildly, especially if you tried to get him to do something that went against his conscience. Everyone who had the pleasure and good fortune to know Avram came up against his knotty side. (See the Avram Davidson Symposium for interesting Davidson anecdotes.)

Of course *I* have a story.

Avram refused to let any of his work be published in Germany. He felt that after the holocaust, that was it. I didn't agree with him then and don't now. I don't believe you should punish the children for the sins of the parents, and I think the way one changes

10

things is by interacting. What would Avram say to that? You don't want to know. But some twenty years ago I received a call from my German agent, who began the conversation by explaining that every minute he spent on the phone with me was costing him the equivalent of a Volkswagen, and then he asked begged pleaded with me to ask beg plead with Avram to allow said agent to reprint a story of his. Just one measly story. Being young and callow, I agreed to try. The conversation went as follows:

"Hello, Avram, this is Jack."

"No, Jack, don't even ask. I won't let that agent whateverhisnameis have the story."

Click.

Don't ask me how he knew, but he knew. At least he didn't cost me a Volkswagen in long distance phone bills.

I remember writing Avram a letter when I was having a difficult time. I was full of angst and self-pity, and he dutifully wrote back and told me what a little self-indulgent prick I was, and that I didn't have the slightest clue about life, trouble, depression, or joy, for that matter. He told me to shut up and wait until I got older.

I did. He was right. And now that I'm older...I'm angrier.

Thanks, Avram. Thanks a lot!

So, yes, Avram could be difficult. Agents and editors will line up at the rail to tell you that. But those same agents and editors put up with loud-mouthed, boorish *best-selling* authors as a matter of course. That's because literature is...business. And Avram as a writer was delightful, wry, funny, stylish, urbane, folksy, intelligent, deep, knowledgeable, brilliant, and unrepeatable. But he wasn't a businessman. He didn't say the right things to the right people at the right time. He sat in his apartment and wrote...and acted like a curmudgeon. You might think that, well, if he couldn't be nice to people, if he couldn't suck up, then that was his problem; and why should we feel sorry or guilty or filled with angst for him?

Read the stories. If you can't forgive Avram everything after reading his work...well, don't call me. I have an unlisted phone number, a difficult to remember e-mail address, and I live in Australia! And I guess I'm a curmudgeon too.

Unlike most writers, best selling or otherwise, Avram was a

one-off. You can't sit down and write an Avram story in the way you might, say, write a Fitzgerald story. (In fact, an entire magazine flourished for many years publishing stories in the style of F. Scott.) Avram was one of those serendipitous "sports" that appear ever so rarely. There are other unrepeatable writers: the master short story writer Howard Waldrop, the tellers of tall tales R. A. Lafferty and Harvey Jacobs, T. Corgehessen Boyle, and the brilliant and almost forgotten Henry Roth, who wrote *Call It Sleep*, one of the defining Jewish American novels of the 20th Century. Their work is joyous, humanistic, humorous, sometimes difficult, eccentric, resonant, numinous, and it does what art is supposed to do: make you uncomfortable, stretch your consciousness, give you more life than you had before you turned the pages.

Avram's work does all of that…with a vengeance, and it also does something that's become all too rare in these data-days of websites and Internet surfing: it merges style and content. Listen…

"It was a goslin day, no doubt about it, of course it can happen that goslin things can occur, say, once a day for many days. But *this* day was a *goslin* day. From the hour when, properly speaking, the ass brays in his stall, but here instead the kat kvells on the rooftop – to the hour when the cock crows on his roost, but here instead the garbage-man bangs on his can – even that early, Faroly realized that it was going to be a goslin day (night? let be night: *It was* evening *and* [after that] *it was morning: one day.* Yes or no?)." But that's just one of Avram's voices. Some of his stories are layered dreams, difficult to discern but worth every bit of concentration, while others are transparency itself. As you read these stories and essays and poems, you'll smell challah baking, you'll travel to the distant places of the imagination and places that made up Avram's past; and you'll be shocked and oddly comforted by these visions.

These quintessentially Jewish visions.

For Avram was a quintessentially Jewish writer. Even when he wasn't writing overtly Jewish stories. Even when he was writing fantasy and science fiction…constructing the fabulous. His way of being was Jewish. His approach to knowledge and information, the legal *pilpul* of ideas, the breadth of education (and he was self-educated), his use of language, the rhythms of his style, his obsessions and concerns and, yes, even his blind spots were all part and parcel of his Jewishness.

This collection is a celebration of that Jewishness; it's a block party on Avram's street. It brings together for the first time *almost all* of Avram's overtly Jewish works in short form. For that alone we should celebrate.

But it's more than that. This book is an attempt by your editors to right a wrong. Avram's glittering, shimmering, beautiful work was neglected during his lifetime. His work did not become part of the *canon*, that body of literature considered essential by those educators, critics, and literary lights who have gained the power to say who's *in* and who's *out*. My co-editor, Grania, deserves kudos and hugs for keeping Avram's work in print. In fact, thanks to her Promethean efforts, his work has gained more "top-of-mind-awareness", as they say in marketing, than when he was alive. (And while I'm busy thanking, I'd also like to thank Ethan Davidson for his insightful and personal introductions and Henry Wessells for his detailed introduction to *Of Making Many Books*.)

So you, the reader, and we the editors, contributors, and publisher can share in this celebration of Avram's work by getting the word out. And if we tell enough people, if we are *in-your-face* loud enough and create enough of a *tummel*, we can do our small part toward righting a wrong and pushing Avram's work into the canon where it belongs.

So, now, you should all live and be well, on to the important stuff. But before you go, I should like to tell you that everything Avram Davidsonian and everything Jewish-and-Avram Davidsonian isn't included in this volume. In fact, there's a wonderful story in this book about the relationship between a dentist and aliens from outer space. (So nu?) That story is a sequel to another story, which can be found in a book I highly recommend, *The Avram Davidson Treasury*, edited by Robert Silverberg and Grania Davis. (*Gottenyu*[5], that last name sounds familiar!) And if you want to read the story that Barry Malzberg refers to in his Symposium piece, you'll have to go searching. Avram is all over the place.

Go and ye shall find.

I should also mention that if you're like me and don't know

Yiddish and Hebrew well enough to carry on a conversation with the Grand Rabbi, you might encounter a few unfamiliar words. (Avram took it for granted that we all know all words!) I recommend Leo Rosten's learned and funny dictionary – if it can be called that – *The Joys of Yiddish* and the sequel *Hooray For Yiddish*. You might have to search around in used bookshops, but I guarantee it's worth the effort. (Trust me, I'm a writer.)

So now you can breath communal sighs of relief. Finally, I'm done introducing. Enjoy what's ahead. It was a joy to be a part of this project.

Avram, if you can hear me, was I angry enough?

Alright, alright, I'll stop doing *shtick*[6] and get out of your way!

---

[1] *Lokshen* means noodles, which go in the soup, sort of like spaghetti with soup sauce. So maybe the Chinese invented noodles, and the Italians made it a national dish...but the Jews...ah, well, if you haven't tasted *lokshen* pudding or *lokshen* in home-made chicken soup (Jewish penicillin), then *you* just haven't lived.

[2] A tummler is someone who makes a lot of noise, one who drives everyone crazy, and tummling is the act of driving persons crazy and making a fuss. The redoubtable Leo Rosten called the ideal tummler a cross between Milton Berle and Jerry Lewis. You, however, can just think of me as a rather humble, sophisticated, gray-haired, square-jawed, devil-may-care Jewish Arnold Schwarzenegger. It can't hurt, and it will make me feel a hell of a lot better.

[3] I don't mean the kind of kishka you can eat, but my intestines, my very guts, if you will.

[4] Beans!

[5] A handy-dandy, all-purpose exclamation. Means: *Dear God.*

[6] Comes from the German word Stück, which means *piece*. To quote Mr. Rosten, it's "a studied, contrived or characteristic piece of 'business' employed by an actor or actress; overly used gestures, grimaces, or devices to steal attention." Oy, this doesn't sound so good. So...I'll stop already!

GRANIA DAVIDSON DAVIS has lived around a lot. She has dwelled in a mountain village in Mexico, on a primitive sandbar in Belize, and on a beach in Hawaii. She has taught in Tibetan refugee settlements in India, and worked as a military historian in neon-lit Tokyo.

She has traveled extensively and her travels inspired a series of fantasy novels based on the myths of the orient. *The Rainbow Annals* is based on Tibetan legends. *Moonbird* uses Balinese myths. *Marco Polo and the Sleeping Beauty* written with Avram Davidson (who is himself a legend), is set in China. Her many short stories reflect her sojourns abroad. She was married to Avram Davidson, and collaborated with him on short stories and novels, and a son. Since Avram Davidson's passing in 1993, she has worked on publishing his immortal works.

The posthumous Davidson/Davis collaboration *The Boss in the Wall* was nominated for the *Nebula Award*. The story collection which she co-edited *The Avram Davidson Treasury* was nominated for the *World Fantasy Award* and the *British Fantasy Award*, and won the *Locus Award*.

She has settled down recently, dividing her time with her family and cat, *Laptop* in Marin County, California, and on the north shore of Oahu, Hawaii.

Foreword
by Grania Davidson Davis

Avram Davidson (1923-1993) said, "I am large, I contain multitudes." This was true in his widely traveled life, in his many levels of spiritual observance, and in his literature.

He is best known as an award-winning fantasy author. His prolific writing spanned a wide range from science fiction to nonfiction, from magic realist fantasy to mystery. He won major awards in many literary fields. Whatever he wrote, at different times in his life, had a Jewish flavor and subtext, a Jewish essence. In his Judaic stories, and in poignant morality tales like "Now Let Us Sleep," we see Avram's essential concern for *ethics*.

One of his earliest Jewish-themed fantasy stories became his most famous. *The Golem* was published in 1955. It's about a *Golem* and a devoted old couple in Hollywood. Author Damon Knight called it "a perfect story." It became Avram's best-loved story, and has been reprinted countless times all over the world. It draws on the traditional Jewish fantasy heritage of Golems and *Dybbuks* and divine fools, that has been handed down by Sholom Alechem and the Singer brothers. Avram Davidson has been called "an American Isaac Bashevis Singer."

Avram lived as an observant Jew in New York and Israel, and wrote his early Judaic stories for nearly a decade before *The Golem* was published. He wrote under the byline of A. A. Davidson after WWII, for the periodicals *Orthodox Jewish Life* and *Commentary*. He wrote about Jewish ethical conflicts in America, and tales of the Diaspora. His stories ranged from China, where he served in the U.S. military during WWII, to brilliant snapshots of Israel, where he served in the military, and lived after the Israeli War of Independence in 1948.

His later fantasy fiction, written for a wider audience under the Avram Davidson byline, spoke of the vanishing cultures of eastern European immigrants. Michael Dirda, editor for the *Washington Post Book World*, recently called him "a prose laureate of 'the old country.'"

He loved the old Jewish customs, the Shabbat and holiday songs. Whenever friends went on a journey, he gave them *messenger money* for charity, a *mitzvah* to insure a safe trip. Avram was indeed as large as the far-flung Jewish people, and contained as many multitudes.

A number of people contributed to this book in a number of ways. I especially want to thank Tom Doherty and Teresa Neilsen Hayden of Tor Books, for permission to use *The Golem* and *Goslin Day* from the story collection *The Avram Davidson Treasury*. I want to thank Avram's dear friends in New York, Simmy and Nancy Klein, for sending copies of Avram's letters from Israel and elsewhere. I want to thank Davidson bibliographer, Henry Wessells, for retrieving the *Jewish Life* stories from the New York Public Library, and I want to thank *Jewish Life* and *Commentary* for their use. I want to thank my gracious co-editor, Jack Dann, our kindly editor at Pitspopany Press, Yaacov Peterseil, and talented Israeli artist, Avi Katz, for a beautiful cover. I want to thank our beloved friends who helped us along the way, and of course I want to thank the wonderful authors who contributed essays for this book.

So go enjoy already –

Grania Davidson Davis

Introduction to
THE GOLEM

THE GOLEM SHOULD HAVE BEEN Avram's breakout story. It should have alerted the literary establishment that here was a writer as brilliantly original and idiosyncratic as Isaac Bashevis Singer, Bernard Malamud, or Cynthia Ozick. Although *The Golem* was enthusiastically received and was included in several important literary anthologies, it seemed to be a *"one-off"*. Avram went on to make his reputation as a fantasy and science fiction writer...and kept producing brilliantly faceted gems of Jewish fiction, such as *Goslin Day*, which were not seen by the larger literary – and Jewish! – audience that should have been his.

In *The Golem*, which was first published in 1955, Davidson magically and poignantly transports one of the most potent Jewish legends from the dark and winding streets of medieval Prague to the warm and beating heart of modern America: Los Angeles.

It's just your typical nice Jewish couple meets Frankenstein kind of story...

It's quintessential Davidson.

Jack Dann

THE GOLEM

THE GRAY-FACED PERSON CAME along the street where old Mr. and Mrs. Gumbeiner lived. It was afternoon, it was autumn, the sun was warm and soothing to their ancient bones. Anyone who attended the movies in the twenties or the early thirties has seen that street a thousand times. Past these bungalows with their half – double roofs Edmund Lowe walked arm-in-arm with Leatrice Joy and Harold Lloyd was chased by Chinamen waving hatchets. Under these squamous palm trees Laurel kicked Hardy and Woolsey beat Wheeler upon the head with codfish. Across these pocket-handkerchief-sized lawns the juveniles of the Our Gang Comedies pursued one another and were pursued by angry fat men in golf knickers. On this same street – or perhaps on some other one of five hundred streets exactly like it.

Mrs. Gumbeiner indicated the gray-faced person to her husband.

"You think maybe he's got something the matter?" she asked. "He walks kind of funny, to me."

"Walks like a *golem*," Mr. Gumbeiner said indifferently.

The old woman was nettled.

"Oh, I don't know," she said. "*I* think he walks like your cousin Mendel."

The old man pursed his mouth angrily and chewed on his pipestem. The gray-faced person turned up the concrete path, walked up the steps to the porch, sat down in a chair. Old Mr. Gumbeiner ignored him. His wife stared at the stranger.

"Man comes in without a hello, goodbye, or howareyou, sits himself down and right away he's at home.... The chair is comfortable?" she asked. "Would you like maybe a glass tea?"

She turned to her husband.

"Say something, Gumbeiner!" she demanded. "What are you, made of wood?"

The old man smiled a slow, wicked, triumphant smile.

"Why should I say anything?" he asked the air. "Who am *I*? Nothing, that's who."

The stranger spoke. His voice was harsh and monotonous.

"When you learn who – or, rather, what – I am, the flesh will melt from your bones in terror." He bared porcelain teeth.

"Never mind about my bones !" the old woman cried. "You've got a lot of nerve talking about my bones!"

"You will quake with fear," said the stranger. Old Mrs. Gumbeiner said that she hoped he would live so long. She turned to her husband once again.

"Gumbeiner, when are you going to mow the lawn?"

"All mankind – " the stranger began.

"*Shah*! I'm talking to my husband.... He talks *eppis* kind of funny, Gumbeiner, no?"

"Probably a foreigner," Mr. Gumbeiner said, complacently.

"You think so?" Mrs. Gumbeiner glanced fleetingly at the stranger. "He's got a very bad color in his face, *nebbich*. I suppose he came to California for his health."

"Disease, pain, sorrow, love, grief – all are naught to – "
Mr. Gumbeiner cut in on the stranger's statement "Gall bladder," the old man said. "Guinzburg down at the *shul* looked exactly the same before his operation. Two professors they had in for him, and a private nurse day and night"

"I am not a human being!" the stranger said loudly.

"Three thousand seven hundred fifty dollars it cost his son, Guinzburg told me. 'For you, Poppa, nothing is too expensive – only get well,' the son told him."

"*I am not a human being!*"

"Ai, is that a son for you!" the old woman said, rocking her head. "A heart of gold, pure gold?" She looked at the stranger. "All right, all right I heard you the first time. Gumbeiner! I asked you a question. When are you going to cut the lawn?"

"On Wednesday, *odder* maybe Thursday, comes the Japaneser to the neighborhood. To cut lawns is *his* profession. *My* profession is to be a glazier – retired."

"Between me and all mankind is an inevitable hatred," the stranger said. "When I tell you what I am, the flesh will melt – "

"You said, you said already," Mr. Gumbeiner interrupted.

"In Chicago where the winters were as cold and – bitter as the Czar of Russia's heart," the old woman intoned, "you had strength to carry the frames with the glass together day in and day out. But in California with the golden sun to mow the lawn when your wife asks, for this you have no strength. Do I call in the Japaneser to cook for you supper?"

"Thirty years Professor Allardyce spent perfecting his theories. Electronics, neuronics – "

"Listen, how educated he talks," Mr. Gumbeiner said, admiringly.

"Maybe he goes to the University here?"

"If he goes to the University, maybe he knows Bud?" his wife suggested.

"Probably they're in the same class and he came to see him about the homework, no?"

"Certainly he must be in the same class. How many classes are there? Five in *ganzen*: Bud showed me on his program card." She counted off on her fingers. "Television Appreciation and Criticism, Small Boat Building, Social Adjustment, The American Dance.... The American Dance – *nu*, Gumbeiner – "

"Contemporary Ceramics," her husband said, relishing the syllables. "A fine boy, Bud. A pleasure to have him for a boarder."

"After thirty years spent in these studies," the stranger, who had continued to speak unnoticed, went on, "he turned from the theoretical to the pragmatic. In ten years' time he had made the most titanic discovery in history: he made mankind, *all* mankind, superfluous: he made *me*."

"What did Tillie write in her last letter?" asked the old man.

The old woman shrugged.

"What should she write? The same thing. Sidney was home from the Army, Naomi has a new boy friend – "

"*He made* ME!"

"Listen, Mr. Whatever-your-name-is," the old woman said. "Maybe where you came from is different, but in *this* country you don't interrupt people the while they're talking... Hey. Listen – what do you mean, he *made* you? What kind of talk is that?"

The stranger bared all his teeth again, exposing the too-pink gums.

"In his library, to which I had a more complete access after his sudden and as yet undiscovered death from entirely natural causes, I found a complete collection of stories about androids, from Shelley's *Frankenstein* through Capek's *R.U.R.* to Asimov's – "

"Frankenstein?" said the old man, with interest "There used to be Frankenstein who had the soda-*wasser* place on Halstead Street: a Litvack, *nebbich*."

"What are you talking?" Mrs. Guinbeiner demanded. "His name was Franken*thal*, and it wasn't on Halstead, it was on Roosevelt"

"– clearly shown that all mankind has an instinctive antipathy towards androids and there will be an inevitable struggle between them – "

"Of course, of course!" Old Mr. Gumbeiner clicked his teeth against his pipe. "I am always wrong, you are always right. How could you stand to be married to such a stupid person all this time?"

"I don't know," the old woman said. "Sometimes I wonder, myself. I think it must be his good looks." She began to laugh. Old Mr. Gumbeiner blinked, then began to smile, then took his wife's hand.

"Foolish old woman," the stranger said, "why do you laugh? Do you not know I have come to destroy you?"

"What!" old Mr. Gumbeiner shouted. "Close your mouth, you!" He darted from his chair and struck the stranger with the flat of his hand. The stranger's head struck against the porch pillar and bounced back.

"When you talk to my wife, talk respectable, you hear?"

Old Mrs. Gumbeiner, cheeks very pink, pushed her husband back in his chair. Then she leaned forward and examined the stranger's head. She clicked her tongue as she pulled aside a flap – of gray, skin-like material.

"Gumbeiner, look! He's all springs and wires inside!"

"I *told* you he was a *golem*, but no, you wouldn't listen," the old man said.

"You said he *walked* like a *golem*."

"How could he walk like a *golem* unless he *was* one?"

"All right, all right... You broke him, so now fix him."

"My grandfather, his light shines from Paradise, told me that when MaHaRaL – Moreynu Ha-Rav Loew – his memory for a blessing, made the *golem* in Prague, three hundred? four hundred years ago? he wrote on his forehead the Holy Name."

Smiling reminiscently, the old woman continued, "And the *golem* cut the Rabbi's wood and brought his water and guarded the ghetto."

"And one time only he disobeyed the Rabbi Low, and Rabbi Low erased the *Shem Ha-Mephorash* from the *golem's* forehead and the *golem* fell down like a dead one. And they put him up in the attic of the *shul* and he's still there today if the Communisten haven't sent him to Moscow... This is not just a story," he said.

"*Avadda* not!" said the old woman.

"I myself have seen both the shul and the Rabbi's grave," her husband said, conclusively.

"But I think this must be a different kind golem, Gumbeiner. See, on his forehead: nothing written."

"What's the matter, there's a law I can't write something there? Where is that lump clay Bud brought us from his class?"

The old man washed his hands, adjusted his little black skullcap, and slowly and carefully wrote four Hebrew letters on the gray forehead.

"Ezra the Scribe himself couldn't do better," the old woman said, admiringly. "Nothing happens," she observed, looking at the lifeless figure sprawled in the chair.

"Well, after all, am I Rabbi Loew?" her husband asked, deprecatingly. "No," he answered. He leaned over and examined the exposed mechanism. "This spring goes here...this wire comes with this one...." The figure moved. "But this one goes where? And this one?"

"Let be," said his wife. The figure sat up slowly and rolled its eyes loosely.

"Listen, Reb *Golem*," the old man said, wagging his finger. "Pay attention to what I say – you understand?"

"Understand...."

"If you want to stay here, you got to do like Mr. Gumbeiner says...."

"Do-like-Mr.-Gumbeiner-says...."

"*That's* the way I like to hear a *golem* talk. Malka, give here the mirror from the pocketbook. Look, you see your face? You see on the forehead, what's written? If you don't do like Mr. Gumbeiner says, he'll wipe out what's written and you'll be no more alive."

"No-more-alive...."

"*That's* right. Now, listen. Under the porch you'll find a lawnmower. Take it and cut the lawn. Then come back. Go."

"Go...." The figure shambled down the stairs. Presently the sound of the lawnmower whirred through the quiet air in the street just like the street where Jackie Cooper shed huge tears on Wallace Beery's shirt and Chester Conklin rolled his eyes at Marie Dressler.

"So what will you write to Tillie?" old Mr. Gumbeiner asked.

"What should I write?" old Mrs. Gumbeiner shrugged. "I'll write that the weather is lovely out here and that we are both, Blessed be the Name, in good health."

The old man nodded his head slowly, and they sat together on the front porch in the warm afternoon sun.

THE NEPHILIM

They were giants in the Earth in
    those days
Men of the caftan and the *shtreimel*
Girt about by *gartels*, robed in *kittels*
Mighty men, men of renown
And they went about from one
    country to another
In the vineyards of Hungary

In the forests of Volhynia
On the plains of Poland and of Russia
By the Dniester's waters, and the
    Duna's
Across the mountains of Carpathia
Amongst the fields they could not till
Upon the land they could not own

Amidst oppression, hate, and scorn
Enwrapt in *Tallis* and *Tephillin*

Afoot, in all the Winter's snows
Afoot, in all the Springtime's mire
Afoot, in all the Summer's dust
Afoot, in time of Autumn harvests
Which they could not reap, they went

The *Torah* slaked them in the heat
The *Mishnah* warmed them in the
    cold
The *Zohar* lit for them a lamp by
    night
The leaves they studied were the
    Talmud's
Not the trees'. For trees die as men
    die

And they were set upon eternal
    equities
Undaunted by the clubs and shoutings
    of the *Goy*
Admiring not his ways, and less, his
    faith
Undaunted by the pluckings at their
    sleeves
Of Edom's ape, the Epikuros
The enemy of their own blood, within
    the gate
(*Enlightenment!* he cried. You have
No soul! Deny God, Be glad to die!
Why will you   live? Or praise Him
In a different key – cut off your beards
And change your clothes, and change
Your hearts – what matter if they
    break?
'Tis good to dwell in Rimmon's
    house!)

  – Bow down! The voices cried. Bow
    down! –

Undaunted, they went on: They would
    not bow
Though Haman stood in every market
    place
And Achashverosh daily set his seal
Upon their doom: They would not
    bow

These same were mighty men that
    were
Of old, Men of renown.

Introduction to
DAN COHEN

AVRAM DAVIDSON SERVED IN THE United States military for three years during World War II. He was a pharmacist mate in the Navy, attached to the Marine Corps in the Pacific. Later he served in Israel after the War of Independence. He knew military life, and he knew the challenges of trying to live as an observant Jew in the American military.

Dan Cohen is Davidson's first known prose publication. It appeared in *Jewish Life* in October 1947. It is the story of a Jewish wartime hero.

Grania Davidson Davis

DAN COHEN

WE HEAR MUCH THESE DAYS OF HEROES, and read even more of them. Two or three great Jewish organizations have set themselves the task of collecting the names, and the number of decorations of Jewish war heroes, and of publishing them. As a serviceman, I knew intimately not a few Jews (as well as Gentiles) who, as Lincoln said, "laid so costly a sacrifice on the altar of Liberty." I only hope to G-d that theirs was not a vain oblation To judge all men in the scale of merit, as the Fathers of the Mishnah told us to do, is difficult. To judge them in the scale of heroism is even more so. I am not here attempting such a judgment. I wish merely to tell you the story of Dan Cohen; you may feel free to judge for yourself.

During the summer of 1943, as I look back on it now, I spent the biggest part of my free time in one USO or another, writing letters. I was still not used to being so long and so far from home, and I took full advantage of the free postage allowed me by a generous Congress. I covered reams of USO stationery describing what was really a dull existence to my parents, my relatives, my friends, and my girl. On one hot afternoon I was interrupted by a very young and slightly drunk G.I. who stopped by my table and remarked, "Feller over there readin' a book in Chinese."

"Chinese?" I echoed.

"Or Japanese," he said, in the tone of one who was determined not to quibble over trifles, and lurched away in the direction of a pretty hostess who saw him coming and beat an unfair retreat to the Ladies' Room. I looked around for an oriental serviceman, but saw none. Indeed, I saw only one man who was reading at all, and as I passed to mail my letters, I looked over his shoulder at the book. It was neither Chinese nor Japanese, however; it was Hebrew. The name of it was not entirely unfamiliar to me: It was *Ein Yaakov*.

Now the Jewish community of this Southern city was such that I truly believe that it would never have built a synagogue if any of the churches had allowed card-playing in the vestry. Their type of Judaism affected me like an incredible dream. Intermarriage was the rule rather than the exception.

The chief religious interest consisted in quarreling over the infrequent *Bar Mitzvahs*. The *reform* faction wanted to hold them on Sunday morning, and the *conservative* faction declared that Friday night was more suitable, or, maybe it was the other way around. Aside from this, there was no difference between them. They had had no Rabbi in years.

Under such circumstances the sight of a soldier reading a Hebrew book – and a *religious* book at that – affected me powerfully. That was how I came to meet Dan Cohen. Before this I had considered myself lucky if the hurried routine of navy life left me time in the morning to say, *Shemonah Esrei*. It's true, I conducted an inquest with the messcooks over every piece piece of meat, lest it should be *chazir* in another disguise, but further than this I did not go, until I met Dan Cohen and saw how far it was possible *to* go.

As a civilian he would have been considered an *erlicher yid*, and a strictly observant man. Incredible as it may seem, he kept – as a soldier – every mitzvah he had kept before the war, and they were many. Most of this information I got from his brother, Murray, who was stationed at the same Army base. The only feature they had in common was their ruddy complexion. Dan was tall and well-built; Murray was short and slender. Murray was always on the go; Dan was grave and quiet. Murray was unconcerned with religious problems; whereas his brother, Dan, he said, "carries a *Shulchan Aruch* in his field pack, and whenever they have a ten minute break, he reads it to see if there are any *mitzvos* he overlooked."

Other Jewish soldiers in the same outfit added information from time to time. Dan kept a glass of *"negelwasser"* under his cot at night, and poured it over his fingers first thing in the morning.

Come what might, Dan *davened* the three daily services. He never ate in the mess hall, but supplied his own chow, and he *took challa* of every loaf of bread mailed him by the nearest Jewish bakery, 100 miles away. He gave his PX rations to the men in the infirmary *Bikkur Cholim*.

"What does he do about *Shabbos*?" I asked.

"He doesn't come in on Shabbos," they told me.

"They give him permission, you mean, not to?"

"Permission, hell! He just used to tell them, Tomorrow is the Sabbath; I won't be here! Now it's taken for granted that he does Sunday duty instead. At first they thought he *wanted* to be court-martialed so he could get out, and the CO said, "I'll be damned if I'll oblige him. We'll see who breaks down first."

After the firing range incident, the CO broke down. What happened was this: That particular morning something had occurred which prevented Dan from saying his regular prayers. So when the men arrived at the firing range, he went into the ammunition tent and began to *daven*

30

Shacharis. Before he was quite finished it came his turn to fire, and the CO sent a man into the tent to fetch him out.

He walked out in his *tallis* and *tephillin*, hitched his tallis over his shoulders, wrapped the rifle sling around his right arm, and began to fire. He fired in the standing, sitting, and kneeling positions. Then he got up, recited *Aleinu* and *Ani Ma'amin*, took off his tallis, tephillin, handed them to the man next to him, and finished firing in the prone position flat on his stomach. Meanwhile nobody said a word. They just stared.

When they examined the results it turned out that Dan had far and away the best score in the outfit.

The CO threw in the sponge right there. "Cohen," he said slowly, I don't pretend to understand your religion. I'm an Army man and I like things done the Army way. But by George, Cohen, any man who can shoot like that, I don't care if he spreads out a prayer rug in the middle of the parade ground and bows down toward Mecca! You're okay, for my money."

Just before *Rosh Hashonah* that year, I was transferred to another Naval installation about 85 miles away and I never got back to that city again.

Some months later, on a bus, I met a Jewish sergeant I knew who was returning there, and the first question I asked was, "What's happened with the Cohen brothers?"

"Oh, one of them is still there, but the other got a medical discharge last month. Psychoneurosis – just couldn't adjust himself to Army life, it seems," he told me.

"Well," I said slowly, "I'm not really surprised. It's the best thing that could happen. Dan is a lot better off – "

"Dan?" he interrupted me. "Who said anything about Dan? It's Murray I was talking about! Dan is still there, made T/4 last week, too. Nothing wrong with Dan!" He began to chuckle.

"You should have seen the beautiful *Succah* he built out at the base," the sergeant said. "He got a *lulav* and *esrog* from somewhere, and he put the lulav to soak in a can of water next to his sack (bed). Just then the charge of quarters runs in and says, 'Cohen, the colonel and an inspecting party are coming around, and you better do something about that stuff.' 'I certainly will,' says Dan, and he ties a note onto the lulav – 'Hands off! Fragile!' The goyim respect him. You have no idea how much.

"He's started a *Talmud Torah* for the Jewish kids in town, and they're holding Saturday morning services in the 'Temple' for the first time since it was built. Just the other day I hear he's trying to make a *mikvah* for the married WACS and soldiers' wives. I'll guess he'll do it, too."

I guess he did, too, I never met him again. I am a pretty active fellow usually; however the thought of calling up every Cohen in the N.Y.C. telephone directory and asking for Dan overwhelms me.

But I have not forgotten what he said to me that afternoon when we first met in the USO, when he was reading *Ein Yaakov*.

"Never compromise – never retreat. If you do, it's a terrific struggle to get back, and you might not make it. Don't forget that the Torah is our only standard of normality. Whatever takes you away from it – or would, if you'd let it – regard those influences, or circumstances, as abnormal. I see nothing in the world about me which convinces me that I can make a better deal if I trade in the Torah for it. Time, place, convenience, difficulty – these things are secondary, or less. Only the Torah is primary."

What happened to him, I do not know. Those dark eyes may be long closed, although I hope not. But I am convinced that Dan Cohen was a soldier before he ever put on khaki. It is the Dan Cohens, I believe, who are the real heroes of the Jewish people, – this I say to you, and also to the JWB, the B'nai B'rith, and all those who collect lists of Jewish heroes: Dan Cohen is our hero, and no Jewish prize fighter or ball player, no Jewish general or jazz singer, can supplant him.

Here, O Israel, is a true hero of Israel.

AVRAM DAVIDSON

YOCHANAN BEN ZAKKAI

Yochanan, the son of Zakkai,
Sat in the gate,
Studying with his disciples
The rule of the Red Heifer
As it is laid down in the Law.

A Gentile, passing by,
heard the lesson and
Would fain inquire, Why
'Twas so decreed, that whoso
Did but touch a corpse,
That one would
Be unclean: nor regain
Cleanliness, until his flesh
Was washed with water
In which the ashes
Of a heifer-red, unblemished –
Were dissolved.

To him the son of Zakkai
Spoke, with patience,
Likening this law
Unto a custom which the Romans
        had –
To exorcize a demon
From a man posses'd;
Before him certain roots
The augurs burned; straightway
The demon took his leave.

In suchwise manner,
Said Yochanan,

Do the Jews
Obey the Law of Moses
On this point; content,
The Gentile went his way.

Scornfully the disciples
Lifted up their voices.
With a broken reed, they said,
Have you pushed away
That man, but what answer
Do you have for us?

Calmly the son of Zakkai
Gazed at them, his
Eyebrows lifted up,
And said, My sons –
The corpse does not corrupt;
The water does not purify;
The Holy One, bless'd be He,
Hath said,
I have decreed a decree –
I have commanded a Law –

It doth not behoove you,
It doth not become you,
To question Me.
Twenty centuries have passed;
The years, grown old,
Have bowed their heads.
Gone are all the augurs,
Gone the astrologers.

In their laboratories
The scientists,
With grave demeanor,
Learned careful research, discourse,
Have made discovery –
Listen well –
Discovery –

That whoso

Does but touch a corpse,
That one shall be unclean:
Nor regain cleanliness,
Until his flesh is washed
With water, Germs
(No trumpets sound).
Bacteria (no cymbals clash).
Infection (no psaltery nor harp),
Say the scientists.

Another twenty centuries
Perhaps will find
The ashes also purify –
Perhaps will find
A thousand reasons
Yet undreamed of.
We will wait.

Was, then, Yochanan wrong?
I do not think so.
Should he have said:
I know no reason for the law;
My science has no answer
To your question;
Therefore ignore the law –
Should he?
Not he. Nor we.

We will not discard
Those laws for which
The scientist has no reply.
We will bide our time in confidence
Ours is an old faith.
We can wait.
We can wait.

Introduction to
THE LAND OF SINIM

AVRAM DAVIDSON WAS STATIONED IN Beijing during the Japanese surrender after World War II. He took the opportunity to learn about Chinese culture, and about the Kai-Fung Jews. These are people whose Jewish ancestors apparently traveled the Silk Road to China. They have largely assimilated into the Chinese population, but they still recall certain rituals, and certain prohibitions such as worshiping idols or eating pork. This story, published in *Jewish Life* in June 1948, is about a Kai-Fung boy named David who wanted to learn our faith.

Avram's sojourn in China influenced his later fantasy writing. Some of his Chinese fantasy stories currently in print include, *Dagon* in *The Avram Davidson Treasury* (Tor), *The Deed of the Deft-Footed Dragon* in the mystery collection *The Investigations of Avram Davidson* (St. Martin's Press), *Dragon Skin Drum* in the upcoming Tor collection *The Other 19th Century*, and *Marco Polo and the Sleeping Beauty*, a fantasy novel written with Grania Davis, which is available through Wildside Press.

Grania Davidson Davis

THE LAND OF SINIM

IT WAS A SPRING MORNING IN THE *YESHIVAH*. An enterprising fly made the round of the rooms, and, finding but scanty nutriment in the pages of a superannuated *Gemora*, buzzed off reluctantly elsewhere to seek his meat from G-d. The Rabbi was talking about the 49th chapter of Isaiah. I listened with half an ear. Through the open door I could hear the noises from the *Beth Midrash* down the hall. The medley of chanting voices reassured me that, unwearied by thousands of years of activity, Reuben's ox was still goring Simeon's cow. It was nice to know there was something constant in an inconstant world. I returned my attention to the class room.

"One of the questions, then," the Rabbi continued, "is what Isaiah means by his use of the phrase, 'the Land of Sinim.' The Jews will return from all over *goluth* and also from there. The usual explanation is that he means China. Some say, no, the prophet meant another country. What other country? Ah, that is also a question!" He continued, but my mind had left him again. Unwittingly, he had touched a chord of memory in me. To me, the Land of Sinim is China. Kung believed it was. I have seen China, but I never saw Kung; I only heard his story, and was deeply moved by it.

Two and a half years ago, at the end of the war, I found myself in a North Chinese city which I will call Chenchow. It has a small Jewish community which supports a synagogue, a school, and a kosher public kitchen. The president of the community at that time was a Mr. Asher Edelman, who treated me with much kindness. Like most of the other Chenchow Jews, he was born in Russia. Because of friendship with the wrong people, the defeat of the Revolution of 1905 brought him a sentence in Siberia. Had he been content, like so many of his fellow exiles, to study the writings of Marx, Engels, & Co., Mr. Edelman might today be a Commissar, able to look back on a long and successful career of having liquidated all his best friends.

Alas for the October Revolution and the triumph of Socialism, he found Marx very dull, and at the earliest chance, escaped into China. He has been there ever since, and has prospered. The Chinese, being a backward race, have never been anti-semitic. Indeed, Chenchow's narrow alleys reminded me of some oriental *Judengasse*. The northern Chinese are taller than the southerners, their noses are not inclined to be flat, their beards are more flourishing, and their complexions are lighter. In the winter they put on round fur hats resembling the *Chassidic shtreimel*, and they wear long black robes. Indoors, they wear black skull-caps.

Once, in joking vein, I suggested to Mr. Edelman that there might be a strain of Jewish blood in the local population. He nodded slowly.

"In Marco Polo's time, there were many Jews in China. Where did they go to? There have never been pogroms here. The Chinese call themselves 'the ocean that salts all the rivers'– meaning that they assimilate every foreign element.

And yet, the last Rabbi of the last community of Chinese Jews died only in the early nineteenth century, in Kai-Fung. Kung was born in Kai-Fung," he said. And he told me this story:

About ten years earlier he had noticed a teen-aged Chinese boy loitering around the synagogue. Once or twice, he offered him some money, but the boy smiled shyly, and refused. Finally the boy plucked up his courage and spoke to him, but Mr. Edelman did not understand his dialect. He continued on to his place of business (he is a fur and hide dealer), but the boy followed him. Mr. Edelman called his interpreter and told him to question this boy.

"Ask him what he wants," he said.

The answer was even more curious. The boy offered to do any labor demanded of him without pay. He had only one request: "Teach me our faith," he begged. Mr. Edelman's *gemora kop* at once observed the use of *our* and not *your*. He asked the boy's name.

"Kung Tafti-teh," was the answer. Now Kung is a very common Chinese name, but Tafti-teh was unheard of. He inquired of him further. The boy said he was from Kai-Fung. He had been named after an ancient king. This King Tafti-teh had written a book, not an ordinary book, but one that rolled up like a picture-scroll. And the name of the book was "Peh-lay-shi-ta". Mr. Edelman surmised that the King was none other than David, and that the "book" was a *Sefer Torah*, and that "Peh-lay-shi-tah" was – *had* to be – *Bereshith*. His interest excited, he asked more questions.

The boy said that his family, which included about ten households, lived just as the other Chinese in Kai-Fung did, with the single – but significant – exception that they never worshiped in the local temples.

"It is our custom that we never pray in the presence of the idols," he said. To whom did they pray? To Heaven.

And once, Kung's grandmother, at a time when there was cholera, forbade them to eat pork until the plague subsided. Her grandmother had told *her*, that when *she* was a girl, "our people did not eat pork, and things were better with us then."

Many times their failing consciousness of being a distinct people had been revived by the enthusiastic efforts of Christian missionaries to convert this lost remnant of Israel.

"But we knew that their religion was different," Kung said. Last year his grandmother had become quite ill, and spoke to him about a matter that had long been on her mind. She said. "For sixty years I have prayed to Heaven that some way be shown us to return to the way of our ancestors. But Heaven has not thought me worthy. The foreign missionaries have said that in the eastern cities there are foreign people of our religion. You ought to go to them, and then you must return and teach us here." Shortly afterwards, she had died. The boy had left his native city and come to Chenchow, and this was why he said, "Teach me our faith."

"I took him home with me," Mr. Edelman said. "He lived with me. I learned with him, and he became like a son to me."

The servant came in twice to replenish the peanut oil lamps while we talked. It grew cold, and the abominable coal that the Chinese call *Ying-mei* spluttered in the stove, but gave off little heat. I rubbed my hands together, but never thought of leaving. Mr. Edelman's voice went on.

How quickly he learned! Hebrew, *Chumosh* and *Nach* – very eager, he was, to learn. He said he had to make up for a hundred and fifty years of not learning. When he wanted to start to put on tephillin, I went to see the Rabbi." The Chenchow Rav was a very old man, whose eyes seemed constantly to weep. He listened to Mr. Edelman's story, and then gave his opinion.

The question (he said) stood like this: At the time when the Kai-Fung Jews first began to intermarry with the Chinese women, were these women properly converted or were they not? If they were, then the young man was a Jew who merely lacked *brith milah*. On the other hand, if they weren't, he required immersion as well. How could we know if the women were, or were not? Obviously, we couldn't. Still, if he was a proselyte, we should call him *ger Tzedek*, but if he were a Jew, we shouldn't. Finally, after the Rav had gouged out hundreds of invisible eyes with his thumb, he came to the conclusion that the young man should be immersed, as well as circumcised, but since he had a "Jewish name" so to speak, he might be called David ben Avrohom, instead of the Avrohom ben Avrohom customary with proselytes. Mr. Edelman was the *sandek* at David's *brith*.

And David continued to learn. He planned to make a Chinese translation of the Siddur for the use of his kinsmen, and one night he discussed with Mr. Edelman certain aspects of the *Aleynu* prayer.

"*'...and the idols shall be utterly destroyed'*," he read, "Think of that! No more crumbling clay idols. No more 'goddess of smallpox,' or 'goddess of cholera', or 'god of this or that', with a painted face! No, but instead, 'the Lord shall be one'!" He paused and smiled at his own enthusiasm. "Oh, I have so much to do!" he cried. "I want to go back now and teach them, and yet I want to stay here and learn more. What shall I do?" he asked Mr. Edelman.

"Right now, you should go to bed. You look tired." They went to bed. Mr. Edelman was awakened by the houseboy's shaking him. The servant told him that David had awakened him by stumbling at the door, and had answered his question in a strange voice and language.

"Then he went out. I think he's sick," the man said. Mr. Edelman dressed rapidly and they went out into the street. A passing policeman said he had seen the young man going into the synagogue, only a few blocks away. And there they found him. He had lit all the candles on the *bima* too, taken out the Sefer Torah, and was chanting it aloud in the empty synagogue. He made no resistance to being led back home. A doctor came finally, and shook his head at the sight of the feverish boy.

"We did what we could, but it was no use. The next day, towards night, he seemed better. He was quieter, and he seemed to recognize me. The houseboy lit the lights and David muttered something. I leaned over to hear – it was the *Shema*. He died in the night."

Mr. Edelman stopped. The dim lights were flickering away their last moments. I pulled myself back to reality, and said good night.

Before I came back to America I visited the *Beth Chaim* of the Chenchow Jews. I saw the stone on David's grave, and read the inscription. Mr. Edelman told me it was a verse that the young man had often repeated. The stone does more than mark the grave of one Jew who returned when so many are fleeing. It may also mark the grave of the last hope of the last Jews of Kai-Fung. How long will they have to wait now? Until the verse of the prophet is fulfilled? For that time. For those Days, we all wait.

KUNG

David, son of Abraham
Kai-Fung 5683
Chenchow 5705

Behold, these shall come from
Afar, and lo, these shall come
From the north, and these
From the west, and these from
The Land of Sinim
Bimheyrah, v'yameynu, ameyn!

Introduction to

THE COUNTENANCE OF THE PRIEST

THE WASHINGTON POST RECENTLY CALLED Avram Davidson "a prose laureate of the old country." This is not because he wrote stories about the people of the Eastern European *shtetles*, which he never experienced, but because many of his stories are about the descendents of those people, the immigrants who came to America, and their descendents who assimilated into American life. These stories have a special poignancy, a sense of the loss of a culture and a way of life.

This story was published in *Jewish Life* in October 1948. It is Avram's first published story that deals with this theme of cultural loss, though in this story the loss is found again. Other Davidson stories that speak of vanishing ethnic life include *The Woman Who Thought She Could Read*, and the remarkable *Slovo Stove*. Both stories (which were almost lost in out – of – print limbo) can now be found in *The Avram Davidson Treasury* (Tor, 1998).

Grania Davidson Davis

THE COUNTENANCE OF THE PRIEST

EVEN RAMBAM, THEY TELL ME, in Egypt, was troubled over the tendency of the Jews to *shmooze* during the synagogue service. (What is the Arabic for shmooze? Anybody know? Well, it's not important). I haven't been in Egypt lately, but in my old home town – in Philipsburgh, this is – we still have the same trouble. You know how it is. I don't say we discuss business on a Shabbos morning, when we should have our attention fixed on the service, but still... You know what I mean? However, there is one part of the *davening* that I have never known anybody to break into with conversation, and that is the Priestly Blessing, the *duchaning*, as we call it. There is something about that ceremony that fixes the attention of the congregation, and – but that's what I started to tell you about.

Our congregation, *Ahavas Chesed*, is the oldest synagogue in Philipsburgh. The oldest members have a tradition to the effect that "Teddy Roosevelt once visited the shul when he was Governor of New York." At any rate, you see our congregation has its traditions. Of them is the chant the *Cohanim* use when they go up to the *duchan*; it is never heard in the other Philipsburgh shuls. A friend of mine, a student of Jewish music, says that he never heard it in any other shul in the country. How it probably came to our synagogue is this way –

Years ago, during Grover Cleveland's administration, the congregation was founded by a group of men who had all come from the same town in Europe. So it is very likely that the melody came from there. They were all related, and interrelated, to one another, and the two biggest families were the Courlanders and the Kahns. They were both families of Cohanim, and they were both big families – so big, in fact, that it used to be a standing joke that on the holy days when the Cohanim went up to the duchan, there were more people to give the blessing than to receive it. I don't believe that this was ever literally true, at least not in my time, but I can remember year after year, when the platform in front of the Ark was packed with Cohanim. And how that ceremony of the Priestly Blessing thrilled me as a child!

The Cantor – old Reb Yossel Anton – it was, when I first began to notice – the Cantor would begin his repetition of the *Amidah*, and we would all teeter on our toes and sing out the responses of the *Kedushah* with loud and uninhibited fervor. For a time then I was preoccupied with wondering, if, when Isaiah saw and heard the *Seraphim* sing *Holy, Holy, Holy,* did they pronounce it *Kawdosh Kawdosh, Kawdosh,* or *Keedeish, Keedeish, Keedeish*? After a little bit, the men who were Cohanim would drift out to have their hands washed, so that they could bless us with clean hands. It seemed to me that half the shul would be going out, and I used to check them off mentally as they passed me:

Old Mr. Abe Courlander, old Mr. Jake Kahn, and old Mr. Nat Kahn; the Grocer Courlander, the Butcher Courlander, the Carpenter Courlander; the Glazier Kahn, the Tailor Kahn, the Peddler Kahn; Courlander *der greisser,* Courlander *der kleiner, der reiter* Kahn, *der blinder* Kahn (he was merely nearsighted), *Hussar* Courlander, and *Gendarme* Courlander. *The Rich One* (he wasn't), *The Clever One* (he wasn't), *The Limping One, The one with the Nose...* and so down to the younger members of the two families who were old enough to *duchan,* but not old enough to establish a *chazakah* on a nickname. I believe that, from time to time, there were non-family Cohanim present, but if they had dared to use an alien *niggun,* I never noticed. They would have been drowned out!

It may seem strange that I devote so much time to that particular melody, but I tell you, it did things to me! That it had no words – unless you call "ahahah" a word – only added to its unique quality, and that the chanting men were not trained singers, detracted nothing. When I heard it, I was caught up, and carried away by it. The time was no longer this century, nor the place that synagogue. I felt myself in the Desert, in the presence of Moshe Rabbenu and the Ark of the Covenant, and Aaron and his sons were lifting their voices to bless the Tribes of Israel. And the chant they were using was the same one. Why not? Weren't the Cohanim the descendants of Aaron? Couldn't this melody have been handed down from father to son, along with the knowledge that theirs was the Priesthood? So I reasoned. Nothing in my life has ever impressed one with the knowledge of the continuity of Jewish history as that chant and ceremony did.

It was my philosophy that *Rosh Hashonah made up for Tisha B'Av,* that is to say: On *Tisha B'Av* we mourn the destruction of the Temple. That splendid place of white and gold, the House of Our Life, where the priests made atonement for our sins, where – on the holiest of days – in the Holy of Holies, the *Coheyn Godol* pronounced the Most Holy Name – the Sanctuary of Israel – Destroyed!

Alilah, alilah! But on Rosh Hashonah the priests came forth again. Do you understand? The eighteen hundred and fifty years were as nothing, as if they had not been; the Destruction, as if it had not occurred. "Where we stand is the Sanctuary!" the Cohanim seemed to say.

There was no longer a sin-offering on *Yom Kippur* – but we still had the Priestly Blessing! There was no longer the rejoicing in the Temple courts at *Succot*, no longer the Drawing of Water, the torches and the dancing – but we still had the Priestly Blessing! No longer a *Paschal* Lamb at *Pesach*, but still – the Priestly Blessing! And Shovuoth came and went without the Bringing of the First Fruits, but not without – the Priestly Blessing! For our sins we were punished, but this was left to us as a reminder that we were sure to be *a nation of priests and a holy people*. I know it says that "Levi hath no inheritance..." Not in the fields of Eretz Israel, but surely, in my heart, Levi had an inheritance.

Well, I grew older. The cycle of the years went on. Another candle in front of the memorial tablets, another empty place in the shul. There were thirty Cohanim on the *duchan* ...twenty-five...twenty. People died, people moved away, people became Americanized – or, at least, Germanicized – and joined the *progressive* temple. Fifteen Cohanim to duchan. Children were no longer being sent to the Hebrew school; instead, a teacher came to the house to prepare the boys for the *Bar Mitzvah Ceremony*. They memorized their *Haftorah*, said their speech, and one saw them no more. Twelve Cohanim on the duchan...ten...eight. The old Rabbi had begun to doze gently in his front seat. The Jewish population, gradually moving to another part of town, decided it could support yet another synagogue. *Ahavas Chesed*, long mellowed, now began to wither. Five Cohanim up to duchan: Old Mr. Sam Kahn, his cousin, old Mr. Joe Courlander, and the latter's three sons.

I went to shul with one of them, Jerry. Everybody in Philipsburgh took it for granted that he would eventually marry Helen Samuels. Helen, however, got tired of waiting, and married some one else. It didn't take her long to find out just what sort of person he was ("A specimen," my Mother called him), and there was a divorce. A Coheyn isn't allowed to marry a divorced woman, but Jerry married her anyway. Four Cohanim up to duchan. They hadn't been married a year, when Jerry's oldest brother, Max, was killed in an automobile accident. These things happen all the time, but we never grow used to them. Old Mr. Joe Courlander bore up well, but Max's widow didn't. Not long after, she went to live with her parents, she and the two little children. Three Cohanim at the duchan of the *Ahavas Chesed* synagogue, and the world went to war again.

During my three years I had two leaves, none of them including a *yom-tov*. The first time, I missed the apple-red face and white goatee of old Mr. Sam Kahn. "Dead," they told me. The second time home, I heard the news about his cousin Joe's youngest son, Jack. "Normandy Beach," they told me. And, finally, I handed back my stencil, and came home again. Came Pesach.

I didn't even notice "Old" Mr. Courlander – no first name necessary now – go out to have his hands laved, but I noticed him return. Old, feeble – how very feeble he seemed! – and so stooped. Slowly he went up to the duchan, and placed his tallis over his head. We dutifully turned away, and the *Chazzan* called out, "Cohanim"! But there were no Cohanim, there was only one old Coheyn, and when I heard him lift up his voice – how it quavered! – in blessing, something tore at my heart.

The Congregation realized that it might soon be without a Coheyn, but what could it do? The matter was discussed at every meeting, but the only suggestion came from the President. "Maybe we could hire a Chazzan who is also a Coheyn?" he suggested.

"And what'll we do with the Chazzan we already have – drown him?" asked the Treasurer.

"Don't tempt me!" the President muttered. And there matters stood. The silver cord was all but loosed, the golden bowl was all but broken. Yet – "Aaron and his sons forever" – the Bible had said.

Last Succot I bought my own *lulav* and *ethrog* for the first time. My hands seemed all thumbs, and I was in mortal fear that I would drop the fruit and make it *posul*. I watched them out of the corners of my eyes, and an attempt to read the prayers with the rest of the eyes wasn't a complete success. We said the *Kedushah*. I looked at the ethrog. Mr. Courlander went out to wash. I looked at the lulav. My uncle nudged me.

"Max's children," he said, pointing to the two boys, about fourteen and fifteen, who were walking past us. "Max who?" I asked.

"Max Courlander – you remember. Well, their mother moved back to Philipsburgh so the boys could be with the old man. Bright boys," said my uncle. "Also, *frum*."

"That's nice," I mumbled. Still, it didn't penetrate. The old man came back, and went up to the duchan. So did the boys. He stepped out of his shoes. So did they. He pulled his tallis over his head. So did they. We looked away. The Chazzan called out, "Cohanim!"

The congregation was quiet. The old man's wavering tones, and the fresh young voices of his grandsons were clearly heard. After each of the Blessings' three phrases – they sang that same melody – that ancient, wordless melody – that chant which I had feared was soon never to be heard again. Their voices soared, their tones were clear and sweet.

When they had done, and they came down, I looked at them, and I saw that they were indeed "Max's children." The same sparkling black eyes. The firm chin. The curls. It is easier to describe their faces and expressions than their grandfather's. Where shall I find the right words to picture his face as he looked at them? Only in the Yom Kippur Machzor are they to be found.

"How glorious was the countenance of the High Priest as he came forth in peace from the Holy of Holies.

"As the canopy of Heaven, was the countenance of the Priest. As the rainbow in the midst of the cloud... As the rose in the garden... As a bright star in the border of the east... As the light that shineth in the windows. As the sun when it rises over the earth... Was the countenance of the priest..."

AVRAM DAVIDSON

THE WATERS OF EDEN

Out of the Garden the four rivers flow,
Their waters cooler than melted snow,
Loving the strands of ancient lands,
Through Havilah, Asshur, Bavel and Cush,
The cool, sweet waters of Eden rush;
Renewing the lands which lie below,
From the Garden of G-d the Rivers go.

Though four streams there are, or four become,
In that good, green Garden the stream is one,
And not till they pass the cherubim's gate
Do the Garden's waters divide their spate.
Ye races of man, though diverse be your course,
May you ever recall that you have One Source.

Introduction to
WHO KNOWETH FIVE?

THESE VIGNETTES WERE PUBLISHED in *Jewish Life* in October 1949, and indeed they are small tales of Jewish-American life at that time. More than half a century has passed since these little sketches were published, but you might meet people like these in your own life today.

Grania Davidson Davis

WHO KNOWETH FIVE?

I. Sherwood Kaufman

THE BIGGEST DEPARTMENT STORE in town is Kaufman's. On its sign, on its letterheads, wrapping paper, in its advertisements, and everywhere else that Sherwood could put it, appear the words, "Marcus Kaufman & Co., Founded 1855." He always felt a thrill of pride when he saw the words. He considered himself – and was so considered – the equivalent in local Jewry of a Mayflower descendant. Not that he mingled much with local Jewry. He didn't have to. He contributed to the Temple, of which his grandfather had been one of the founders, and that was all.

Noblesse oblige.

It came as a rude shock to Kaufman when one of the men at the Civic Club remarked to him. "I suppose the U.N. decision about Palestine must be very gratifying to you?" The shock was even greater because the man was Lewis Porter Franklin, president of the Chamber of Commerce and a Son of the American Revolution. That night he had a dreadful dream in which Franklin arose at a C. of C. meeting and demanded the immediate confiscation of *Marcus Kaufman & Co., Inc.*, and the deportation of all Jews to Palestine. He awoke sweating.

Next day he penned a letter to the *Times Herald* in which he said he voiced the opinion of thousands of his co-religionists to whom America was the only Promised Land in which they were interested. The only reasonable solution to the Palestinian question, complicated as it was by the self-interest of certain politicians of Eastern European origin, was the creation of a *Palestinian* state, to be neither Jewish nor Arab, etc., etc. The caption over the letter was, "Not Interested in Palestine, Says Department Store Head", and Sherwood felt much better.

A few days later he overheard Lewis Porter Franklin talking to a small group in the Civic Club Lobby. "I've been teaching at First Methodist Sunday School for twenty years," Porter said, "and I know the Bible promises the Holy Land to the Jews, not the Arabs. And now that we are finally seeing the beginning of the fulfillment of God's word, I can't imagine how any – any *man* can oppose it. If a man doesn't believe in the Bible, what *does* he believe in?" He gave Sherwood a cold look, and walked away. The numbers 1855-1855 were dancing through Sherwood's head, but for once they failed to comfort him.

II.   Nat Rubenstein

Nat was born in 1900 and from his 13th to 18th years he said his morning prayers every morning that his father was home to see to it. Then he went into the army, and when he came back from France, the old man knew better than to start *that* again.

Nat joined three veterans' organizations; he became a Mason, a Modern Woodman, a Shriner and several kinds of Knight. He dearly loved to put on his uniforms, to don the white spats, the Sam Brown belt, the golden aiguillette, and the medals; or – if it was Lodge night – to fasten on his sash, sword or apron, or put an embroidered fez on his head. Once, some new members walked in between the flag and the altar, and then tried to laugh it off; Nat really gave it to them, but good.

The old man died in '26, and then Nat was able to do what he wanted with Rubenstein's – "The Store with a Tradition." In five years, he had moved the store and bought the new building. He owned the house he and Bella picked out when Stuart was born, and there was some other property as well in Bella's name. One night when the meeting of Sam Greenspan Post was almost over, and the boys were starting to get out the card-tables, some *clutz* got up and proposed that the Post's annual Memorial Service be held at the *Shul* for once.

Nat was on his feet in a second, a heavier figure than in the A. E. F. days, and not so much hair, but the same fighting spirit. "The Memorial Service has always been held in the Temple," he said. "Why should we change a custom of thirty years? Not only that, but who wants to bother with all that ritual they go through in the Shul? That stuff went out with the bustle," Nat laughed. The motion was defeated, and they got out the card-tables like they started to.

III.   Stuart Rubenstein

When he became a *Bar Mitzvah,* his father gave him a check for a hundred dollars."That's for learning your piece so nice, like Gra'ma wanted you, and not making no fuss," his father said. "Now you stick this here check in the bank, and we'll put something to it every now and then, and when you're old enough, you can buy a car."

Stuart liked the idea so much that he put all the other gift money in the bank, too. Then he forgot about it and went about the business of grow-ing up. He learned to dance, he played a good game of basketball at the Y.M.H.A., saw his first burlesque show, kept a scrap-book of aeroplane pictures, flexed his muscles in front of the mirror every night, and got good marks in school without having to work very hard.

After painting his face with merchurochrome and carrying a dead fish down East Main Street, he submitted to an initiation which he found more disgusting than painful, and became a fraternity man. This entitled him to wear a red hat with Greek letters on it, and instruct other boys in the technique of carrying dead fish down East Main Street.

Because Buddy Samson went, and he was Buddy's best friend, Stuart went away to camp one summer instead of going, as usual, to the Rubenstein's cottage at Lake Wippacumago. At camp, he made many new friends, few of whom could read Greek, but all of whom could read He-brew. He was surprised to see how quickly the letters came back to him.

After his return he found a job for his after-school hours, and saved his earnings. True to his promise, his father put something to it every now and then. When Stuart was eighteen, Nat gave him another check and asked him how much he'd saved up for his automobile now. Stuart told him. His father whistled.

"Why, you got enough to buy a truck!" he said.

The truck is a beauty; Stuart spends much of his spare time taking care of it, and twice a week he loads it up and drives it from Migdol Mosheh to Tel Aviv, and back.

IV.   Isidor Glass

Before his son was born, Isidor remembered how the boys at the *Hochschule* used to torment him about his own name, so the baby was named Siegfried. Somebody who should have known better suggested to Herr Glass that he might care to have a tree planted in Palestine in honor of the event.

He and Ottillie had a good laugh at that one. Herr Glass was a regional official of the *Deutschesisraelitische Nazionalgesellschaft*, and frequently contributed money and articles to their newspaper. The news-paper (its editorial board consisted exclusively of men who had the Iron Cross) constantly urged the government to take sterner measures to restrict the immigration of Polish Jews, who were, it said, as great a menace as the Zionists.

The National Socialists came to power.

"I give them one year," said Herr Glass, "and then, if we see Hitler on the street, we will say, 'Ach, there goes Hitler, *nebbich*'." Quite a number of their neighbors said various things when the Glasses left their native city, but none of them said nebbich. They would have preferred to stay in New York, where so many of their *landstleute* lived, but the distant relative who sent them the affidavits and the passage-fare wanted to see what he was getting for his money, so they went to his hometown. The distant relative was not particularly impressed, but the Glasses were, after all, a living reminder of his charity – much better than a posthumous marble plaque in a synagogue – so he made the best of it. He had a large credit-payment furniture store, and he gave Isidor a job collecting the payments on a commission – a very small commission – basis.

Siegfried went to the local public school, where he was nicknamed *Siggey*, lost his accent, became a Boy Scout, and was quite happy. Ottillie learned to do her own housework, but, finding it difficult to make friends, had no one to talk to all day. And Isidor, after ten or twelve hours of touring the city, climbing up and down stairs, suffering snubs and insults from foreign-born and native-born alike, – Isidor didn't feel much like talking. He ate his supper, took off his shoes, and fell asleep over the newspaper.

Ottillie was in the kitchen when she heard Isidor begin to gasp, and, frightened, she ran inside. The gasping turned to roaring laughter as he showed her a newspaper item captioned "Not Interested in Palestine, Says Department Store Head." He continued to laugh until tears rolled down the creases in his cheeks; it was the first time he had laughed since they had come to America.

V.   Molly Goldhizer

One of the women was late that afternoon, and even after the meeting she was still angry. "Those kids of mine!" she protested. "They eat me up alive! Sometimes I wonder why I bothered. They told me I had till Wednesday for the costumes, and this noon they come home and tell me the teacher wants them ready by tomorrow. So I first had to get the material –"

"What costumes?" Molly asked.

"For the Christmas pageant," explained the other woman, irritation subsiding into pride. "Linda is an angel, and Garry is one of the uh, oh yes, one of the wise men. Miss MacDonald says they're the best children in the whole pageant. She couldn't believe they were Jewish. 'Why, I never would have known it!' she said to me. She could not get over it." Pride had utterly vanquished annoyance by now, and her voice grew smug. Molly who was usually so good natured, felt vaguely annoyed, although she didn't know why. But by the time she left, other things were on her mind.

She picked up her chicken at the butcher's, called for Debby at the kindergarten, gave her her milk, and started to kosher the chicken. The kitchen was large and furnished in the most modern fashion. Irv Goldhizer told her, when they got the house, "You can even have an electric fly-swatter if you want to, and you can keep even six sets of dishes if you want to; so long as my supper is hot on the table when I'm ready for it."

Molly's mother had never learned to read. Molly's brothers had gone to the *Talmud Torah,* but she had not been sent. "All that a Jewish woman needs to know, I will teach you," Mama Selig used to say. Laws of *kashrus* and *Shabbos,* family recipes, old legends, rules of mourning and *yahrtzeit,* lectures on modesty, and methods of confuting the *ayin ho-ra* – the evil eye – comprised mama's version of all that a Jewish woman needed to know.

That afternoon Molly had an unexpected caller – a strange young man. He explained that he represented an organization interested in starting a *Yeshivah Ketanah* – an all day Jewish school – in town. The young man had been carefully coached in his methods; he had been warned not to tell the parents that such a school would make their children more religious, because that might frighten them away. Instead, he was to talk vaguely of "Jewish culture," "the advantage of small classes in promoting a well-rounded personality," "spiritual training as a defense against anti-semitism," and so on. But, emboldened by the *mezuzah* on the Goldhizer doorpost, he ventured to speak up for the necessity of more Jewish education for women. Molly agreed with him at once; she would be glad for Debby to go to such a school. He departed in a pleasant daze.

Molly found herself thinking of the woman at the meeting, the mother of the angel and the wise man, and she, who was usually so good-natured, felt vaguely annoyed, although she didn't know why.

Introduction to
REDISCOVERY

BY THE SUMMER OF 1950, when this story appeared in *Jewish Life*, Avram Davidson had lived in Israel, and had returned to the United States. Israel became a focus of his writing during this period, and his writing matured a great deal, moving from relatively simple sketches to fully developed stories.

This story about the subtle tensions between the Sephardic and Ashkenazi Jews measures the depth that his writing attained during the 1950's.

Grania Davidson Davis

REDISCOVERY

ONCE IT IS REALIZED THAT THERE IS no part of the world where anyone can go with a perfect assurance that he will meet no one who knows him, encounters with once-familiar people in the most distant places no longer astonish.

Accordingly, when I met again, this time in the Machaneh Yisrael quarter of Jerusalem, my old school friend, Henry Rodericks Bono, I was pleased, but, as I've explained, not surprised; I said, "Hello, Hank. Glad to see you." He gave me his hand, said he was glad to see *me*, and asked how long I planned to be "in town." I told him. He had not changed at all. His tall figure was as thin as ever, no lines marred his long face, and his eyes were – as always – clear. I thought them his best feature; they were a distinctive shade of violet (never mind how it sounds, it looked fine), and made up for the fact that his teeth were rather irregular, and that his lower jaw did extend just the slightest bit beyond the upper. However it was, Bono had *mien*.

He also had, at that moment, a very small, rather dark, and somewhat dirty boy hanging onto his right leg. Jerusalem is filled with these little boys. They go about bawling the names of evening newspapers, or protected with rubber gloves, they peddle *sabras* (prickly-pears) which they skin open with large knives, or they shine shoes which are first lathered with shaving brushes. They also appear out of the air when a bus pulls into the crowded central station, and trot away with cases and valises larger than they are. These are the children of the *Frenks*, or *Oriental* Jews. Henry Bono had had quite a different childhood. I know, because I shared part of it with him, although I could not, of course, ever have shared the experience of being Henry Rodericks Bono.

As children, we lived "just around the corner" from one another, not far; it was possible to run from his door to my door while holding one's breath, a fact we both verified. But there was a difference vaster than space. We – my family – lived in a large, newly-built block of apartment houses. With elevators and uniformed employees. The Bonos lived in a three story brick house with white stone facings, one of three rows of such houses that formed a triangle enclosing a smaller triangle of a park. Around the park was a high fence of ornamental iron-work, and the entrance to the park was by an ornamental iron-work gate. In the gate was a lock; those who lived in one of the small brick houses had keys to the park; those who lived elsewhere had not. Even the President of the United States had not a key, but Henry Rodericks Bono had a key. Fortunately, I was a friend of his. I can't even remember when I first met him.

As I search my memory, I find no trace at all of jealousy because I had no key. On the contrary, I felt only the superiority of having a friend who did.

The question of any further distinction came up when my parents were deciding which school I was going to attend. My mother favored the School of the Society for Cultural Ethics. My father called it "the Society for the Deodorization of Jews." He favored the nearest public school. My mother murmured something about the lavatories. "*Terrible!*" she concluded, making her face a mask of horror. "You don't know *what* types he might meet," she warned, but her tone indicated that she knew only too well.

"You don't know what types he might meet going through life. Let him start now," said my father. At this point I interrupted. Hank was going to the public school, I said. And I wanted to go. My father laughed.

"There you are," he said. "Phillip Rodericks Bono, whose family has been in the country about six hundred years, sends his son to the public school. A former president of the Board of Aldermen, a trustee of the Castilian Synagogue, an ex-member of the Electoral College, a Director of the Niew Amsterdam Society; the public school is good enough for him and *his* son. What kind of *yichus* do you have? Of course, my father said, warming up, "your father is a big wheel in the Bialystoker Cemetery Association; and if I'm not mistaken, he once received a testimonial dinner from the Attorney Street Republican Club."

"All right, all right," my mother said. Then she told me I could go to bed. I also went to the public school, where I did, indeed, meet all kinds of types. When I asked Hank if his family had been in America six hundred years, he said no; two hundred and fifty years, he said.

Thinking of this, I re-examined Bono now as we stood in the street called Agrippa's Way. He was wearing khakis without military insignia, and shirt, trousers, and cap (the kind with the neck-flap that folds up and fastens with snaps) that had been bleached by the sun and softened by repeated washing. I saw that although his brown buckle shoes were polished to a gloss, the backs had been cut down to the soles. He wore no socks.

His father, Phillip Rodericks Bono, kept, in some respects, to the styles of his young manhood (he had married late in life) his shoes were always high, and so were his collars. The only times I ever saw Mr. Bono in his shirt-sleeves was at their summer home in upper Westchester. He wore sleeve garters. Both his grey hair and his grey beard were parted geometrically in the center. It would be a mistake to think that Mr. Bono was either stiff or stuffy – he was actually a very kind and gentle sort of man. Nothing could have been more amiable than his manner in convincing me that a baseball cap was not a proper sort of headcovering to wear when accompanying the Bonos on my first visit to their synagogue, and that I ought to wear one of Henry's hats. I realize now that it could not possibly have fitted, Henry's head being narrower, but at the time that never occurred to me.

My parents were not particularly observant, and the only synagogue I had previously visited was a highly informal congregation on the lower East Side, the one favored by my grandfather. My visits there had hardly prepared me for the Castillian Synagogue. So ancient is this venerable body that Trinity Church is, by comparison, a parvenu. It has more traditions than a wharf has barnacles. Unkind and probably jealous souls have been known to murmur that only the minutest proportion of the Synagogue's membership is actually of Castillian descent, and that the bulk of the congregation consists of ordinary Ashkenazim who have reached a degree of affluence or prominence which allows them to wear upon their brow the borrowed garlands of Sephardic splendor.

At my grandfather's synagogue I had been dimly aware that there was a man on the central platform reading something aloud, because the conversation occasionally died down long enough for me to hear him, and every now and then there would be a general cry of "*amen*" – presumably in response to something he had said. With the Bonos, everything was different. There was no conversation. I could hear the voice of the cantor (I soon learned to call him the "minister") clearly. The solemn hush of the congregation was interrupted occasionally by – or rather, blended into – a solemn chanting which in no way resembled the jolly and rather raucous melodies of my grandfather's *Polisher shtiebel*.

Presently Mr. Bono left his seat and approached the central platform. He went up. He bowed to the minister. The minister bowed to him. Mr. Bono said something. The congregation responded. The minister continued his reading. Then Mr. Bono said something else. He bowed to the minister. The minister bowed to him. He returned to his seat. The service continued, with diverse bowings and processions, and more solemn chanting. I could see Mrs. Bono in the women's gallery; her eyes, unlike mine, were on her book. After some time we went back to the Bonos' house, where Mr. Bono said the *kiddush.*

Deeply impressed, for weeks I spoke at home of little else. My mother said she could not understand how people so long in America happened still to be orthodox. My father thought he understood it. Most Jews of recent European origin were anxious to become Americanized and socially superior. They associated the religion they knew in Europe with everything else European, and (he said) thus hastened to discard it. The Bonos (and here he was correct) had so long since passed that stage that they no longer even remembered it. They were beyond question Americans. Their synagogue dated back to colonial days, and had a historical *hecksher* on it.

And so it was. Bono the elder held almost feudal views on the subject. Whatsoever was good in Jewish life, whatsoever was gracious and dignified, was Sephardic. That which was coarse and undignified, that which was untraditional, was characteristic of, was the fault of, the Ashkenazim. Sometimes he called us *the Tedescos*, using the Spanish word.

Mrs. Bono, the former Charlotte Acosta – that was the name written on the flyleaf of her prayerbook – was descended from that group of Jews who had come to New Amsterdam from Pernambuco when the Dutch lost it to the Portuguese. So had the famous Menasseh Bono, progenitor of the Bonos, and so had Joseph Aboab Rodriquez, ancestor of the Rodericks', Mr. Bono's grandmother's family. Sometime before the American Revolution (in which figure so prominently the names of Captain Augustus Bono and Major David Rodericks – or would, if it were not for the prejudice of Gentile historians) the Acosta family moved to the West Indies and there remained until Mrs. Bono's childhood. According to Henry Bono's account, his mother and grandparents had arrived in New Orleans two days before *Rosh Hashonah.*

Grandfather asked, naturally, as the first thing, where the Sephardic synagogue was. And they told him there wasn't any! And hadn't been for years! So he went to an Ashkenazic synagogue, and when he came home he said, "It's no use! I can't understand a word they say!"

"Your people," Henry remarked, "have such a confused way of pronouncing Hebrew. My people pronounce it just as in Biblical times."

Eventually the Acosta family settled in New York where they were comforted by the accents of a minister who lisped in the best Castillian fashion – *sav* becoming *thav* – and transformed *ayin* into *ngayin* in the approved manner. That first New Year's Day, however, they spent in solemn isolation in their hotel suite, Mr. Acosta himself reading the prayers and blowing the *shofar;* alone, but not lonely, these heroic Iberians.

The last time I saw the Bono family as a complete unit was at dinner one evening the summer after Henry and I graduated from Governor Tompkins High School. Besides myself the only other guest was a tiny, fragile great-aunt, a Miss Gumprecht, who wore, I recall, a cap or bonnet of antique design, with violet ribbons. Gumprecht is, I believe, a non-Sephardic name, but I never cared to ask possibly embarrassing questions about racial purity. The silver – so Henry had once told me – had been copies after the pattern of the original family service when that had grown too weak from generations of use and polish. The china was very old, and, since only enough of the set remained to serve five people, it was used only when five people were at dinner. I believe that on occasions when Mrs. Bono wished to use that particular set, her guest list was pruned accordingly.

There were candles burning in a massive candlelabra. Mr. Bono carved. As he flicked off the slices, Mrs. Bono told me that the next house had been taken by a Jewish family. The previous owner, a recluse of many years standing, had been found dead in his study. The newspapers made much of the fact that, although a rich man, he had lived for years on nothing but bread and mustard.

"It wasn't that he was a miser at all," Mrs. Bono said. "He used nothing but the most expensive brand of mustard; he bought it at Charles and Company."

"What sort of people have taken the house?" Miss Gumprecht asked. Mrs. Bono said she had never visited them.

"I should hope not," Mr. Bono said. "In the first place, the man's name is Cohen, but he calls himself Coe. And in the second place, he put a huge Christmas tree in his front garden, covered with gaudy electric light bulbs; a display which would have been almost vulgar even if from a Christian, but from a Jew – " he left the sentence unfinished.

"You must remember, Phillip," said Mrs. Bono, in the tones of one determined to make allowances, "that he is not one of our people. He is a Tedesco."

"That helps to explain, Charlotte," said Mr. Bono, "but it is in no sense an excuse. There are many Tedescos who, if not as observant as one could wish, still have a very good sense of what is proper. Another slice, Aunt Emily?"

After dinner we sang Grace according to the Sephardic ritual, a drawn-out proceeding. Away from the table, and in the comfortable living room, looked down upon by pictures of Bonos in long beards and Rodericks in long periwigs, I smoked – for the first and last time – one of Mr. Bono's Havana cigars; and listened to his stories – alas, not for the first time – of the Spanish-American War, in which, as a very young first lieutenant, he had acquired his taste for Cuban tobacco.

"Dear Pappa always loved his cigar after dinner," Miss Gumprecht said, and added – through what mental gymnastics I know not – "Phillip, I have meant to ask you what position Mr. Levi has now. Mr. Levi," she explained to me "was formerly one of our assistant ministers." I said I remembered.

"Mr. Levi was in Canada or Chicago the last I heard," her nephew said. "He may be all very well out there, but not here in New York. Do you know what he did on *Tzom Gedaliah*, Aunt Emily?"

"Just exactly what *did* he do on Tzom Gedaliah?" Miss Gumprecht asked. "I've heard such stories!"

"On the Fast of Gedaliah," Mr. Bono declared, "Mr. Levi went up the *tebhah* – where everyone could see – despite his robe – that he was wearing tan trousers – not black, but tan – *tan* trousers – on Tzom Gedaliah!"

"Dear me," Aunt Emily murmured, and clicked her tongue. Mr. Bono nodded with gloomy emphasis. Mrs. Bono sighed. Shortly afterwards I left.

Many things acted against my meeting with the Bonos again. I went out of town to college, my family moved, the war broke out. After the war, I spent two and a half dull years doing nothing in various ways. Then I went to Israel. I have since realized that, to most American Jews, Israel consists of vague, exotic areas called *Tel Aviv*, *The Negev*, and *The Kibbutz* – all of which consist of little white houses surrounded by orange trees. I see no use, in these circumstances, of trying to explain where I was before meeting Henry Rodericks Bono in Jerusalem (*Jerusalem* my reader nods. He knows all about it. The Wailing Wall is there – surrounded by little white houses and orange trees, and overlooking *The Kibbutz*.)

"How long do you plan to be in town?" Bono asked.

"About a week," I said.

"Good – come to supper tomorrow. I want you to meet my wife. I've been married a month tomorrow." He bent down and plucked the little boy off his pants leg. "Rachmiel," he ordered, "*ten shalom l'adon*." Rachmiel, by means of a very grubby hand, gave peace to the lord – namely me. "One of my brothers-in-law," Bono said. While I was digesting this, he took me by the elbow and turned me about to give me street directions.

At six the next evening, I walked up Agrippa's Way to the Street of the Great Assembly, where I turned left and walked as far as the shop of the man who makes straw saddles for donkeys. Here I turned left again and entered a court with trees, through which I passed, coming out on a hillside. The slope was sprinkled with houses according to no discernible plan. "The house with an automobile in front of it," Bono had said. I looked about, but could see none such. An old woman was sitting on a rubbish heap, plucking a recently deceased chicken.

"*Yesh kan bayit im auto lifnav?*" I asked, in my fluent Hebrew which so often causes me to be mistaken for a sabra by visiting Argentinian businessmen. The old woman gestured with the chicken toward a pulsating mass of children. As I came closer, I saw that beneath the children was an automobile. It had no wheels, no engine, and no upholstery, but still, it was beyond question an automobile. One of the children detached himself from the chassis, and, running over, clasped my leg. It was Bono's young brother-in-law, Rachmiel. He took me up an outdoor staircase to the second storey, and as we walked along the veranda, Bono came out of a room.

"I've told my wife and in-laws all about you," he said, as we went into the room. "This is Ruchamah – my wife." Mrs. Henry Rodericks Bono was a rather young and altogether beautiful girl. She was, like her brother, dark, but her fine skin seemed translucent, and I noticed with surprise and pleasure (aesthetic) that there were still women who not only blushed, but looked lovely while doing it. Her glossy hair was not entirely confined by a green silk kerchief, and she wore large gold filligree rings in her ears. She greeted me shyly in Hebrew. Bono continued his instructions.

"My father-in-law, Mr. Abraham – " A stout, genial man in a grey robe wished me *Shalom Aleichem* – about a baker's dozen of brothers and sisters, meeting whomever took us up and down the room, until we came to the end. Four or five primus stoves hissed busily, and two middle-aged women, wearing more elaborate arrangements of kerchiefs than Ruchamah, were popping things into pots. The cooking smells were unfamiliar, but promised much.

"Ruchamah's mother," Henry gestured to one of the women, who beamed. "My mother-in-law," he gestured to the second woman, who also beamed.

"I didn't quite get that, Hank," I said.

"My father-in-law has two wives," he said.

"But Rabbenu Gershom's decree outlawed that," I said, feeling exceedingly confused. Bono's answer put everything in place again.

"Rabbenu Gershom," he said firmly, "was an Ashkenazi."

Supper began with *falafel*, a delicacy sold on a thousand Israel street corners, but nowhere prepared so well as here. One of the Mrs. Abrahams – I never straightened them out – dipped her fingers into a bowl of ground bean-paste, rolled a little ball, rolled more of them, and dropped them into a caldron of hot oil. When they were browned and crisp she seigned them out and drew towards her a pile of *pita* and two bowls of hot sauce – one white, one red. She cut each *pita* (the Levantine bread, looking like a large flap-jack) in half, anointed it with sauce, and rolled up several of the balls in each. The sauce trickled down my chin and on my shirt; trickled down my wrists and into my sleeves. Bono showed me the knack of folding the end of the *pita* and sealing in the sauce. There followed stuffed grape leaves, there followed mutton in various forms, new combinations of eggplant, and all the delicious alchemy of Near Eastern cooking. And with everything, *pita*. *Pita* took the place of plates, *pita* was used instead of napkins. The innumerable Abrahams laughed and joked and chattered in Hebrew, Arabic, and Spanish and Bono laughed, joked and chattered with them. In Hebrew, Arabic, and Spanish.

Since we started together in Spanish I at Governor Tompkins High School, I knew just how much of the language Bono had known, and I was amazed to find that he had become fluent, and amused to find how his accent had shifted from the modern to the medieval. The Balkan and Levantine Sephardim, as is well known, cling to the dialect of 15th century Spain. Henry's *h* had become *f*, his *j* was now *zh* and not *hh*, and his *c* and *z* – previously lisped – were both *z* as in English. I gave up the attempt to follow the conversation, and concentrated on the food.

After assuring everyone I could hold no more food, and convincing Mr. Abraham that two glasses of *arrak* was all I could safely take aboard, I fell into conversation with Bono. He told me he had been in the army, in the same *plugah* with Ruchamah's brother, Uriel – Uriel flashed a smile and licked his fingers – and that he had come to know the family that way.

We – Henry and I and his father-in-law-had been sitting on a divan with the table in front of us, but the rest of the family had eaten curled up on various sections of the rug-scattered floor. Mrs. Abraham brought us tiny cups of sweet, black coffee, and the other one brought Mr. Abraham a water-pipe. As he gave a few preliminary gurgles and rearranged the hot embers on top of the tobacco, I thought of Mr. Phillip Rodericks Bono, his Havana cigars, and high collars. I though of Mrs. Bono and the family silverware; of Aunt Emily Gumprecht, and the Minister. I recalled how, on *Purim*, when the name of Haman was read from the *Megillath Esther*, the seat holders of the Castillian Synagogue used to tap sedately the carpeted floor with the tips of their shoes. I also remembered Mrs. Bono's excusing the vulgar Mr. Coe (*geboren Cohen*) who had set up the blatant Christmas tree.

"What are you thinking of?" Henry's voice broke into my reverie. I looked up. Rachmiel surveyed me with round eyes over the rim of a leaking coffee-cup. The two Mrs. Abrahams – neither of them wearing shoes – were squatting companionably in a corner, and cackling happily to a story Uriel was telling with many gestures. The other children were tumbling about, or singing out of chorus. Ruchamah leaned her head on Bono's shoulder and smiled at him with her splendid eyes.

"I was thinking about something your mother once said about the Ashkenazim."

"Ah, the Ashkenazim." His tones were indulgent. He put his arm around his wife and looked at her as if to say, "They never produced a prize like this."

Mr. Abraham passed the tube of the *nargileh* to Henry who released Ruchamah and put a cushion behind his back and folded his feet under him.

"Of course, the Ashkenazim" – he sucked at the pipe – "are wonderful people. Wouldn't have the State of Israel without their help. But don't you think" – he took another puff – "you must admit" – *puff* – "that they *are* rather" – *puff* – "just a trifle" – he sat back, crosslegged, smoke curling around him – "stiff?"

Introduction to

THE FISHERMAN...A TASHLICH LEGEND

THIS VERY SHORT STORY is very important. It was published in *Jewish Life* in the fall of 1950, and it is the first published story by Avram Davidson that is pure fantasy. In 1950, he would have been around 27 years old, still a young writer and a young man. Now he began to let his imagination roam, and it was in the realm of imaginative fiction that he found his true genius as a writer. Soon he would be writing for a larger audience in the fantasy and science fiction magazines, but at this stage his mind was still focused on deeply Jewish themes.

Grania Davidson Davis

THE FISHERMAN...
A TASHLICH LEGEND

HE CAME AROUND THE CORNER into Dock Street and at once I noticed something odd about him – something I was aware of noticing, but was unable to pin down. The late September sun bathed his well-knit figure in soft light, and played warmly on his dark, keen face. As he came up to me, he looked at me rather intently, and would have continued by, but I suddenly put out my hand and stopped him. Then I wondered why. He gave me a sharp glance – something like the glance Mr. Cook, the High School principal, used to give the boys as he passed them in the street.

"Don't I know you?" I asked. He put down his suitcase slowly, and pushed his hat back on his forehead.

"*Attah Yehudi?*" he asked me.

"Oh, you speak Hebrew!" I blurted out.

"I speak English, too," he said. "I just wanted to make sure you were Jewish. Since you are, I am bound to tell you that you stop me at your own risk." And with that, he raised his eyebrows, as if to say, "We-e-ell? And *now* what do you want?"

"What the devil do you mean?" I asked.

"Call me by my Jewish name," he said, and then I realized *whom* it was I had stopped on the street so familiarly. He nodded his head gravely. I groped for words, and stammered something about not wanting to keep him from his business. He chuckled scornfully.

"Don't give me that," he said. "Right now they all want to keep me from my business. Blowing *shofars* every morning, distracting me with their prayers – and all the rest, just to keep me from gathering evidence." This to me took on an aggrieved note. "I've got my job to do, just like anybody else. I've got my rounds to make, and my reports to turn in, too. And now *you* stop me with that silly pretense of having seen me before. Just be careful you don't see me again, that's all." And he made as if to depart. I put out my hand again.

"One more word out of you, and I'll say the *Shema* right in your face," I warned. He blanched and gnawed his lips.

"What have you got in that suitcase?" I asked him.

He looked at me slyly. "I've been fishing," he said.

"Let's see what's in the suitcase," I directed him in pontifical tones. He started to protest, but I only got as far as "*kel melech ne –* " when his fingers were busily undoing the straps. He threw open the lid, releasing a briny odor – briny, and yet – inside was a net, and a wicker creel. He opened the creel and I peeked in. At first I could see nothing, but then as they took shape, I withdrew a little.

He reached in his hand and pulled one out. It was spikey and had a hard shell, and thousands of little hands.

"Look at this beauty," he said. "Spawned yesterday from the cast-off *aveyrah* of a communal dignitary. And this one – " he pulled out one that had no shell at all, but many tendrils that wrapped themselves around his hand – "this one came from the old mother of a middle-aged and un-married daughter." He disengaged his hand and put these back in the creel. His next step was a curious one: he put on a pair of leather gloves. He carefully inserted one hand in, and pulled out another specimen of his catch. Its upper surface was beautifully iridescent, but the lower surface contained a double-row of ugly suckling mouths, sharptoothed and gaping. "Here you have something that a pillar of the community shook into the river. One of the most well-esteemed philanthropists that ever sweated his employees." Back it went, and he took off the gloves, removing the rest with his bare hands.

There was one in the shape of a rosette with a single petal missing: a faint pulse of life still beat in it. "Young girl whose sweetheart told her that his intent to marry her was the same as if they were actually married. She believed him – for a while." The next one resembled a slug, but had several sets of claws that continued to tear feebly at its own body. "Head of a merchants' association – almost all Jewish – that decided to close their stores on Monday each week. They could have chosen Saturday, but they didn't." He gave me another sly glance.

"Want to see some more?" he asked. I had enough. I didn't even ask to be shown my own – I was afraid of what it might look like. He packed his catch up again and fastened the suitcase.

"Well, I'll be running along now, if you don't mind. I've got to bring these in to headquarters." He went down the street, casting no shad-ows in the late September sun. As I watched him, I thought of the sins which had *not* been cast away, and my heart grew heavy.

Introduction to
OF MAKING MANY BOOKS

HARDWARE AND SOFTWARE

READERS OF AVRAM DAVIDSON's writings have long known of the importance of books and the written word in his work. There are examples almost too numerous to mention where the physical book (the hardware) or the intellectual content (the software) is at the heart of his stories and essays – a few telling instances are when Vergil's friend Clemens yearns to possess manuscripts in the collection of the Magus, "the works of the music masters of Chandraguptas and Asokas" (in *The Phoenix and the Mirror*); the consequences of Doctor Eszterhazy consulting the Baconian Fragment (in *Duke Pasquale's Ring*) or visiting a library to read Basil.

Valentine's *Twelve Keys,* while his own copy is at the bookbinder's (in *The Ceaseless Stone*) and, perhaps the most bookish of all, that splendid short story *And Don't Forget the One Red Rose* (reprinted in *The Avram Davidson Treasury*). The series of essays collected in *Adventures in Unhistory*, the last book published during Davidson's lifetime, is rooted in his more than six decades of eclectic reading. This notion of reverence for books and learning is a constant in Davidson's writing irrespective of genre, and the volume you hold in your hand, demonstrates how closely the theme is intertwined with his Jewish heritage.

As *Of Making Many Books* shows, Davidson was no stranger to libraries and their function as repositories of knowledge. If he was not a trained bibliographer, he nonetheless had an eye for the potential for story and history that an odd volume represents. Davidson opens volumes that evoke the London of Dr. Johnson and France before the Revolution, as well as 19th-century Jewish communities in the Western Hemisphere (many now vanished). This essay (as well as many others in this volume) is spiced with comments that touch on Davidson's travels in the late 1940s and early 1950s.

Provenance is one key to understanding the significance of rare books, and Davidson's notes on a copy of Don Isaac Abarbanel's *Proclamation of Salvation* (printed in Koenigsberg in 1860) discuss the ownership stamp of *Orthodox Rabbi Lazarus Greenspan*, whom Davidson identifies as a *wine-Rabbi* active during Prohibition. In the realm of old books, truth is often stranger than fiction, indeed.

The original publication of this essay in *Orthodox Jewish Life* was almost simultaneous with that of My Boy Friend's Name is Jello in *The Magazine of Fantasy & Science Fiction*, the short story that marked Davidson's first appearance in the science fiction field, where his polished and eccentric fiction made an immediate mark. Davidson's talent was mature from the start, however, as the earliest pieces in this collection show. *The Land of Sinim* (June, 1948) and *The Fisherman...A Tashlich Legend* (Sep.-Oct. 1950) may be seen as part of Davidson's literary apprenticeship, but they are full-fledged gems with strong fantasy elements reflecting themes that would preoccupy him for much of the next half century. Both as a devoted reader and as Davidson's bibliographer, it was a tremendous surprise and pleasure to discover these stories as I turned the pages of bound volumes of *Orthodox Jewish Life* in the New York Public Library on a hot summer day in 1999 – a pleasure and surprise that readers of this volume can now share.

Henry Wessells

HENRY WESSELLS is a freelance writer, translator, and editor. He is the publisher of *The Nutmeg Point District Mail: the Avram Davidson Electronic Newsletter* and the *Avram Davidson Website*, which can be found at http://ad.kosmic.org/. (Requests to be added to *The Nutmeg Point District Mail* mailing list should go to wessells@aol.com.) With Grania Davis, he is the editor of *The Other Nineteenth Century* by Avram Davidson.

OF MAKING MANY BOOKS

THE SYNAGOGUE IS BARELY FIVE YEARS OLD, and, like a healthy child who outgrows his clothes, is already starting to erect a new building; when it moves it will, of course, have to move its library. That this library should have in it books older than the synagogue is nothing – but many of them are older than City, State, or Country. These are not just the usual *Siddurim, Machzorim, Chumoshim*, which are the basic (minimal, if you will use the current jargonalia) requirements of a *shul's* library – or, perhaps I should not say, "not just".

Here is a *siddur-cum-machzor* from Metz, quaint and picturesque old city in easternmost France, where *glatt*-kosher *pate de foie gras* may still be had. *Imprimateur ordinaire du Roy*, it says on the title page – the use of the older form instead of *roi* should have warned me *Presse de Joseph Anton*: Here I must confess that I am so unstable in the calculation of *gematriya* that I date all old books by the reign of the monarch prayed for, instead of trying to figure the date properly. My first guess was that the *Roi* – the king – was fat, bourgeois Louis-Phillippe. I turned to the *Hanothen Teshua* prayer, savoring as I did so the scent of old leather, printers' ink, and old linen paper (sorrowing that books printed today will crumble in decades like, *le-havdil*, so many newspapers: text: "And how dieth the wise man? As the fool.") I saw the name of *Louis* leap up, but before I could affirm my guess, I saw the words *Melech Tsorphath-Navarre*; and realized that there has been no Navarre since Dr. Guillotine's invention abruptly ended the life of its last king. "*Louis He-chamesh-essre*" declared the yellowed page, "*V'eth adonenu Ha-Dauphin*" – and the faint echo of the proud Capet: "*Apres-moi, le deluge...*"; was Louis XV also among the prophets?

I felt my breath go; I heard the tumbrils in the narrow street. *Put not thy faith in Princes....*

There is no end to what can be learned in synagogue libraries, from their old volumes. I once knew a man who taught himself to read the Russian alphabet by comparing the Hebrew titles of the books in his shul with their Russian transliterations. One might almost do the same here,

and learn a little history in the process. Previously the abortive Polish revolt in the '60s had been known to me only vaguely, as the subject of a
short story by Conrad. Did Jews, in any great part, figure in this revolt? I
still do not know, but the old books – the volumes of *Chaye Odom* and
Shulchan Oruch – bear, prior to this period, censors' imprimaturs in Polish
only; afterwards, in Russian only.

Here is a book containing the *Tractate Eruvin*, from what the translator and commentator – the Rev. W. Wotton, D.D. – calls the "*MISNA.*" It
was printed in London, in 1718, full of interior *ss* like *fs*, and done in a
mixture of Latinized English and Anglicized Latin: *THE MISNA*, then, *AS
HELD BY THE SCRIBES AND THE PHARIFEES*, in which *Chachomim
omrim* becomes *Sapiente dictum, Bikkurim* are *Primitiva*, or Firft Fruits;
and *Terumah, Primitiae*, or Primeft Parts. All moft (sic), curious.

Here is a translation of David Kimchi's commentary on the prophecy of Zechariah, *by A Clergyman of the Church of Ireland and Sometime
Fellow of Trinity College, Dublin...Your fathers, where are they? And the
prophets, do they live forever?...*and in the darkness which lay suddenly
upon the earth, in the bottoms, by the sycamore trees, the vision of a man
riding upon a red horse....

Samuel Rodriguez Mendez, Nathaniel Zarphaty, Isaac De Eliahu
Ha-Cohen Belinfante...notes sounded upon a trumpet filled with dust... *The
Book of Prayers according to the minhag of the Holy Congregation of the
Sephardim at Amsterdam...1769* by the vulgar reckoning...and, at the back,
a *KALENDARIO* (again, the archaic *s* like *f*; which is which, in a language
so strange to me as Portuguese – if it is Portuguese! – I cannot say, but let
the reader hazard for himself.) "*Kalendario, Que ferve para 115 Annos,
Que fao feis giros; cada giro de 19 anno, comeffao do A*5530 a the o
Anno 5643...*" and so on, with reference to *minha* and *Harbith* (*maariv*) as
well as *Ros. Asana, J. Kipur, F. Pesah, R. H. Yiar... Tubeab*, and also,
Purim Pequen. I assume that "*Medianos*" are the days of the *Chol Ha-
Moed*, but what is (are) "*Je jum*"? – as in "*Jejum de Ab, em Domingo fe
rezu a teph.*" *Hehum, yeyum, zhezhum* – won't some learned Portuguese
take pity on me?

Other lands, other times, other questions. Everyone knows that
Geo. IV, in his rage against Queen Caroline, ordered her name struck out
of the prayer for the Royal Family; but it is commonly agreed that his
successor, William IV (he of the pineapple-shaped head) and William's
Consort, were on excellent terms. Why is Queen Adelaide's name, then,
not mentioned in that prayer as printed in THE FORM OF DAILY

PRAYERS/ACCORDING TO THE CUSTOM OF THE GERMAN AND POLISH JEWS/AS READ IN THEIR SYNAGOGUES, AND USED IN THEIR FAMILIES, why? This book, "Carefully Revised by Isaac L. Lyon, Professor and Teacher of the Hebrew Language", and "Printed And Sold by H. Abraham, 25, Houndsditch London, A.M. 5596," mentions King William as King William in the English text, but in the Hebrew he appears under the classically anonymous style of *Ploni*. It is not my intention to do Professor Lyon (to say nothing of Mr. H. Abraham) an injustice, but – the third book from the end on the bottom shelf is also a *siddur*, also *minhag ashkenaz*, dated in the reign of George IV, and translated by David Levi (who mended boots in the old London ghetto of Aldgate on the side): *Je regrette, messieurs* – but the translation is the very same. It seems that Mr. H. Abraham (or perhaps Professor Lyon) merely substituted, on the English page the Fourth William for the Fourth George; quite forgetting to add the name of the former's Queen. Poor "D. Levi, Esq."! – all through the years of the century publishers in several countries play fast, play loose, with his translation. But never again do we see his lengthy Orders of Services for the Fasts of Monday and Thursday, for the Fast of the Eve of the New Moon, "Which Is the Lesser Day of Atonement": *Pizmon* succeeding ponderous Pizmon, like elephants following one another in procession and holding their predecessors' tails in their trunks....

It is curious that the pages most thumb-marked in this book are the weekday and Sabbath morning services, and the "FORM OF READING THE KERIATH SHEMAH BEFORE RETIRING TO REST AT NIGHT." Sabbath afternoon is fresh and unmarked and there are neither wine-stains nor candle-drippings at the Havdolah. I conjecture that the owner kept this Siddur at home, that he lived too far from a synagogue to walk there and back, but that he did walk there for Sabbath Minchah, and rode back – in a hackney – coach, perhaps, or an early horse – drawn omnibus (perhaps the man at the reigns was the Jew of Gilbert's "Bab Balads," the one "...who drove the Putney *bus/ For flesh of swine, however fine/* He did not care a cuss...") In the absence of the evidence to the contrary, this is what I intend to believe.

"A Jewish calendar for fifty years, containing Detailed Tables of the Sabbaths, New Moons, Festivals and Fasts, The Portions of the Law Proper To Them, and the Corresponding Christian Dates, FROM A.M. 5614 TIL A.M. 5664, together with AN INTRODUCTORY ESSAY on the JEWISH CALENDAR SYSTEM, and tables for the continuation of the Calendar till the year 5776, A.M. bring for a period of six lunar cycles containing 114 years. With tables of the *parashoth* and *haphtaroth* as read by both Portuguese and German Israelites, &c., &c., &c. BY JACKQUES J. LYONS, Minister K. K. "Shearith Israel", New York, &c., and ABRA-HAM DE SOLA, Minister K. K. "Shearith Israel", Montreal, lower Canada, Professor of Hebrew and Oriental Literature in the University McGill College, Montreal, &c. MONTREAL: Printed by John Lovell, at his Steam Printing Establishment, St. Nicholas Street, 5614-1854."

This, believe it or not, is the *title*, and not the first chapter, of a little green volume cracked and peeling at the spine. I understand that it is still in use at the 70th Street establishment of the *Portuguese Israelites* in New York City. I am not, you understand, expressing surprise that it should still be in use; I am merely surprised that a work a mere hundred years old – a modern innovation, so to speak – should have gained favor in this fortress of tradition: "What, pray, Sir" – I can hear the indignant voices – "What, Sir, pray, is the matter with the good old Mendez-Mendez-Zarphaty-Belifante Calendar of 1769?" I can prove nothing. I suspect politicks (sic). I desire to hear *no excuses*.

Tamooz (I do not know if Lyons or De Sola is responsible for this yam-in-the-mouth accent) "*Tamooz*. Extremely hot. Ther. 76° a 80°, afternoon ver. 84° and 92°. Winds generally from the West. Rice, early figs and apples, plums, cherries, mulberries ripen palm produces opo-balsamum (not just ordinary, no-account balsamum, but *opo*-balsamum!): melons gathered."

Lists of fascinating Fasts and Feasts (samples: Simon took Gaza. Feast. Murder of Simon ben Gamliel. Fast. Apostacy of the Golden Calf. Fast. Death of Herod the Great. Festival &c., &c.) all – alas – marked "Discontinued". Or perhaps discontinued only by German & Polish Israelites...eh? Who knows?

List of all then known Jewish congregations in the Western Hemisphere! Who can bring us tidings of the present condition – if any – of the Jewish communities in Bolivar (Tennessee), Clarborne (Alabama), Clinton (Mississippi), Colluma (California, on the Yuba River), Bridgetown (Barbados), Nevada City (California. The number of Israelites in the city in 5613 - 1852 was thirty), Porto Cabello (Venezuela), St. Thomas (Danish West Indies; Minister, Revd. Solomon Levee Maduro), and Talbottom (Georgia)?

I note that among the list of subscribers is Capt. Phillips Levy, U.S.N. – by courtesy, Commodore. I would like to think that in some distant ocean, under an alien breeze, the doughty old veteran would retire to his cabin and hammock and book and read that in the month of – let us say – *Elool* that "figs, olives, and pomegranates ripen" in the Holy Land; that "the shrub *al kenna* blossoms (and the) first clusters of vine (come) to maturity"; that "The *Selichot*, or Propitiatory prayers are commenced from the first of this month, according to the Portuguese Custom," but that Fast for the death of the Spies (Numb. XIV, 36), formerly kept on the 17th, has been discontinued.

The American socio-political scene intrudes an antic note in, of all works possible, the *Proclaimer of Salvation of Don Isaac Abarbanel* (Koenigsberg. Gedrukt bei albert Rosback. 1860). An owner's rubber stamp is firmly imprinted to inform the world that it belonged to "Orthodox Rabbi Lazarus Greenspan" – the name is fictitious. Inquiries produce a tolerant smile and the information that the long late and orthodox gentleman was "a wine-Rabbi": that is, during the days of the 18th, or Prohibition, Amendment to the Constitution of the United States, Rabbi Greenspan had a license to sell *sacramental wine*; that he interpreted *license* as widely as could be; and did not concern himself overmuch as to the orthodoxy (or, indeed, the Jewishness or non-Jewishness) of cash customers who applied to him for the sacrament. There is something baroque in the thought of "Orthodox Rabbi Lazarus Greenspan" gaining his bread by defying American puritanism, meanwhile consoling himself by reading the words set down about the Coming of the Messiah by the great Don Isaac in his own exile and old age, in Italy.

Also from Italy, though another city and epoch, with a gummed label affixed to show that it was rebound in distant Baltimore, Maryland, a generation after its publication, is the *nouveax dialogues sur la kabbale/ou refutation critique, hisorique, et theologique/des dialogues sur la meme/ de m. le prof. (Samuel David) luzza to de padoue/ par elie ben -amozegh/ rabbin predicateur a livoourne/ chez l'auteur et c./ 1863*. The book is a credit even to the justly-famous Hebrew press of Livorno ("Leghorn" to *forestieri*), being printed from a most clear and beautiful font of *Rashi* type. Benamozegh peppers and salts his *refutation* with copious references to such non-Kabbalistic sources as Eusebius' *Preparation for the Gospel*, Plotinus, Enneades, Cuddworth, *Natura Plastica*, Numenius, Kepler, Clement of Alexandria, and the *Univers Israelit* for December, 1861: Luzzato's reply (if he made one) is not in our library. I bet it was a scorcher.

After the sun of Abarbanel had set, and long before the sun of Luzzato arose, the brilliant if erratic orb of Leone de Modena streaked across the Italian skies, as witness the first American edition (and perhaps the only one) of his *Tsmach Tsadiq* with *Axplanatory Notes* (sic), produced shortly after the Spanish-American War, on the Lower East Side of N.Y.C., where the said war was generally interpreted as a belated comeuppance for the decree, 406 years earlier, which sent the sturdy old Don into exile. There is no translation, but there are illustrations, and curious ones at that: Cain slays Abel, the two being clad in the costumes which Renaissance Italy impartially ascribed to both classical and Biblical times; unicorns are captured and gentled by comely maidens; mermaid-sirens, holding their tail-flukes in their hands, arise from the sea and sing enticingly to passing mariners, after which incontinently devour them: a moral point vigorous and vivid, which the old Rabbi of Modena (in the illustration, copied from the 1st Venetian edition, he is already bald and wrinkled) could make better than he could, for any great period, keep. And yet – and yet – while the thought of the aristocratic Don who, losing to Torquemada the struggle for Ferdinand's mercy, lost office, homeland, wealth, but neither faith nor honor; writing in distant places in his ancient age his great religious works – while the thought of him fills us with a vast awe and reverence, it does not draw us near to him; it cannot, he is too high, too fearsomely exalted for us to reach. But Aryeh Yehudah Modena, *b'la'z, Leone*, that man of many faults, like his Biblical namesake "unstable as water," hot-tempered, full of humours, spending his money as fast as he got it (and often not getting it), losing at cards and writing a book proving that card-playing is a cardinal sin, winning at cards and writing that card-playing is an amiable and harmless pastime, wandering here, wandering there, "with age, with cares, with maladies oppres'd," yet always throwing himself with fresh enthusiasm into the struggle and never losing heart – I think we can feel very close to this man. I know I can.

A slim and prettily-bound little book, in golden-brown leather, smooth, with traces of gilt still adhering to the cover: "ELEMENTS OF FAITH, for the USE OF JEWISH YOUTH, of both Sexes." So says the author, Rabbi S. I. Cohen, but it would seem that E. Justins, 34, Brick Lane, Spitafields, who printed the book in London 139 years ago, had one particular sex in mind. Rabbi Cohen, who wrote the Hebrew text (with vowels) – the translator is unnamed – used the form of a catechism to "impart the sublime comprehension of things imperceptible to the mere corporeal sense" and incidently drive arrows in Satan's eye and counteract the work of the missionaries who enticed impoverished and wavering Jews from their religion.

"Q. Were the idolaters prosperous with their belief?

"A. No; their actions became excessively destructive and abominable, and their folly invented strange and disgusting idols; nay, they even committed their children to flames as a sacrifice to their idols, *and otherwise occasioned great injury to society*." Italics, as they say, are mine.

According to the custom of the time, the back of ELEMENTS OF

FAITH, etc., lists the subscribers, i.e. those who paid for the work before its publication. The list is strictly alphabetical, but strictly: under "A" is listed "Anonymous, Per Mr. Beyfos" – Mr. Beyfos himself is not listed, unless, indeed that is he who appears under "C" as "Cosmopolitan, a", under "G" as Gentleman, a", or under "U" as "Unitarian, an." We all know what comparisons are – (odious), but it is an inescapable fact that Moses (late, Lord Rothschild) is down for three. Who knows but what, had the figures been reversed, it might have come to be Montefiore who was the baron, and Rothschild the lesser baronet?

Crossing the Atlantic, again, here is a censored Bible, produced during the '70s by a gentleman who was afraid that "the modest daughters of the Israelites, lest they encounter passages which would cause them to blush... (might) turn away from the study of the Sacred Scriptures." Accordingly, the editor left numerous such passages untranslated. I refrain from comment, but pass on to a work whose title page is missing, but which came apparently from the hand of the Rev. Dr. Joseph Krauskopf, minister of a reformed conventicle in Philadelphia during the '90s. Dr. Krauskopf was also franticly concerned with maintaining a chaste pallor in the modest daughter of the Israelites, and was particularly embittered by a certain religious and surgical ceremony, "of which (he said) we cannot speak in the presence of our wives and sisters without a blush mantling our cheeks, and whose only excuse is that is was supposedly instituted by Abraham...."

Which will serve as well as any as a place for me to point out a curious and significant thing. Most of these old books (and I have not mentioned a fraction of them) formed a collection in the possession of a single family. As the dates grow later, the titles change. Bibles with traditional commentaries give way to the emasculated versions noted above. Prayerbooks and holyday machzorim undergo a metamorphosis. Names such as Isaac M. Wise, Dr. Mertzbacher, David Einhorn, Benjamin Szold and Marcus Jastrow appear. The Scriptures are bowdlerized, the Siddurim wax thinner and thinner; finally there appears the 1st edition of the Union Prayerbook: after this there are no later dates. And finally the whole collection is donated to a communal institution, subsequently dissolved, from which it found its way hither.

One can learn a lot, as I said in the beginning, from a synagogue library.

Introduction to
CAPHTOR AND OTHER PLACES

CAPHTOR IS THE BIBLICAL NAME FOR CYPRUS. Avram Davidson visited the island when he traveled by ship from Israel to Europe. Cyprus made a deep impression on the young Avram, and he used the island as the setting for one of his earliest and eeriest mystery stories, *The Ikon of Elijah*, which can be found in *The Investigations of Avram Davidson* (St. Martin's Press, 1998).

From Cyprus, he sailed to Turkey. Avram was impressed by the hospitality of the Turks, and so was I when I recently visited that country. In Istanbul, I saw the site of a synagogue that has been used for uninterrupted Jewish worship since the time of Byzantium. Jewish refugees from the Balkans now use it. That's rather impressive, compared to the sad history of the European Jews.

This story of Avram's travels in Cyprus and Turkey was published in *Jewish Life* in the summer of 1952. Here we see his early use of dialect, which became such an important element in his style. We also see the first reference to the "Bazaar of the Horse Jewelers." This later became the *"Street of the Horse Jewelers"* in his classic Vergil Magus novels.

Grania Davidson Davis

CAPHTOR
AND OTHER PLACES

OBSTRUCTED BY BUREAUCRATIC difficulties right up to the last minute. I finally hopped into a launch and was conveyed to the *Abbazzia*, an ancient and cozy Italian vessel. As I climbed down into third class, the steward asked me, "Kosher?" I nodded. He pointed heavenwards and said, "sta Masgee." The *Masgee*, or *mashgiach*, the supervisor of kashruth, a trim little chap with a trim little beard, a beret, worn grey suit and sweater, not particularly mashgianic in appearance, assured me that he got his meat in Trieste from a sympathizer of the *Naturei Karta*. I recalled my only close contact with these stubborn saints, which resulted in my being kicked out of their Jerusalem chapel for appearing in a straw hat and similar vestments – savoring (to them) too much of the ways of the General Zionists and other Canaanites. However, supper was *milky*. I slept well and was up early the next day to disembark at the small Cyprus port of Larnaca, whence I took a taxi to Nicosia, the capitol (5 shillings).

First impression of Cyprus: Imagine – or shall we say, now conjecture a vision of a time – when, by a twist of unoccurred history, the Arab conquerors had been early repulsed from Eretz Israel and the Jews had not returned. The Greeks had stayed on, the Turks had conquered and remained, and the British had come and stayed: This is Cyprus, the *Caphtor* of the Bible.

Everything is familiar, but with a difference. Like Israel, the palms and eucalyptus, the old mudbrick villages, the new houses of cement blocks, same red tiles, Spinney's Stores and Barclay's and Ottoman banks in the cities. In the country, between Larnaca and Nicosia, a replica of the northern Negev – desert, erosion, scorched vineyards, sheep and goats grazing, oxen and donkeys plowing, grain being apathetically sown by hand, wadis, distant mountains, etc. The driver was a greyhaired mulatto, I sat next to him. In back, the following: an elderly peasant, wearing baggy, saggy black breaches which descended only to the knees, looked like a dropsical stork; a middle-aged man with gold teeth and a badge reading *Mukhtar* (village headman); and a young swarthy fellow. I took off my hat and put on a skull cap –

Chorus from rear seat, on rising note: Aaaaahhhh.
Driver: Toorkeeyah?
I: Falasteenah.
Chorus, on descending note: Aaaahhh.
Driver: Yahoodee?
Chorus, on long, drawn-out note: Aaaahhh.
Driver: Oogle-boogle franis Ahrabee (chops with hand). Kaahlas!
Chorus, with satisfaction: Aahh
Driver: Yahoodee scannis ahrabee. (Laughs scornfully. Makes
pushing, sweeping gestures with hand.)
Chorus, scornfully: Aaaahhh.

End conversation... haven't the faintest idea what language we were all talking. Later met driver in town, got big smile and tiny cup of sweet black coffee. I do not know if this is a gesture of Anti-Arab League solidarity or gratitude for the shilling tip. Put up at hotel New Cleopatra and dined on bread and butter, raw salad, coffee. Commenced letter...

Decided to take bath, explained decision to clerk, Mr. Cleanthos Karageorgides. He called out something in Greek, at which a midget came out of a telephone booth. I wish to emphasize that I am not making this up – so help me, a midget came out of a telephone booth and beckoned to me. I followed, feeling quite sure that even Walter Mitty never had to put up with anything like this. I followed up a flight of dark stairs lined with high wicker-work tables, down a half-flight, along a dark narrow corridor where loose tiles clinked like castinets under a long grass carpet, past an alcove hung with portraits of the royal Georges of Britain and Greece, all culminating in a Room with Bath. Chirping like a cricket, my little guide explains to me how it all works: *First* you put in the plug, *then* you turn on the water. I shake my head in wonder at it all. He beams, we shake hands, he departs. I sit down in my first horizontal bath in nine months, soak sybaritically in hot water and read a Penguin novel.

Next day: All these people who shout "Shalom" to me in the street are not, it seems, Jews after all. One of them explained to me that they were mostly Armenians who had either been in the RAF in Palestine during the war, or had been in business there at one time or another. Tony (as he calls himself) doesn't look like the stereotype of an Armenian – fair, blue-eyed, short nose. Ah, he says, for the Good Old Days in Tel Aviv! Tony says that an Armenian potentate called Dikran the Great carried away "Jewish technicians" to build up Armenia. Cyprus, says Tony, is very dead.
Next day: Heard Yiddish for the first time from a Turkish banana

peddler who used to live in Jaffa: "*Vie geht es yetzt in Yoffa?*"

Next day: Rain. All week: Rain... At last the rain lets up. I decided to leave Nicosia at once; I said to Cleanthos, "Name some nice villages in some nice mountains." He began naming; I counted up to five and stopped him at "Plattres," this being the first one I could pronounce. "Can I get a bus to Plattres?"

"Oh, yes: I call up... Okay: one o'clock, bus to Plattres."

"But it's one o'clock now."

"Never mind. Only after some minutes. I send now with you one small boy." Hastily grabbing my tephillin and typewriter, I surrendered the latter to the small boy, and off we went to the bus depot.

"Can I get a bus to Plattres?"

"Oh, yes: that one there. Leave one o'clock." It was then 1:15.

"Have I time for a cup of coffee?"

"No, not have time. But leave soon. One o'clock. Never mind: Drink coffee half-road." Meanwhile the stevedores were loading on top of the bus various huge wicker baskets, small barrels of wine, sacks of produce, a tin trunk, a live pig in a crate, etc. The bus left at a quarter to two.

The Cyprus bus is not very long and not very wide and has leather-padded seats arranged in various directions, some across the width, some along the sides, and some as in other buses. There are three doors and one goes up by a kind of stirrup. The sides of the bus bulge out, the windows are either open to the winds or closed by canvas flaps with *isinglass* windows like the old touring cars. The driver's seat is on the right, over it is fastened a calander and an ikon. It all seemed reminiscent of the Ipswich stage coach in the days of Mr. Pickwick, or the Ostia diligence in which, a hundred years ago, Rollo went from Rome.

The bus stopped at every village crossing and ox-forge to take on or discharge passengers, to lash or unlash their gear, to enable the travelers to buy peanuts or oranges or large, grey, eviscerated hares....

Now I saw the other side of Cyprus; beside the gloomy, eroded terrain, there is much well-cultivated land with a variety of crops and many orchards, ranging from oranges (the largest groves of which are owned by a Jewish planter, a Mr. Slonim, near Limasol) to apples (baskets of which are often sent to Israel as gifts), depending on the height of the land. At Lefka, the "half-road," I learned from the man next to me that the bus did not go to Plattres at all, but only to Prodromos, a tiny hamlet nine miles short. I received this with my usual quiet calm, but made a mental note to have the bus people beaten across the soles of their bare feet with the bastinade, if a single scrap of Ottoman law remains on the Cyprus statutes.

At one mountain village an old and toothless man climbed aboard, groaning and creaking, his head wrapped in a knitted helmet, all the passengers echoing his moans in sympathy. Subsiding finally, he looked at me and said something in Greek; I said I couldn't understand.

He: English?

Me: American.

He : And where are you going?

Me: To Prodomos.

He: Where? Where?

The whole bus: *Prodromon! Prodromon!*

He: You are not from Cyprus?

Me: No.

He: You are not from Syria? You are not from Turkey? You are not from E.Jeeps? You are from *America*? You have come all the way from *America*, and you – are – going – to – *Prodromos*? To PRODROMOS?

Me: Yes.

He: (crossing himself) *Kyrie eleison!* (Lord have mercy on us) *Kyrie eleison! Kyrie eleison! –*

Voice from behind: These old man is dentist. He like to make joke.

(The idea of a toothless dentist may seem strange, but is probably good propaganda.)

Voice: You know where is Las Vegas, Nevada? I have uncle there. All the American womens are coming to divorce their husbands.

Ancient dentist: *Kyrie eleison!*

Prodromos was shrouded in mist and darkness through which I stumbled along to a cold, stone-cold room, later – at my tooth-chattering request, supplied with a charcoal brazier. I dined on raw cabbage and coffee and said *maariv*, shaking, I fear, far more from outward cold than inward heat. On the table I saw a curious object which was identical to that described by D. H. Lawrence as "...the sacred patera (of the ancient Etruscans)... the round saucer with the raised knob in the center, which represents the round germ of heaven and earth. It stands for the plasm, also, of the living cell, with its nucleus...the germ central within the living plasma, the symbol of eternal maleness etc." I thought it very clever of Mr. Lawrence to know all this inasmuch as the Etruscan language has never been described; almost as clever as for the Etruscans to have invented the microscope, which they obviously must have... I said to the old woman, she of the charcoal brazier, "Is this the sacred patera of the Etruscans, ancient symbol of the germ-cell plasma and eternal maleness?"

Answered she, "Is very nice ashtray. You like?"

Up next morning to see the mists vanish and watch take shape a landscape such as that which Galilee or high Judea must have had before their glorious forests were cut down and the soil – the flesh of the land – washed away and left only the stones, the rocks, the gaunt bones...

"Hello"

"Ollo"

"Speak English?"

"Sure. What you want?"

"I want to go to Plattres. Where is the taxi-man's house, please?"

"'e's no 'ouse. Go 'boom'."

"The taxi-man's house has blown up?"

"No blow up. 'e's go mountains. Ber-um ber-um. Fall down. Finish."

"The taxi-man has been killed by a landslide in the mountains?"

No landslide. Woods. Ker-ash. All dead."

"The taxi-man's been killed by a falling tree?"

"No tree. No landslide. No blow up. 'e's take gun, 'e's go mountains, 'e's go woods, 'e's shoot partridge. Today, no taxi."

Some days later: Finally located a real live Jew. In Roman times there were several hundred thousand Jews in Cyprus, but they joined in the rebellion against the Imperial power and were finally expelled. In the last century the ICA settled a number of Jews here, and some more came during the '30s; but of all these only a few hundred remain. Mr. Alef (as I shall call him) painted a gloomy picture of Jewish life here: no Jewish education, no synagogue, no Rabbi, intermarriages and assimilation. He complained that British and American Jews took no interest, but admitted that Cyprus Jewry could afford to maintain the needed institutions if it wanted them.

A week later. At sea, S.S. Campidoglio: After a two-days sail through the Greek archipelago, we put into Izmir (Symrna) about 8:00 A.M. of a wet and chilly day, with snow showing on the mountains and distant housetops which ring the inlet whereon the city sits. With few formalities we went ashore, muffled in our scarves, *We* being myself and an Englishman with the rank of second officer (mate) in the Panamanian merchant service. He had taken a ship to the old-rich island of Bahrein in the Persian gulf, had been given a ticket to fly back to England, had *flogged* – sold – his ticket, and with the money and his wages had a sailor's good time throughout the Camel Belt countries. Now, broke and thinly clad, but with no regrets, he was taking just about the cheapest passage back to

London: 20 pounds. I, for 23 pounds, had a slightly less crowded cabin. Reason it is so cheap is that we are traveling as part of a party of emigrants from Cyprus to Britain.

In Haifa a friend had given me the address of a cousin in Izmir, and – naturally – I'd lost it, but remembered the name and district. I approached a passing Turk and said "Yemnis Tcheshar?" (fig market). He very kindly went blocks out of his way to show me the district. Once there, the second mate and I reconnoitered and, over a shop with an open front, saw in red letters the good Turkish name of Avram Kohn. Mr. Kohn was a young iron-monger and spoke French. The second mate knew some Spanish, and – the Jews of western Turkey being of Spanish stock – with his bad Spanish and my poor French, we made our wants known. Mr. Kohn made a few telephone calls and brought us Turkish coffee while we waited. Presently the cousin came along, also a young man. He took us through the labyrinthine ways of old Izmir (more of them later) to his place of business (olive oil and dried fruit export), which was not like an American office. Picture a tiled floor, the inevitable picture of Kemal Pasha, a rectangular stove, and two huge roll-top desks; behind each one of which was sitting a tall, grey-suited, grey-haired gentleman, each with spectacles and a large paunch. These were the uncles. There was also a small office-boy (referred to as *le petit* – the little one) who periodically threw chips of wood into the stove and then went out for coffee. Ah, the coffee of the East! No resemblance to the wretched stuff of the same name which one has to put up with elsewhere. Here it comes in tiny cups with little brass covers.

I explained my needs: The ship has no kosher kitchen, and I'm very, very tired of sardines. *Le petit* is given directions, we muffle up again (neither of us is dressed for winter) and go out into the streets, which are greasy with mudslick. We trudge through streets and alleys, through the Bazaar of the Horse Jewelers – for here the horses wear their own sort of jewelry; brass tags, studded bridles, blue bead necklaces, plumes – tassels, pompoms of red, yellow, green, and indigo – underneath old and broken greengrown archways, past beautiful old mosques and their attendant water stands (like huge tiled pomegranates spouting faucets; the Moslems always wash before prayer), brushing past whole skinned sheep sitting calmly – all passion spent – on butchers' stalls, dodging carts and donkeys piled one story high with baskets – and suddenly turned up next to a pen of turkeys – this was the kosher poultry market. There were two young *shochtim* there, thoughtfully preparing their knives, and hey-presto, I'd bought a chicken for less than a dollar and one of the two had gotten a woman to cook it.

"Now," saith he, "I will show you the synagogue." It was large, cold and empty. I expressed admiration and murmured something about food. We then went to the only kosher eatery in Izmir – I cannot call it a restaurant; it was too tiny – let us call it a cook-shop. In this tiny room were a large man and a small boy (cook-owner and son-waiter), a window, side-board, and two up-against-the-wall tables. The stock was in the window and the stoves (charcoal) on the side-board. There was also a *mizrach* picture of Moses and Aaron, and a picture of Kemal Pasha.

We dined at once on stew-and-stringbeans, beans-and-rice, crusty bread, and mutton and sausage grilled on skewers. For some moments there was only a soft, slushy sound heard. Presently, three muffled-up characters, rather greasy about the mouth (for we had fed *le petit* as well) followed the shochet out into the streets. To the accompaniment of friendly cries of "shalom" and "baruch habah" we passed through the Bazaar of the Goldsmiths to another place where we had cognac and coffee. Guess what was on the wall? A picture of – you guessed it.

"Now," saith the shochet, "I will take you to another synagogue." This one was small, bare and cold; and it was 1:00 P.M. – time for the *Minchah Gedolah*. With no pause in the psalm-chanting, the congregants provided the second mate with a chair and a charcoal brazier in an adjoining room, "lest" (as they put it, with infinite delicacy) "he should feel cold while the Jews are standing in prayer." After minchah we chatted a while, in Hebrew, French, and Spanish, and I remembered that Izmir had given birth to one of the more outstanding False Messiahs in Jewish history. I had the temerity to ask about him. The tremors of an ancient excitement stirred the old men faintly and they cast swift, sly glances out the corners of their rheumy old eyes. "Yes," they said. Yes, Shabettai... who in all the world (they asked) had not heard of him?... even the place of his dwelling was still remembered; the owner had sold it to a non-Jew and had gone to Israel.... No, there were no followers of that man in Izmir now; in Salonika, in Stambul, yes: but they were grown just like the Turks... The old men grew confidentially boastful and muttered that the family of Attaturk (Kemal Pasha) was said to be in part related to those Jews who had followed the False One into Islam. But it was too cold in the synagogue, and all that had happened too long ago, and the old men sighed and tottered home.

One chap, hearing of my dietary difficulties on the ship, offered me, in French, advice based on his own experience: "I say to the steward, 'I suffer from the stomach. Give me, therefore, not of the meat, but of the milk and vegetables.'" He seemed to think this quite clever. I should have thought it cleverer to tell the truth, but then, I had not grown up in a country which massacred Greeks and Armenians. The Turks never did that to the Jews, but one might pardon the Jews for feeling some desire not to be conspicuous. Only a few years ago the government (later defeated in free elections) levied impossible taxes on the leading businessmen of the kehillah and put them in prison camps when they failed to pay; whence they were released at the time the late American President visited the Near East: "*ah, ce grand Monsieur Roosevelt!*"

"And now," quoth the shochet, "I will take you to another synagogue." The poor second mate was perishing with the cold, but he was game, and muttered something about being the only authority on Izmirian synagogues in the Panamanian merchant-marine. Presently, the guide ran out of synagogues or had to go *shecht* or something, so we rejoined the cousin, who said he would show us the town. This was done in two parts. Part one: we took a bus up the mountain, then we took the same bus down the same mountain. Part two: we got into a taxicab which dashed madly down the street, now on the right side, now on the left, and now in the middle; while the cousin pointed out passing blurs as follows: "This is the house of my cousin Menasheh. Regard the Great Synagogue (the second mate flinched). In that residence dwells my grandmother... here is the military hospital... this is the palace of the Governor of the City..." The taxi spilled us out and we immediately hopped on a two-part trolley car and proceeded to cover the route we had just taken, only more slowly. Comment from the cousin: "This is the palace of the Governor of the City... here is the military hospital... in that residence dwells my grandmother... Regard the Great Synagogue... this is the house of my cousin Menasheh."

One curious thing about Izmir is that the houses seem so near the water. We saw no fences, and the streets run practically into the bay; automobiles drive under the noses of ships tied up at the waterfront. The old, romantic Oriental Turkey is largely gone since the drastic reforms of Kemal Pasha, but we saw few young women in the streets. We are told that the Moslem women are still not accustomed to move around freely in public. The Turks have no particular national characteristics which one can mention and say, The Turks look thus-and-so... and the Jews here look just like the other Turks. It is estimated that more than half the local Jewish population has gone either to Israel or the Americas, North and South. Jewish life here is certainly not what it was under the Sultanate, when the *Chacham Bashi* (Chief Rabbi) was a government official with police powers, and the Turkish army commissioned shochtim so that Jewish soldiers could have kosher meat (a much more sensible idea than commissioning *chaplains* who often as not eat non-kosher food themselves, as we do in the United

States). In particular, religious education is in a rather bad way, even in the school supported by the community. The synagogue classes seem very ill-attended, and in the old Yeshivah I saw, only two students came regularly, young men in their twenties, and they only part time. Still, I do not think we can say that the Turkish Jews face assimilation as we usually think of it. I do not think they fully understand the concept, and I hope they never will.

Introduction to
A SONG OF DEGREES

THIS STORY WAS PUBLISHED IN *Jewish Life* in summer, 1955. It is the last known piece that Avram wrote for that magazine until the 1970s. During the early 1950s, most of his Jewish writing was focused on his sojourns in Israel. This story is set in Jerusalem, and tells of carps in bathtubs, and Sabbath peace that is not always peaceful.

In August 1949, Avram wrote in his journal about the Sabbath in Jerusalem: "On my first Sabbath night in Jerusalem I was so struck to the heart by the vehicular traffic, which scarcely bothered me in Tel Aviv or Haifa, that I went straight from my meal to my room. By my second Sabbath, I had gathered strength to go afield from the main streets and into the Meah Shearim quarter. Words fail me. Time and space lost their meaning. I wandered through dim streets and dusky courts, not knowing my way, not caring. I passed troops of Jews singing Sabbath hymns on their way from synagogue to home. My feet carried me into areas where every house resounded with the melody of Kiddush and *zemirot* and grace, where every window looked in on scenes of classic beauty, where old books and pictures came alive. Were they real, these white-bearded grandfathers blessing children? These grandmothers in snowy kerchiefs? Stalwart tall sons and fathers and sweet-faced children, still daring beards and unashamed of *peot*? In what century was I now…?"

Grania Davidson Davis

A SONG OF DEGREES

IF I MENTION TO MY FRIENDS that such-and-such a thing happened when I was living in Jerusalem, they laugh, and then they ask: Was that when you were staying at the place that had the carp in the bathtub? By this time I have grown rather tired of the story, almost sorry I ever told it; so my smile is brief and weak. Yes, I say, it was at that time. That was the place where I was staying.

It was cheap. It was quaint, for the hotel was in one of the oldest buildings in Meah Shearim, which is the second oldest part of the New City of Jerusalem. Concrete blocks had, I suppose, not been invented when it was built – fortunately – so it was erected of the beautiful tawny stone used locally. There was a shop on the street level, and you entered the hotel from the side, by a flight of stairs which pierced the thick masonry. There was no drawbridge nor portcullis, but neither would have seemed out of place.

At the head of the steps you emerged into open air onto a sort of patio-courtyard effect. To the right was a series of storerooms whose doors would have given serious resistance to any of Mr. DeMille's battering-rams; over them (reached by wooden steps) were several apartments, on the communal veranda of which were such useful implements as three-quarters of a bicycle, a pile of used bricks, some tin tubs with holes rusted in them, a horse-collar, a windmill-vane and a large detached sign (upside-down) whose faded letters read:

St. Petersburg
Famous Tailor From
M. Tomashevsky

The hotel proper was a series of rooms in L-shaped sequence. The fourth side of the square had a parapet which looked over the neighboring backyards. In the square was a chicken-coop, a dovecote (both provided with live-stock), a lavatory and a shed containing a bathtub. In the bathtub was a large carp, swimming slowly back and forth.

"Live fish are scarce," said my host, in answer to my questioning look. "You think this is America? Ha! Ha! Ah *fragge!*" His grey beard, when he sat down, reached the table. "So we save them for *yom-tov*. Next yom-tov, if The Name wills, you'll have with us a pretty piece of sweet-

and-sour fish."

The next yom-tov was a month off; I might do without fresh fish, but I didn't feel I could do without a bath all that time. I asked if there was another bathtub in the hotel. "Ha! Ha! *Ah fragge!*" chuckled Mr. Karapapakh. He rose and beckoned. The belt at the back of his snuff-brown *kapotte* hung, swinging buttonless. I followed. There was, indeed, a second bathtub. In the bathtub, though, was a large carp swimming slowly back and forth.

"Live fish must be *very* scarce," I said. Mr. Karapapakh demanded to know if I thought this was America. "Ha! Ha," I said, "*Ah fragge!*" Quaint. Also, cheap. Also, clean. (For those not desiring to share a bathtub with a carp there was always the public *ambatya* a few blocks away.) My room – that is, one of the four beds in it was mine – was large and airy. The plastered walls were tinted a cool blue in the Arab fashion and on the one near my bed was a calendar picture of a light-heavyweight Turkish lady whose veil had slipped its moorings, revealing a *fin-de-siecle* leer which might conceivably have been very exciting to the *hepcats* at the Court of Abdul Hamid.

I had no money to speak of; Sabbaths I fed upon the bounty of the most generous of friends; weekdays I ate – when I was on duty, at the hospital where I was employed – when not on duty, in a tiny restaurant on Rechov Meah Shearim: *The Street of the Hundred Gates*, and was glad to have the bread and margarine and sardines the menu afforded. (Once, on a day when I was affluent and asked if there was anything else to eat, the proprietress called me *feinshmecker*.)

Just to be in Jerusalem was paradise *now* – "pray for the peace of Jerusalem" – and it was very peaceful there at that time. It was like lying or floating at ease in a sun-warmed pool. Days, I walked the tree-lined streets and breathed the clear, sweet air. Nights, particularly Sabbath nights, I wandered through the maze of courts and yards and lanes of Meah Shearim, lost in the intoxication of a life I never before knew still existed. I gazed, unashamed, in windows where every family group was like a Szyck painting come to life, where time stood still and might still have been the time of Luria, Alkabetz or Azulai – scenes in which no modern note intruded, where candle-light or oil lamps illuminated antique synagogues or Sabbath tables where bearded patriarchs in robes sat with kerchiefed wives and children who had the faces of angels (if angels wore *peyoth*).

I listened in joy to the songs sung everywhere to the Sovereign Lady, Queen Sabbath. The same songs woke me the next day and I went to my window to watch the groups of people singing on their way to the synagogue; people in fur hats, in velvet hats trimmed with fur, people in knee breeches and white hose and low pumps, People in colored robes – blue or gold or rose or green – and long striped waistcoats, people carrying *tallithoth* in velvet bags, or wearing them across their shoulders. I listened. I followed. I sought the peace of Jerusalem.

Not all who dwelt in Jerusalem sought or prayed for that peace.

In Haifa or Tel Aviv one learned to tolerate the traffic of automobiles in the streets. In Jerusalem it was much, much rarer to see a car profaning the Sabbath – and thus much more noticeable, more painful. There were the automobiles of the *Corps Diplomatique*, representatives of all those foreign nations which did not lift a single finger to help Jerusalem in her hour of agony. There were government vehicles, military and civil, bound on such errands of necessity and emergency as picnics, dove-shoots or shopping expeditions to the Arab town of Abu Gosh. They were brave, these drivers: if someone shouted, "Shabbos!" (or "Shabbat!") at them, they cried – with scorn and contempt – "Nu, 'Shabbos!' Mah, 'Shabbos'?" and sped on their way.

There were tourists, some of whom visited the Russian or Ethiopian cathedrals, where they courteously removed their hats. Later, returning through the Jewish streets, they lit their cigarettes and pretended – what fun! – to snap pictures of the picturesque old-style Jews, who hid their faces or sometimes – ha! ha! – scurried away. Sometimes they did *not* hide or retreat, sometimes there were angry words, blows were struck from both sides, stones flew in either direction. Next day the newspapers carried stories of the dispersal or arrest of "religious zealots." Irreligious zealotry was, apparently, not illegal.

Such incidents made me very low in spirits. One Sabbath, sad at heart, I wandered through the streets and met a friend, whose invitation to walk with him to the Tomb of King David I accepted at once. It seems that half of Jerusalem had gotten the same idea. For six hundred years no Jew had been allowed to enter the tomb-site. *Y'feh nof, m'sos kol haoretz, har tzion* – "Beautiful in elevation, the joy of the whole earth, is Mount Zion"; and even after that tiny corner of Mt. Zion passed into Jewish hands, general entrance had been forbidden "for security reasons." Now it was open to all.

We went along King George Street ("Rechov Ha-Melech *King*-George," it was locally and redundantly called); we went past the circular Yeshurun Synagogue and the Jewish Agency buildings, past Terra Sancta College, a huge gilded statue on its apex, where some of the Hebrew University classes were then meeting, past Beth Meir, the Mizrachi headquarters. We were part of a stream of people... an old stone windmill and then another one, the last in a field entangled in barbed wire – No-Man's Land – then a deep descent, a deep fold in the earth's surface. A thought: Was this perhaps either the Vale of Jehoshephat ("The Lord Judgeth" – among the Judged doth He judge, too) or GeyHinnom – the Valley of the Sons of Hinnom – anciently, a place of burning – which name, Gehinnom, Gehenna, is given to the condition of the souls condemned. Some cite Ezekiel: *Where their worm dieth not, and their fire is not quenched;* others say, it means *to be cut off, as the beasts are cut off...* Then down, into the sun-baked gauntness, and up... up... a steep hill, a line of people filing like ants, old men and women being assisted to ascend Mt. Zion, the joy of all the earth, the Navel of the World.

Those cigarettes which had remained so far were now thrown away, as we approached the entrance where young soldiers were on guard, with an eye on the walls of the Old City nearby – the walls so close we could see heads peering over at us. Inside we went with the throng, through a series of cave-like rooms, dark and disordered, containing as yet nothing much but scraps and rubbish... We passed through a room with a court or large airshaft off to one side, with a well... into a chamber roughly fixed up as a synagogue. Here there was a wait, a press of people, silent, or murmuring quietly. Finally we were inside a small room, with tiles fitted halfway up the walls, a rather slip-shod and decadent-looking Arabic design, but who had eyes for it?

Over the tomb-site was a large wooden structure, and over this was a cloth cover. The *Frenks* and the *Temanese* were kissing it, pressing their faces to it, murmuring, weeping, whispering... Back in the synagogue once more, we began to read psalms from the *Siddur*, the Songs of Degrees (or Ascents), the Pilgrimage Psalms... lights were flickering in glasses and oil-lamps... Suddenly, powerfully, for the first time in my life, I had the awareness of being in a *Holy Place*... It made no difference that some people said that David was not really buried there: If it was not his tomb, it was his cenotaph... The deep and pure feelings, the prayers, emotions, sacrifices, of all those here now, had hallowed and sanctified the place. It seemed *right*, very right, that we should be reading the psalms David wrote about Jerusalem *in* Jerusalem, "city where David encamped"; his love-letters to Jerusalem, loved by all the Jews, loved so much, so long, reading them in Jerusalem, at the site dedicated to King David, to David the King, to the earthly David, the psalms of love and joy and praise dedicated *by* the earthly David, Elchanan, to the Heavenly David, Ruler and Creator and Savior,

Ancient of Days...

...And when, after a while, someone asked – no words: a look, a gesture, a thought, from heart to heart a prayer – for the Siddur, and I passed it over... it seemed that I could not endure not to be saying the psalms, the *tehillim*, praises; and I pressed close to the man, a dark Sephardi man with a stubble of beard, and the man made a brief glance, and with a smile of pure love he offered to share the book, and we each held it with a hand and we read the psalms together... people, place, praise, verse, reader, writer, G-d, for once, at last, together, joined, united, one. As it is said, by *gematriya*, *echod* equals *ahavah*...

But then it was over, we were out in the World of Illusion once more, away from the World of Reality. In silence we returned to take up our lives once more in the world of barbed wire and tourists and jeeps and carps which lived in bathtubs.

Introduction to
THE VARIOUS JEWS OF ISRAEL OR SIX SKETCHES OF ISRAEL

THIS STORY WAS PUBLISHED IN *Commentary* in December, 1950, under the editors' title *The Various Jews of Israel.* On the copy we located, Avram had written, "Not my title!" So I changed the title to *Six Sketches of Israel.* That's not Avram's title either, but maybe it's closer to his original. Who knows? It is a glimpse at Israeli life of that era, in the afternoon hours from twelve to three.

In a letter to his mother dated January, 5709, Avram wrote, "I am, thank G-d, quite well and happy over here. I think you would like it very much. It is something like Florida and something like California and even a little like Paris. The weather lately has been very fine along the coast (from Tel Aviv to Haifa) and everything is bright. The streets are clean, the trees are being trimmed, even the donkeys trot with animation – for donkeys, that is. The sea is blue, the skies are clear, everyone is in good spirits and confident of the future…"

So let's see what life was like (by whatever title) from twelve to three in the Israeli afternoon.

Grania Davidson Davis

THE VARIOUS JEWS
OF ISRAEL

OR

SIX SKETCHES
OF ISRAEL

The Lads from Casablanca

TWELVE NOON TO 3 PM IN ISRAEL... the government offices which opened at nine, and which will close at five (with a half hour from ten to ten-thirty and another one from four to four-thirty for tea and *ugot*) for the day, are now practically abandoned for the three-hour lunch. If lunch were cut down to an hour, or even an hour and a half, these offices could operate on a five-day week. But suggest it. Just try. You will get a ferocious eye-rolling, brow-lifting, shoulder-shrugging cry of, "But we are a Young Country! Our economy cannot stand a five-day week!"

Twelve to three... at this time, all over the country, a multitude of governmental, institutional, political, and other varieties of officials, are entertaining foreign visitors for lunch, and telling them identical stories. Every official remembers when everything between Jaffa and the Gymnasium was sand... when everything between the Gymnasium and the Yarkon was sand... when everything between the Gymnasium and the sea was sand... "Sand! Sand!" they cry, waving their arms, and looking like people who remember when Wall Street was considered uptown... one gets the impression that the Gymnasium stood stark and aloof in the midst of the dunes, like the statue of Ozymandias, and that it was attended only by Bedouins. And not only that. Each official remembers the Old Days, when "we made five piasters a day. Five piasters! And we saved three!" But progress has been made. For the same work, laborers now get 140 piasters, and can't save anything. And who has done this? Who has put all these buildings up between the Gymnasium and Jaffa (or the Sea – or the Yarkon)? Here fill in the name of the Fund, Office, or Party the official represents.

Twelve to three... a few months ago the army in one sector went unpaid because the payroll was stolen. The money was in a safe, under guard, but from twelve to three, the guards went to lunch, and someone stole the payroll... from twelve to three cows cannot calve, the Arabs cannot attack, Messiah cannot come... in short, the crime was not so much that the pay was stolen as that it was stolen between twelve and three.

Twelve to three... everything is quiet and peaceful on Ha-Yarkon Street... quiet in the Machal club, quiet in the Gachal club... in each one, the servicemen and ex-servicemen are drinking *gazos* and reading their mail.... The difference between the two clubs is one of more than distance. *Machal* means, *Mitnadvei Chutz L'Aretz* – Volunteers from Abroad. *Gachal*, in turn, means, *Gius Chutz L'Aretz* – Mobilization from Abroad. Of course, Israel has no authority to mobilize anyone abroad, so both groups are really volunteers. *Nu, az ma yesh?* The rock-bottom difference is that the *Machalniks* came from countries where things are not bad, where one would not mind returning, if one had to. Great Britain, America (North and South), South Africa, France, Switzerland, Benelux, Scandinavia – these are Machal countries. Central and Eastern Europe, the Near East, and most of North Africa – these are Gachal. There are exceptions. Australians and New Zealanders are neither the one nor the other. Algerians, being citizens of Metropolitan France, are Machal.

These differences aside, there are yet differences among the various Gachal groups. The *Poilisher Yidden* are seldom seen in the Gachal club. Either they have relatives to visit, or *landsleit*, or jobs, or connections with the ruling parties, or *something*. The Iraqi Jews are off somewhere else, too, quietly going about their tasks. The Yemenites have not yet adjusted themselves to sitting on chairs – in a club, or elsewhere. Who, then, is to be found in the Gachal club? Moroccans.

I had first made their acquaintance in the transit camp in France, the kind of place the British would call "a beastly hole," where I grew to like them for their good spirits in adversity (most of them had left Morocco by plane, in the night, with no baggage to speak of), their willingness to work – a willingness not shared in very large part by the European DP's – and for their amiability and simplicity. In Israel I found a different picture. There the Moroccan was pictured as a sort of wild man, a knife-flourishing Goum. The President of the state had reproved them for (he said) wanting to open little shops. The Histadrut resented their unwillingness to be collectivized. The Orthodox at this time largely ignored them because they studied *Zohar* instead of *Gemara*, and ate rice during Passover. Neither did they fit into the European middle-class pattern of the General Zionists and Progressives.

So the young Moroccans drank lemon gazos in the Gachal club and scrawled, *Vive Menahem Beigin-a bas Ben Gourion* on the walls of the lavatory. But from twelve to three they didn't even scrawl. Just sat and drank and smoked, and languidly offered to buy or sell their own or one another's shirts, and talked about the bad old times in the Mellah ghetto of Casablanca.

Between the hours of twelve and three one afternoon, a very unorthodox proceeding took place. Two carloads of military police drew up in front of the Gachal club, and the MP's secured the doors and began to screen the men inside for deserters. They found no deserters, but at last they did find an American without an identity booklet. He was an American, one of the Machal, and the MP spoke to him civilly.

"Why haven't you an identity booklet?"

"Because I don't want one."

"Why don't you want one?"

"Because," said the American, "I'm an American, and if I don't want an identity booklet, I don't have to want one!"

The MP glanced nervously at his associates, but they had no advice to offer. He then asked for a passport; it was shown him, and he professed himself satisfied, and went on to the next table, where he found a Moroccan with no papers at all.

"Stand over there," the MP ordered. The man remained seated, the MP jerked him to his feet; he threw himself upon the MP, the other MP's threw themselves upon him, and he was dragged to the street, followed by everyone in the club. In the street he continued to struggle, and struck one of the MP's. One of them gave him a blow to the jaw which knocked him out completely, and the military tried to make a quick getaway. In his haste and confusion the driver started the car before the unconscious man was completely in it, and his head dragged along the ground for a few feet. When his comrades saw this, they gave a shout of anger, and encompassed the policemen. Someone picked up the man, threw him over his shoulder, and ran away with him. Just like that. The police, utterly disorganized, ran about in little circles, but did not follow.

The Moroccans then began to chant, "Ge-sta-*po*! Ge-sta-*po*!" and one of them attempted to put his fist through the window of the police car. It cracked but did not break; the policemen swooped towards him, but he disdainfully climbed into the car himself, and lit a cigarette.

Meanwhile, another American was taking pictures, and one of the

MP's gestured towards him to the other MP's, with the face of one about to break into tears. They started towards the photographer on the run, but he regarded their coming with such calmness that they slowed to a walk, and civilly asked him to come along, which he did. The cars then drove away through the crowd, which parted for them, with jeers and boos.

While the Gachal men gathered and talked together in excited French, the Machal men compared accounts of the techniques of the military police of all their respective ex-outfits, with additional comments as to how these things were better handled in South Boston, the Gorbals, or Spadina Street, Toronto. An Old Resident with white hair and a seamed brown face listened to everyone. Then he gave his opinion in slow, careful tones.

"Bismarck said, 'There is nothing in the world heavier than the hand of a British policeman.' *Shoter angli*. Let us be glad our *shotrim* are not too good at these things."

At this point, to everyone's astonishment, the crowd suddenly burst into the *Marseillaise*, and marched away to the French consulate down the street, to the representative of a nation which did not even regard them as citizens. Nobody followed. It lacked half an hour of three o'clock and, after all, from twelve to three it is lunchtime in Israel.

The Surgeon

"I'm sending you a new assistant," the doctor said. "He's taken the first-aid course and you can teach him the pills."

"All right," I said. By "the pills" I knew the doctor meant such *materia medica* as the ship's sick bay included and such knowledge of dispensing it as I possessed. We were well stocked on battle-dressings and my cabinet contained at least six separate kinds of rectal suppositories, but I could never obtain enough antiseptic to last the month out. Currently the ship had no medical officer, and I was thankful we were in port.

The new man was quiet, clean, and intelligent. He listened with respectful attention to everything I told him. I was rather jarred when he said that he had been in the Palmach, the Israeli commandos, had been wounded, and was now in the medical service because the duties were less onerous; it was disconcerting to know that the medical service was looked on as a sort of rest cure, but I said nothing. His name was Shmuel and he was a Polish orphan. I asked him how old he was, and he said he was nineteen. His bearing was open and dignified and he spoke soft, drawling Yiddish.

Among the several *moadonim*, or service clubs, in Haifa, there was one that served as a sort of gathering place for the "Anglo-Saxons," as the men from the English-speaking countries were called. I found it not a little amusing, having been a Semite in the Diaspora, to have to come to Israel in order to be called an Anglo-Saxon. Several times I met at the club an English boy whom I knew slightly, and he always took it upon himself to attach himself to me. I don't think I am being unjust when I say that he was not particularly bright. His mates had soon found this out, and made a habit of telling him the most fearsome stories, which he always repeated to me, adding – invariably – "But I don't believe that, do you?" It was always clear that he did believe it.

"Do you see that fellow?" he asked one night, and it was Shmuel he pointed to. "He said he's a medic, and I asked him what experience he had, and do you know what he told me? He said that in the war they were hiding from the Germans in the woods, you know, in the winter. And there was one fellow whose toes on one foot were frozen and they began to rot. So this chap said he took a pocketknife and cut the fellow's toes off, and the fellow was afraid to cry out because of the Germans. Cut them right off with a pocketknife, he said; but I don't believe it, do you?"

That night Shmuel and I got back to the ship almost together, and I got into my "berth" first. He combed his curly black hair and took off his clothes, folding them neatly, while we chatted of this and that. Then he climbed into bed, and I saw, as he rested his left foot for a second on my bed, that the foot had no toes.

Albert and the Louisiana Purchase

At three o'clock in the afternoon a kibbutz is very quiet. Everyone has long since finished dinner and tea is more than an hour away. The older children are in class and the younger ones are taking naps. The men are almost all in the field or workshops. A visitor at this time has the place to himself, and, if no one appears to give him a conducted tour (as is usual in books and magazine articles), at least no one comes out to bother him or prevent his going where he wishes. Now and then the donkey cart rattles slowly by, or the mule wagon comes ponderously up the slope from the fields, with *Nimrod* and *Chazak* curling their lips at one another, and taking vicious snaps of air with their large yellow teeth. Baruch, the teen-age driver, smooth-faced, in short pants and high boots, sits on the crates of new-dug vegetables. Whenever he thinks discipline is in order, he tugs the reins and shouts, "Hoiss-'Ah!"

This time is a good time to talk to Albert, and Albert is a good man to talk to. About seventy years ago his grandparents moved from Algeria to Southern France. His parents, in turn, went to Turkey, but returned to Marseilles when Albert was a boy. He speaks Spanish and Turkish as well as French and Hebrew, but no English. Nevertheless, he is well informed about American history; his sources are the popular French press and French moving pictures. Over his buckets and brushes (he is the kibbutz painter), he has told me more than one fascinating item.

During the Occupation, Albert found it expedient to leave Marseilles. He does not resemble the popular Nazi caricature of a Jew; he has a pair of very blue eyes, a light complexion, and a nose that turns up just a bit at the end. But he had the handicap of having a *carte d'identite* which not only showed his last name to be Levi, but also had stamped on it in large, red letters the word *Juif*. This last piece of forethought on the part of Petain's Secretary of State for Jewish Affairs helped many thousands of French Jews along the road to Auschwitz. Albert was luckier; he got away in time and hid in various odd corners of Provence, aided by hundreds of Frenchmen (and Frenchwomen). All this while he had nothing to read, of course, but the fascist-controlled newspapers, and he is a man who believes what he reads. He is convinced, for example, that the late President Roosevelt was a Jew.

"But it's true," he assured me, surprised that I was not as proud of it as he was. "Isn't his son named 'Elliot,' same as the Prophet?" I tried to explain the difference between *Elliot* (with a silent "t") and *Elias* (with a silent "s"), but Albert was not convinced. Surely I would at least admit M. Truman to be of the chosen seed? No? But had I not seen the photograph of President Weizmann giving President Truman a Sefer Torah? And could I imagine that M. Weizmann would give the Holy Scroll to a Gentile, who might not even know how to care for it properly? No – incredible. One day he asked me if I had ever been in *La Nouvelle Orleans*. Had I seen the house of Jean Lafitte?

"*Ah, il etait un brave type, Jean Lafitte*," Albert said admiringly. "But for him, Louisiana would not be part of the United States.... What, they did not teach you that at school? My poor fellow! Everyone in France knows it. *A cause de Josephine*," he explained.

The Empress Josephine, it must be understood, was not a woman cheap to maintain. The clothes, yes? The jewels, yes? These things ran into money. Even the Emperor of the French had to call her attention to the bills. *Alors*, Josephine had an idea of great brilliance. She went to an American official then in Paris – "Not Benjamin Franklin?" I asked fearfully – But no, M. Franklin was then a very old man; it was not likely he would leave his Philadelphia farm to visit Paris. No, no, the American was a M. Jefferson – one has heard of him?

Well, Josephine simply proposed that M. Jefferson should arrange for the United States to buy Louisiana. The American was dubious, but she convinced him. She knew how to make herself agreeable, that one, is it not so? There was, however, one great obstacle: the General Washington. He was no longer a young man, he was stubborn, he did not wish to buy Louisiana. What to do? Regard at this point the importance of Jean Lafitte; a brigand, it is true, but he wished to become *serieux*. He journeyed to see the General personally, he made him generous gifts – *tiens*! The affair arranges itself! Louisiana became American. Of course, there was the matter of the duel between Lafitte and the General Jackson, but happily honor was satisfied without bloodshed: M. Lafitte fired into the air, and Jackson did the same; then they embraced. *Naturellement* M. Jefferson had to leave Paris, the jealousy of Napoleon being well known.

And when, in the face of such evidence, I remained doubtful, Albert offered me the final argument:

"But, my friend, I read it in a *journal*!"

Naturellement!

A Garden Shut Up

The Bukharan quarter of Jerusalem is in the New City – new by Asiatic standards, that is. Not all the people are from Bukhara; there are Jews from Tashkent, Meshed, Kabul, and Teheran, besides the more prosaic run of Oriental Sephardim in general. The younger people are mostly all *sabras* and so disdain to wear the picturesque garments of their fathers and grandfathers.

The Frenk, in long robe and cloth-wrapped fez, is a person of dignity, worthy by his manners to be the heir to that Isaac of Baghdad whom Harun-al-Rashid sent as ambassador to Charlemagne. One can picture Isaac coming home, rather weary, to tell his Rebecca... What! All the way to France? Heavens!... and of course, Rebecca demands to know what presents Parthia is sending Rome, so Isaac mentions the bales of carpets – soft as down – for the rush-strewn stone floors of the drafty northern palaces, the jewel-studded golden plattery, the crystal flasks of balsam and attar, the Damascene swords, "and of course," he adds, in what he hopes is a matter-of-fact tone, "and, of course, the elephant." Shrieks and wails from Rebecca. How will he ever get an elephant to France? Suppose it should die? Suppose – "Never mind, never mind," says Isaac, resignedly. "We are in *galut*; it cannot be helped."

But the young Frenk will not wear the old style of dress; he lounges about in a battered felt hat and a suit of torn khakis, wears – instead of slippers – shoes, but not socks; feels disoriented and discontented, and fancies slights where none are intended.

Bukharim – as it is called – is not much different from the Machneh Yehudah or Meah Shearim quarters. There are the same one – and two – story buildings of tawny stone, the same open-fronted little shops, the same herring barrels, spice canisters, and sweets stalls. And, buzzing over everything, the same flies.

There passes a young woman – a girl, rather – tall, slender, in a long dress. Golden wheels dazzle in her ear-lobes and her black hair hangs in two long braids behind, and, wonder of wonders, she balances a water jar on her head. I turn my head just in time to see that she turns hers – but in a flash she turns it again, and slips into a doorway.

The doorway is below street level and over it is a sign announcing a Bukharan synagogue within. Bukhara! My heart leaps. Caravan city on the route to Samarkand and China! City of amirs, caravansaries, and stone synagogues of incredible antiquity! I turn aside and enter, stopping by the door until my eyes accustom themselves to the dim light. The floor of the synagogue is covered with rugs of all colors, overlapping one another, and brightly upholstered divans are along the walls. The walls themselves are tinted with a blue wash. There are no chairs. Here and there is a Cabalistic diagram in a frame, and oil lamps, no two alike, hang from the ceiling. Open on a table is a volume of *The Mighty Hand* of Maimonides.

"*Ken, adoni*" A man has come in by a side door and, before I have time to answer, he strides over and gives me his hand. "*Vus macht a yid?*" he booms. "*Fin vanen kimt ihr?*" The caravan city vanishes in a flood of Yiddish.... The Bukharans, it seems, having other synagogues, have rented this one to a congregation of dispossessed Hasidim.

And the maiden with the water jar? Oh, yes. She was married.

The Socialist

The Polish *motor-ship* (New York, Cannes, Genoa, and Naples) was not a luxury liner; its passenger classes were First, Cabin, and Tourist, and the Tourist cabins contained berths for ten people. Most of the passengers were Italian-born, returning to visit their families in Italy. Some of them had been waiting and saving a long time. There was an old woman with a goitrous neck and no teeth, who always wore black and sat the whole day on a bench below-decks. To anyone who cared to look, she showed a manila envelope stuffed with documents and family snapshots. In America for thirty years, she knew no English, and when I asked one of the Italian passengers where she was going, he said that he couldn't understand her.

"She speaks a dialect," he said.

The weather was fine as far as Gibraltar, and when, a few nights out, there was a concert given in the Tourist salon, it was well attended. The ship's band played, several of the passengers sang, and a young man from New York City gave us several Palestinian songs. His instrument was a long wooden flute, called a recorder, and he played quite well. The audience applauded politely and I went over to speak to him. Our acquaintance became rather close and it did not end with the voyage, but continued in France and in Israel. His name was Ben Jacobs and he was a practicing socialist.

I don't like people who assail me with their opinions. It makes no difference to me if these *nudniks* happen to be atheists who ask, "But how can you believe that nonsense?" or if they are of some sect of hairy saints who demand to know why I trim my beard "like a *goy*." Jacobs was never like that. He answered all questions put to him, and gave a very good defense of his beliefs if they were attacked, but he preferred to talk about music. He was going out to one of the very left-wing kibbutzim and he had brought eighty albums of phonograph records and a record player with him. They included "everything from Brahms to Bartok," he said, with such performers as Burl Ives and Wanda Landowska. He was very fond of music; he called it "half my life."

This was Jacobs' second trip to Israel; the first time he had gone, it was still Palestine and the British had put him in Acre Jail for illegal entry. They had had a short tussle in which he had lost two teeth; later, he was deported.

The political party with which he and his kibbutz were affiliated had the merit of sincerity: they practiced an intense form of socialism themselves instead of just urging it on others. Not only did they have a common purse, they even owned their clothes in common, and no one was allowed to wear any clothes except those bought by the kibbutz through the purchasing cooperative.

"In order to prevent exploitation," Jacobs explained, "you've got to prevent selfishness. As long as one man has nicer clothes than another, you've got pride on his part and resentment on the part of the other – class hatred in miniature. We don't want that. I spent two months at K'far Ananot the last time I was over there. It was wonderful, living in a society without exploitation, without selfishness. The *chevra* is just like a larger family. I can't wait to get back. I can just see the place now." He smiled fondly as he thought of his Land of Heart's Desire, and I could see the two gaps in his teeth. He had had to fight and to wait in order to achieve his goal, but it had all been worth it.

He brushed a long lock of brown hair off his smooth forehead and took out his recorder and began to play a shepherd's song.

He was in the kibbutz less than a week when he returned from work one night to find that the record player and records had been moved to the communal culture room and the kibbutz rubber stamp placed on each album. He left the next day with all his things.

A Small Queen

In Jaffa, just a block or two from the corner of King George Street and the Tel Aviv-Jaffa Road, is a large concrete building called the Bet Chen. Literally, Bet Chen means *House of Grace*, but *Chen* is also a word like Wren or Wave; it stands for *choyl nashim*, the women soldiers of Israel. The building is typical Tel Aviv-Jaffa architecture. It is concrete, shabby, and ugly, but it cost the *Z'va Haganah Le-Yisrael* dear before the Arabs were dislodged.

By day and night there burns in the tiny lobby (the door is cut off from light by a tall wartime battlement) a small, naked electric light bulb. Sitting under it at a table is a gray-haired woman with a jaw that could bite the heads off rattlesnakes. She knits away the hours and if so much as the shadow of a man falls on the pitted floor – "*Ken, adoni*" – her voice falls like a portcullis between the adon and the staircase. Bronzed, bearded Palmachniks, *up from the Negev*, pause uncertainly and stroke a wing of a mustache to restore self-confidence before they inquire for *geveret* Sarah, or Zippora, or Zahava. The knitting dragon says one word – "*Tekif*" – (right away) and one waits. She has no telephone, she sends no messages, but presently, down comes the *geveret*, greets the *adon*, and says good night to the watchwoman. The latter is an old pioneeress – one might have known as much – veteran of many battles, ambuscades, and night attacks; and is known to the awe-stricken Arabs as *the Mother of Ifrits*. An ifrit, I believe, is even fiercer than a *djinn*.

In this unlikely place lived a queen. Her name was Malka. Malka means *queen*. The word *petite* has a special connotation in English that it does not have in French, so let me say that Malka was petite. She was an ex-Chen and she wore her unruly black hair trimmed short. I do not know how old she was; she could not have been very old, but she had been in Haganah before it became the Army of the State, before there was a state, and she had had her share of death and fighting.

It was fashionable at one time to laugh at the Chens' appearance, to say that they never combed their hair, that their uniforms were surplus from the Chinese Eighth Route Army, and that they had better mustaches than the Palmach had. There were (and are) some determined viragoes who thought it as reprehensible for a woman to be feminine as for a man to be effeminate; just as there were others who got lipstick all over the rifle stocks. Malka never wore lipstick or rouge, but there was no face more glowing in Israel than hers.

She spoke English effectively but not perfectly, and when she felt herself short of words, or was excited, she broke into French, and then, what animation! She received letters from France and Belgium and often spoke of having lived in Switzerland, so I was surprised when she told me that she had been born in Frankfort on the Main. She emphasized, proudly, that her parents were Polish Jews, and that she was never legally German, and felt no regrets. I was glad. The German Jews make solid and substantial citizens; their daughters, it is true, tend to be rather solid and substantial too, but there are no better housewives. However, they can never forget past glories, they all come from excellent families the like of which are nowhere else, and one is not allowed to forget it.

So, before the debacle, Malka and her mother and sister got to Switzerland, and later to France and Belgium. Almost half her life had been spent among French-speaking peoples, and it was in that language she felt most at home. She had had an excellent French education, too, for part of the war years she spent concealed in a French convent.

"The sisters were so kind to us, so sweet." Malka made this point again and again. "How loving they were to us Jewish children. '*Mes enfants*,' they would say, 'how terrible that you should suffer. But here you are safe. No one can hurt you here.' And a young priest came to teach us, and he brought us little gifts. Such a kind, handsome young priest! We idolized him, we looked on him and listened like to a – how should I say? – to a God. We held on to his hands and sat in his lap, and he would talk to us. To tell us what? That why we suffered, all the Jews, why? Only because we were so stubborn and not accept Jesus. And he told us verses from the Bible, and from here, and from there. Who could answer him? What did we know, we children?

"So the girls began at last to ask one another, 'Perhaps it is so, as he says. Perhaps it is true.' We heard only the priest and the sisters; our parents were dead, or we didn't know where; and it is so easy to forget. I used to cry to myself at night. I knew I am a Jew, I must remain a Jew. Before also, in the old days, Jews suffered, and then it was easy to escape by becoming a Christian. But then there were great men, wise, who knew more than we about it, and they said, 'Rather to suffer and to keep our religion.' But I am only a child myself – how can I teach other children?

"But I always tried to remember my prayers as my father taught me. My poor father! Every morning he wanted my brother to say his prayers, and he didn't want to. Such quarrels, and where are they now, my poor brother and father? I don't know. Oh, the sisters, they were so troubled with me. One day I went to my room to say my prayers – my Jewish prayers – and I hung my handkerchief over the crucifix so that I could pretend I was home again. And then the sister came into my room. I was so frightened, and she saw the handkerchief – oh, do not ask!

"So then they sent me to another place, because they knew they could do nothing with me, and I think they were afraid for the other girls. And soon the war was over."

"What happened to the other girls?" I asked, as we walked through the dimly lit streets of Jaffa's Old City.

"Some became Catholics, one girl is a nun now. And some say they do not want to do with any religion." Then, as we came to the section on Ajami Street where the French religious orders have their houses, hospitals, and schools, Malka pointed out to me a building.

"There is where one of the priests is now, who was in that place in France. I come sometimes to see him."

"You come to see him?" I was surprised.

"Oh, yes," said Malka. "He was very kind. And it was not his fault, he was not a wicked man. He wanted only to help me, but I was a bad child – oh, such a bad child – and I would not be helped!" and Malka's happy laughter rang out in the dark street between the convent and the church.

Introduction to

IN ISRAEL'S GREEN PASTURES
FOUR TALES BY A REFLECTIVE SHEPHERD

THESE VIGNETTES WERE PUBLISHED IN *Commentary* in June 1952, with the subtitle, *Four Tales by a Reflective Shepherd.* Avram's grandfather had been a chicken farmer in New Jersey, and Avram hoped to follow his muddy footsteps by practicing agriculture in Israel. Before he journeyed to Israel, Avram studied at Pierce Agricultural College in California, where he became interested in breeding improved varieties of sheep. After he arrived in Israel he wrote in an undated letter to friends, "I am now thinking of a combination dairy farm and ice-cream factory...Of course cows are terribly expensive, and I daresay the machinery must be too, let alone land, buildings, etc..."

The *Commentary* editor quotes Avram in his story notes: "'Believing that cities corrupt and large cities corrupt largely, and that it is not permitted for Jews to live in Galut when they can live in Israel,' he has put his beliefs into practice by emigrating to Israel, where he is engaged in animal husbandry."

On the copy we found, in Avram's own handwriting, we discovered this note: "I changed my mind a lot. AD"

We can all be perhaps relieved that he changed his mind often enough to give up shepherding and devote himself to his writing.

Grania Davidson Davis

IN ISRAEL'S GREEN PASTURES
FOUR TALES BY A REFLECTIVE SHEPHERD

We Had Some Fine Times Then

MAURY NISSIM WAS A SMALL, TRIM, dark-blond fellow whom I knew slightly in France before I went to Israel; knew slightly in Israel the first time I was in Israel, and next heard of again shortly before I left Israel for the second time. He was said to be living in Tel Aviv, and since it was in Tel Aviv that I heard this, I went around to see him. He was staying in a typical Tel Aviv house: two stories high, cement blocks overlaid with peeling plaster, washing strung across the court, shingles advertising *Diplomated* teachers of all languages, and every bit of electrical and plumbing installations visible on the outside in a variety of pipes and tubes and discolored leaks. My knock was answered by a colored girl in gold jewelry and an advanced stage of pregnancy, we spoke in Hebrew and she asked me to come in, then called out to Maury in French that he had visitors.

He came in from an adjoining room wearing only trousers and undershirt, but my quickly formed opinion about the nature of the menage was wrong: the young lady was the wife of a friend.

"Well, for Christ's sake! Come on in!" he said. "Jesus, what a surprise." Maury speaks a very fluent brand of American English, learned chiefly from expatriates in Paris. He also has a first-rate command of French, German, Hebrew, Ladino, and Bulgarian. He brushed some soiled linen and a roll of film off the sagging couch, and invited me to be seated. The young person said goodbye, Maury patted her paternally on the belly and on the behind, kissed her cheeks, and closed the door behind her. Then he repeated his opening remarks. Then he asked what I was doing.

"Getting ready to go back."

"You too? So am I."

"To Bulgaria?"

"You think I'm *nuts*? Naa. To France. To civilization."

"Cecil Ginzburg said you were in a fishing co-op."

"Cecil Ginzburg is full of it. A fine fellow, but full of it. I *was* in a fishing cooperative, yes. No more. I mean, no more cooperative. I couldn't care less. But still, we had some fine times while it lasted. If I had an English accent like Cecil's, I might have gotten a government job, too; but I figured, what the hell. Build up the country. Supply food. Rugged outdoor life, all the rest of it. So I joined this co-op. Y' wanna hear about it?" He got up and rummaged around until he found a pack of cigarettes. We lit up. "I can only afford Matossian now," he said.

"*I* can only afford Matossian now."

"Well. You remember Herbert Sam?"

"The Egyptian? Yes."

"That's him. I met him right aftesr I got my *shikrur* from the army. The Israeli army, not the Bulgarian army. And he told me about this co-op. The *Misrad Dayag* – the, how d'ya call it, the Bureau of Fisheries, was going to give us a permit and help us get a loan and so on. And I met the fellows and everything seemed swell. You know where Jubjuba is? On the coast? It's down near the Egyptian line, and there used to be a little Arab settlement there, not even a town, just about seven or eight houses and a well. And nearby a British barracks of some kind. There's a nice beach, too. So we moved in, just waiting till we got everything fixed up, in the meanwhile. We pooled what money we had and bought a dory so we could practice rowing anyway. Hell!" he said, suddenly and explosively. He rubbed his chin.

"It all seemed so important at the time. Now – I couldn't care less. The set-up was like this: Herb and a Turkish fellow we called Izmir, they were the brains, the liaison people with the Misrad Dayag and whoever the hell it was that was making the loan. They used to stay up in Tel Aviv and come in on weekends. So that left me, Hannah, Nate, Freddy, Sue, Amnon, Igor, and Jack. Hannah was living with Nate, Freddy was a Moroccan, Sue was living with Amnon, Igor was a Ph.D., Jack used to be in the Foreign Legion. I guess that takes care of everybody. While we were waiting for the Misrad Dayag to fix things up, what we did for a living was this: The *Agudat Ha-Shomrim*, the Watchmen's League, paid us to guard the pump at the well. The police paid us to guard the old barracks. Somebody paid us to post a lifeguard at the bathing beach, I forget who. People were always coming there on bathing parties. So we had enough money to get by while we were waiting, and we took each a turn on guard duty. And believe me, there was plenty to guard."

"I believe you," I said.

"The Arabs used to come sneaking around every few nights. They knew we had women there. Once they shot the electric light bulb – what am I saying? The kerosene lamp, the chimney, shot in my room, right off the base. Boy, did we ever duck! Except Jack. Jack was mad. He lit a cigarette and he walked outside with his rifle. Slowly. They shot at him, he shot at *them*, they ran. We found blood on the sand next day. They left a boat and a net, so we had more practice. And visitors, did we ever have visitors. From all places. Women used to bring us wine and talk about how romantic. Boy. We had some fine times. But no permit, no loan.

"Then one night we threw a party for Amnon's birthday. He's a sabra, you know how they are, they've never been outside the country and they feel they've got to show that they're just as hep as everybody else. So he brought in lots of liquor and we all got as drunk as owls. And Jack got really drunk, crazy drunk, and he at once got the idea he was back in the Foreign Legion.

"He started to yell, '*A l'attaque! Suivezmoi!*' and we did, first, because we were all drunk, and second because he said he'd shoot the first man he caught skulking. We charged out the door yelling and just our luck! We saw some figures on the road, so we started to shoot. We kept on shooting till our ammunition gave out. And then we forgot all about them and went back into the house and started singing. What did we sing? '*Aupres de ma blonde*,' I think."

"But the people you were shooting at – ?"

"Oh, yes, them. Well. That was embarrassing. They turned out to be a patrol from the Agudat Ha-Shomrim, checking up on our guard. They were real mad," Maury sounded almost puzzled. "Not like anyone was hurt, I mean. Well, they took away our guard job from us. Then the police decided it was cheaper to buy a padlock for the barracks than to pay us to watch it. And then it came on winter and the lifeguard job went away, too. Then Freddy went to Tel Aviv and got a job with some American airline he used to work for in Casablanca, he was in seventh heaven."

"I can imagine," I said. Without meeting him, I felt I knew Freddy. He was one of a long line of Freddies, Dickies, Jackies, from Morocco on up the Mediterranean, who learned English from the U.S. army and can never again be happy with their old way of life. Most of them are doomed. Freddy was lucky. For the female Freddies there is no hope at all.

"And then Hannah and Nate split up. They still live together in the same room, but she says to him, 'Don't think you can touch me any more. That's finished,' she says to him. Then she says, 'Give me five pounds.' 'Give me ten pounds.' And he does. Then he cries. He's crazy, that poor bugger. And Igor left for Australia, and so one, two, three, no more co-op. Only Jack stayed on. He used to go out in one boat with a naked Arab and throw detonation in the water and sell the fish that were killed, but the police stopped him."

"And after it was all over, I suppose you got the permit and – "

"*What*? You nuts or something? Never got a thing. Let me tell you the pay-off of the whole business. It seems the Misrad Dayag is a *Mapam* enclave in our *Mapai* economy. And none of us had the slightest affinity for politics, let alone being good Mapamniks. They never had the slightest intention of helping us at all. One of them told me so later on. Not that it matters now. I couldn't care less."

"So you're going to France?"

"Betcher life."

"When?"

"Pretty soon. I've had enough of the East. I was raised in an Oriental country and now these three years here. Enough. I'm waiting for the war to start, then I'm going into the American army as Bulgarian interpreter. I'm so happy Bulgaria is with the Russians because she is always on the side that loses. Then I will get even with all those sonsa-bitching fascists that turned Communist so quick. Then – well, we'll see. But I'm through with small, Oriental countries."

He rubbed his chin again and looked dreamily out the window.

"Still," he said, "we had some fine times."

Doctor Basileus

"The true homeland of the Jew is the Exile. His people has spent a great deal more time in the Exile than in Israel itself. Can the Jew, then, not be at home in Israel? Yes; for in Israel he is in exile from the Exile itself."

Dr. John Anthony Basileus (Dr. Med., Gen. Practitioner, said the brass plate near the gate – the one now green with *vedrigris* and the other a hazard of rusting iron and falling masonry) put down his pen and closed, without blotting, the ledger which currently served him as commonplace book. He sat for a moment in silence trying to remember something. A soft, bubbling noise in the corner of the room told him what it was, and he got up and took the sterilizer off the *petiliah*, the single-burner asbestos wick kerosene stove. The flame, forgotten, continued to burn – or, rather, smolder, as Dr. Basileus took a small egg from the sterilizer and poured the water into a teapot. In his dietary habits he gave great scandal to the plump, serious Rumanian nurse who assisted him in his clinical work.

"Honestgod, *Doctore*," ran her opening lines, "why you are not eating more?" and her fingers scurrying to thrust in a scrap of escaping hair or fix an undone safety pin or an undone button.

"Eating much is bad for thought: it causes humors to arise to the brain, Sister Goldman."

"It is not so. How you can believe such thing?" She would turn her round, red, serious face at him and scan the thick nose, the spectacles with one opaque lens and the bridge mended with adhesive tape, the straggling gray mustache and irregular teeth.

Or – "Honestgod, *Doctore*, how you can cook food in this sterizer? Where you have put before dirty instruments, diseased thing?"

"If I trust my patients' lives to sterile technique, Sister, I may also trust my own."

He put two lumps of sugar in his tea (tea and sugar alike a gift from the police; probably smuggled; ask no questions John Anthony, but take what the day brings. In the past the day had brought a rich father and a foreign education, a spendthrift brother, an unfaithful wife, a loss of faith, and a calm compassion which passed no judgments and made no demands. Take what the day brings) and cracked the egg against the littered desk. Several times a day Dr. Basileus would buy a cornucopia of peanuts in the village and he always saved the paper, which – always – was a document or form or notice of some kind from "the late Mandatory Government" which the winds had scattered about the same time as they had scattered most of the local Arabs across the Jordan. It pleased Dr. Basileus to read these while he ate, and then to use the backs of them for writing up his records. There was a most pleasing variety. Criminal trial reports, testimony from civil suits, statistical accounts, orders and decrees, whatnot. It pleased Dr. Basileus still more to think that these papers in the distant future might be used to reconstruct the history of the times. He saw himself as a clerical scribe of the past, going every day to the monastic lumber room and idly picking up separate leaves of parchment or papyrus, and then – on the back of a fragment of a rare Latin history or a leaf of a lost apocryphal Gospel, setting down in his cramped and corrupt script the daily accounts of the abbey. To make any systematic attempt at collecting these papers would altogether spoil his pleasure.

At such times he regarded himself from afar as, also, a civilized scholar surviving into the times of the barbarians (although who were the barbarians, the Moslems or the Jews, or both, he was not quite certain). Calm and forbearing, he goes about his daily tasks amid the ruins. He was also capable of regarding from afar this observer himself, and of smiling at him; for this attitude might have been taken at any time during the last eight centuries by any member of the family of Basileus.

His cousin Christopher had sat in this same room the night before he fled with the others. Tears ran down his face.

"We have lost our country," he had sobbed.

"That is not news," Dr. Basileus had said. "We lost our country when the Kingdom of Jerusalem fell to the Turks. We have lost our language, we have lost our culture, some of us have lost our religion as well. It is Antoninus's nonsense that has persuaded you that you are an Arab. 'The Arab Awakening' indeed! They are walking in their sleep.

"Really, I have no patience at all with you, Christopher." But he said it gently. And uselessly.

Dr. Basileus remained in his crumbling house and had never been molested. Instead of treating illiterate Arabs for trachoma he now treated, for the same complaint, illiterate Jews who spoke the same language. As before, he read Dickens in English and Balzac in French, and wrote epigrams in old ledgers. A new pleasure was the collecting of records on scraps of empire. Nashashibi and Husseini, Latin church and Greek and Evangelical, were replaced by Mapai and Mapam, Sephardim, Ashkenazim, Yemenites. The sun scorched in summer and the roof leaked in winter. Take what the day brings, be it quarreling Christians, feuding Moslems, or discontented Jews.... "We wept when we remembered Zion." ...Who weeps now? The Moslems may, but is it not rather late for the descendants of the Crusaders to weep?

"Honestgod, *Doctore!*" Sister Goldman had said; "I cannot to understand why you are staying. Yes, I am content that you stay, but how is it you are not going away with your others?"

"'Go ye not unto the Gentiles,'" Dr. Basileus had quoted; "' – nor unto any city of the Samaritans, but go ye unto the lost sheep of the House of Israel.'" And he had peered at her to see if she recognized the source or the irony of his quoting it. But – "You are good man, but I cannot to understand you."

Doctor Basileus smiled and finished his egg.

Don't Talk About Money

Only as far as Beersheba, said the man sitting next to me in the bus.

In Beersheba I am going to pick up my things and go back to Lydda. If they are there, I mean. I hope they are there. A chappie I know from Eilat promised that he would leave my things off at Beersheba when he came up with the lorry, and he was supposed to come up last week, so they ought to be there by now.

I had great plans for Eilat. It was Solomon's dowry present from Pharaoh, king of Egypt, you know. Even when I was still in Calcutta I used to dream about Eilat, because you see, from the map it is quite obvious that Eilat is the key to the Indian Ocean. I saw there – in my mind only, of course – a great, new city, something like New Delhi, only *ours*, of course; and something like Calcutta. But with no slum quarters. I have studied something of engineering and something of architecture, only I did not take my certificate. My word, my grandfather was angry with me because I did not take my certificate.

Well, then you must come into the business once and for all, he said; and I did not want to go into the business, so I went and spoke to Granny. Granny is Cochinese, you know: not the black Cochinese, but the white. They come from Spain, I think. Anyway, my grandfather is very proud to have married a Cochinese, because his parents were Baghdadee. She said, Silas, do not force the boy to go into the business, he is not a businessman, he is a scholar, he should be a scholar.

He will not learn to be a scholar by gadding about in the Himalayas when he should be studying, my grandfather said.

Then let him go to my family in Cochin, Granny said.

Cochin, my grandfather said. In Cochin they know everything, he said, but not how to make money. I am here for that.

And you must give the boy a decent allowance, Granny said.

My grandfather said, Do not talk about money.

Look, there is Masmiyah, see all the new houses. When I came here there was not a new house. But they were built too hastily, look: already, cracks.... You must move slowly when you build or what you build will not last. In India the ancient ruins are in better condition than the new houses here... Perhaps I will not stay in Lydda, perhaps I will settle in Ascalon and raise fowls. I think I should like that. Best of all, I should like to found an *ashram*, but the people here are not ready for that, they have no interest in things spiritual. Once, in the Himalayas, in an ashram, I asked the yogi why the *Baghavad Gita* begins with a negative; and this is what he said. You must first be negative with the world before you can be positive with the Divine.... Of this I am not sure, but here I see they strive for the opposite, which is surely wrong also. Now my *grandfather* has a more simple philosophy: he says, If you want to be a millionaire, you must act like one. That is just what he did, he set up one of the very first places in Calcutta for motor cars, all his money and the rest borrowed, and he dressed up like a man owns ten jute mills, and in a very short time he was a millionaire. If he would invest his money in Eilat it could be the city I have dreamed of, but he would not like it there, they are some of them working on *Shab-*

bat and they would laugh at him with his spectacles and great white beard....
No, I did not get a place as engineer or architect, but as bookkeeper. I have
studied accountancy as well, but I did not take my certificate. He was very
angry, my grandfather. Never did I see him so angry except when I said I
was going to be married.

Why do you want to be married so young? he asked. You are only
twenty-five. Look at your Uncle Solomon, he is fifty-five and unmarried.

And then when he heard that my wife's mother is a Bene Israel, he
was enraged, for, you know, the Baghdadees look down on the Bene Israel.
They are the oldest community of Indian Jews, but they are very dark, very
poor, and very ignorant; and my grandfather said, You will never marry a
Bene Israel.

Then you will never be mayor of Calcutta, I said. For many years
it has been my grandfather's ambition to be mayor of Calcutta, and he has
promised the Bene Israel community that if they will support him, he will
allow them to be given honors in the Baghdadee synagogues. And if he
makes a scandal against them, he will not become mayor, and he is very
near, he is already a magistrate. So I said, We will go to Israel.

Go, he said. Go anywhere, but go.

It will cost money, I said.

Speak to Granny, my grandfather said. When he is willing to give,
he always says, Speak to Granny. When he is unwilling, he says, Don't
talk about money.

But Eilat, that's not what I expected. I do not see the possibility
there for the city I dreamed of. There is no respect for the things of the
soul, and a city is more than bricks and plaster. So people come there to
make a little money and they go away again because of the bad condi-
tions.... A few months ago my grandfather came to visit us in Lydda. You
are wasting your time, he said, spraying drains for the municipality all day
and reading your books all the night. You should open a big shop and put
in a big stock and the public will have confidence and your business will
increase.... Then I asked him to sustain me in printing my philosophy, and
he said, Do not speak about money. You have a job with Government, it is
healthy, out-of-doors work, your wife is fruitful: be content. Do not talk
about money.

The Lady in the Cup

At three-thirty in the morning, the guard came in to get Rory up.

"Wakey, wakey, rise and shine," he said, tumbling the blankets.
"'Arise, shine, awake, awake; the glory of the Lord is revealed upon thee,'"

he said, bending over the bed. Rory shot up.

"Got it," he said, bent down, poured water over his fingers, and hopped out and into his clothes and shoes while the guard held the flashlight for him. They went out together into the cold and the stars. The settlement was so high up and the hills were so abrupt, that they seemed to be really among the stars and not just under them.

"Had your breakfast?" Rory asked, huddling into his jacket.

"You mean my dinner," the guard said. "No, I'm going now."

"Who's the *shomeret* this morning?"

"It's Sally, thank heaven. Gerda's done."

"Amen to that," Rory said.

Who the *shomeret* was made all the difference in the world. Sally, now, was a pleasure to everyone because everything was a pleasure to her. The children were all darlings and never gave a bit of trouble, the guards were all lovely boys and there was always hot coffee fresh and she made the sandwiches the way you wanted them. Gerda, on the other hand, was hell. She made the coffee when she first came on duty, and then let it get cold; cut the bread before it was needed and let it get stale; made sandwiches any which way – and woe to him that complained!

"You've got a lot of cheek!" she'd spit. "I've got twenty-four babies to care for and worry about," she'd jaw at you. That was it, she was afraid of the babies – afraid they'd smother, take fits, fall out, anything. When she was on duty they always cried, and no wonder, with that face on her, and that heavy hand. Poor kiddies! And the parents! Pity the girl if a mother took it into her head to come have a spy and found her precious crying and the girl away in the kitchen for a cup of coffee or making a bite for the *shomer*.... All the mothers would talk about nothing else for days. Suggest, if you will, that they put *two* females on duty in the nursery, then, instead of one – ah, no, that wouldn't do, either: More work. They would not admit you can't have it both ways; and as for the idea of putting the kids in with their own natural mother – oh, Lord. Heresy. Destroying the foundations of the *kibbutz*.

But this morning everything was fine, just fine. Cheerful, capable Sally had a nice, hot breakfast for the guards and the driver and the shepherds, those whose work had them up so early; and all quiet in the nursery.

"The top of the morning to you," said Sally.

"The top of the morning to *you*."

"Isn't it lovely, the way he talks so Irish?" Sally asked the *shomer*. "It comes from sitting on what's-his-name's tomb. Thomas Fox" (– Wolf Tone – Rory corrected.) "Wolf Tone, I mean." She had to sit down to finish her laugh at the mistake. "Solly Clein is Irish, too, but he didn't ever sit on Wolf Tone's tomb, that's why he talks like the rest of us."

"Now you're making things up," said Rory, happily. "It's true, as children, we did use to sit on Wolf Tone's tomb, poor man – "

"Well, if I am, you just let me. I didn't make that up about the lady in the cup, did I?"

Rory turned to the guard, who was eating eggs. "She's told the girls that there's an old Irish legend, if you look into a teacup long enough you'll see your true-love's face. All I said was, at home we had teacups that had pictures painted on the inside bottom, and the people did say, if you could see the lady in the cup, it was a sign the tea wasn't strong enough."

"Never mind; I like my way better," said Sally.

The sun hadn't come up yet when Rory reached the sheep pen, and only the kerosene lamps hanging in the *dior* gave a faint light to the yard. The pre-dawn silence was broken only by the occasional clatter of hooves on a rock, by the snuffling of the ewes and the grunting of the rams, or by Ezra's or Fred's calling from time to time, "Here's one," and "Take her in." A ram had been selected as "teaser" and a canvas apron fastened loosely on him. He moved freely among the ewes and when he found one in heat, attempted to mount, but was prevented from coupling by the apron. At this point he was seized by the horns and pulled away: his attention once diverted, he instantly forgot the ewe and began searching for another. The ewe, meanwhile, was dragged or pushed unwillingly into the *dior*, where her back was painted for identification. After the search, the ewes in oestrus were bred and given extra rations; the rams were forcibly fed with milk after each mating. At noon the mating was repeated to ensure results, and then the ewes went back into the flock. The whole business took about an hour each time. Rory was sure – quite sure – that no one would make jokes about perversion among shepherds who had ever joined in such a morning's work. Drenched with sweat, the three men struggled to control the animal sensuality which – if controlled – meant better lambs, finer wool, more milk. The darkness, the smells of sweat, suint, and urine, the gurgling and panting of the beasts in the darkness – it was either the epitome of sensuality or its utter denigration.

It was a scene from some inferno; it was not conducive to promoting lust in men.

But it was over at last – at least for the time being – and Rory was able to take the Flock out to *mireh*, down the rocky slopes ("...a good sheepfold should always be on a rocky slope for the sake of drainage," Ezra said), across the road that led up to the kibbutz, along the dusty path through the fields, and over to the hills that made tip the morning pasture.

He jogged back and forth, avoiding – when possible – the dusty side of the column. It was astonishing how long a column one small flock of sheep could make when they were stretched out single file. When in front, he sang; when behind, he whistled, or clapped his hands; when the sheep stalled and were loath to budge, he crooned to them in a low, tremulous tone. And when the poor wittolds scattered in panic, as they did for such slight causes as a lizard's scuttling across them, or a bird's starting up from the grass, he rounded them up and spoke quietly and soothingly.

"Our Shepherd, the Shepherd of Israel..."

(Ezra said, "A good shepherd should always be in front of his sheep to lead them, but a good shepherd should always he in back of his sheep to keep them from straggling.")

On the hills were whole groves of *sabras*, the native prickly-pears, now in fruit; orange-pink, egg-shaped fruit: the devil's own job to get the spines off them if you didn't want a nasty lot of ulcers. What you did was, you cut off the whole fleshy leaf, on which the fruits grew like fingers; you pronged it onto a stick, and you rubbed it in the dust until all the prickles were off. Then you made two cuts and popped out the inside and ate it, pips and all. There were plantations of olive, fig, and grape. "Grape trees," Tabib called the vines, Tabib being the Christian Arab who rented the plantations from the *Apotropos*.

"What you wish, eat," Tabib said; "but do not let the sheep eat the trees."

About nine o'clock the sheep stopped grazing about and gradually collected in one place, where they lay chewing their cud, or standing with their heads under one another's bellies for the coolness. Rory looked about for a nice flat rock and for a moment paused in choice between one covered with white and green lichens and one that had the penny – bits in red and brown. As a good Irishman, he chose the green, looked carefully for scorpions, and sat down and looked about him. To the left was the Sea of Galilee, blue in its deep pocket, bordered with Syria and Jordan. Northwest were the "Horns of Hittin" – you daren't go there, for it was still mined, they did say. Behind towered Mount Hermon; to the south, rising from the low hills, rose Mount Tabor.

He opened his knapsack, Rory did, and took out his *tallit* and *tephillin*, and said his bit of prayer. Then he had a sandwich and poured some tea out of the canteen into his pannikin. He glanced at the sheep: all quiet – a far cry from this morning's messy work. He turned his attention to the cup.

From the slight movement of his hand the liquid was a bit atremble and he gazed at it as it calmed, and in the lessening ripples of its surface he saw an image take form.

Then he spun his head around and he broke into a delighted grin and jumped to his feet.

"Well, I wondered if you'd turned to stone and if I'd have to roll you back down the hill by myself," she said. And, "Will you show me what it is you do out here?" she said, fussing with her long brown hair and smiling.

"Sally, darling," said Rory, laughing with pleasure, "I will that."

And he showed her the personalities of the flock, and the view, and how to fix sabras, and the colored lichens, and the hand-cast bronze bell on the old wether's neck. And he showed her the vines and the plantations, and they ate the soft, ripe, purple figs until their tongues were nearly rasped with the sweetness of them.

Introduction to
THE TOMB OF JETHRO

AVRAM WAS A KEEN OBSERVER OF THE various cultural and ethnic groups that live in modern Israel. In an undated letter to friends he wrote, "There was rain this morning, and after it the Arab women came in selling flowers. Tattooed faces. Picturesque."

This story was published in *Commentary* in November 1952. It is about a cultural group, who are said to be descendants of the followers of Jethro, Priest of Midian and father-in-law of Moses. They are the Druzes, of Israel (and China). Are there Druzes living in China? Read the story and find out.

Grania Davidson Davis

THE TOMB OF JETHRO

"WELL, ANYWAY, THAT'S WHAT he claims," Pinchas said.

"But surely not of *all* the Druzes," I protested. "After all, most of them live in Syria, and there are many in the Lebanon as well."

"I don't know, but if you ask him – in fact, even if you don't – he tells you that he's the Sheikh of All the Druzes. It could be. He looks the part. You haven't forgotten his present, have you?"

I patted my pocket.

"No, it's here all right... but you don't really think, do you, that for a packet of toffee he's going to reveal the Secret of the Druze religion?"

"Ah, the Secret of the Druze religion... I'll tell you...."

I waited, looking out of the unglazed window of the truck at the mountainous country through which we were passing. High, very high up, off in the distance, Safed perched like an eagle on its mountain top.

"The Secret of the Druze religion. I think... is that there *is* no Secret."

"The sanctuary is empty, so to speak? and always was?"

"Something like that. Or – if there ever was anything, they've forgotten it long ago. The people – the lay people, that is – all they know is, once a year or so, they come and kiss the veil in the temple – which they call the Tomb of Jethro. They can't tell you any more, because they don't know, and – not knowing – they don't like to be asked. And the Sheikhs and Kawasses... on that point I'm not sure. I think perhaps it may be like the Emperor's new clothes, only it's gone on too long for them to admit to the nakedness...."

"You get along well with them, do you?"

"Oh yes, fine. No trouble. We have a perfect understanding about water and grazing, and during the season they come and gather our olives and *sabras* on a share-crop basis. We can't spare the men or the time for that. And I think that they appreciate the fact we are a religious community."

The buildings were almost disappointing in their smallness and lack of any distinction, and might have been any country mosque or sheikh's tomb. For that matter, there is hardly an ecclesiastical building of any kind in the Holy Land which can lay claim to much beauty or distinction-certainly not the cement-slab and peeling-plaster synagogues of the coastal plain. It did not matter. One does not think of the Druzes in connection with architecture, anyway. The Baha'is at Haifa have at least their garden, with its rather insipid prettiness. There is a colony of Samaritans in Jaffa, a tiny branch of a tiny nation; but their holy hill of Gerizim is over in Jordan, and so is their annual offering of paschal lambs. The Karaites near Ramleh have only their rather grimy history of opposition to the "Rabbinic" Jews, and nothing else, not even a Sefer Torah. And the Circassians, in their three or four northern villages, having lost their original language, cherish fading memories of ancient conflicts with the czars; cherish their horses and – presumably – the famous beauty of their womenfolk, who may still be seen at times, with blond tresses and painted lips and cheeks, rows of golden sovereigns sewn onto their kerchiefs, swathed from chin to toe in gaudy, Gypsy-like clothes, standing in the bus queues in Haifa, sucking ices.

The Druzes have their Tomb.

Quite a number of people were gathered outside and camped around it, and the good smell of wood smoke came to us as we got out.

"This is nothing," Pinchas said. "Wait till tomorrow."

The Druzes and I looked at one another with an equal shyness. They might have been, I thought, the original "dark and handsome" men whose foreshadowings used to be found in crystal balls by the Romany people before they went in for phrenology and relief checks. The Druze war record – the War of Liberation I mean – is a rather equivocal one. At the very beginning of hostilities the Israeli Druzes fought on the side of the Arabs, whose language they speak and whose culture they largely share. However, they experienced a great change of heart after the capture of Acre by the Jews. The Sheikhs and Kawasses reproved the people for their haste, and reminded them that the Moslems had martyred Druze leaders as recently as six hundred years ago. Obviously a mistake had been made, but it was soon corrected, and the Druzes received Israeli army badges to wear upon their *keffiyahs*. They fought the rest of the war on the winning side.

Some of them came over to greet "*B*inchas" and to lead us to the notables, who were holding a pre-convention caucus in the house of the Guardian of the Tomb. Some of the Guardian's milch goats were milling around in front, with cloth bags tied up around their teats to prevent the kids from taking tithes. An old man leaning upon a staff muttered something as we went past, his milky eyes evidence that the curse of Sodom still lay heavily upon the people of the land.

The room's walls were tinted blue and ornamented with an illuminated sheet of Arabic script surrounding a peacock, and an old calendar advertising Eno's Fruit Salts. In a niche in the wall was a bundle of leeks and a photograph of President Weizmann. I thought these adornments represented a nice balance of powers. Meanwhile, Pinchas was exchanging compliments (I suppose) with a group of dignitaries seated to one side, and then he introduced me. The Sheikh of All the Druzes, or pretender to the title, looked everything that a Sheikh ought to be. He had a white beard, a white turban, long white robe and soft white trousers, white socks, and a black-and-white-striped waistcoat. A white silk umbrella rested beside him.

"*Tov, tov,*" he said; and, "*Ani sheikh shel kol ha-Druzim.*"

I said, "Tov, tov." ("Good, good.")

"*Kol ha-Druzim,*" ("*all* the Druzes") he emphasized. I really wondered if he had not got a rival somewhere. Accept no substitutes, his tone seemed to say. A thin person with a black velvet fez and gray chin whiskers, seated nearby, was introduced as the head man of a Temanee village not far off. In Hebrew which we are told is exceedingly pure, and which I find exceedingly difficult, he explained to me, *sotto voce*, that he was not sure if one was permitted to visit non-Jews on the occasion of their possibly idolatrous Feast, but – for the sake of the ways of peace – he had come to greet his neighbors the day before the main Feast. The Druzes, he said, were very bad people, but one had to be on good terms with one's neighbors.

"Pay attention," Pinchas interrupted. "The old man is saying how much they love the Jews. They love the Jews *very* much, he says. They are very lucky that they have Jewish neighbors. If, for example, a cow from a Jewish village gets into their fields and eats the maize" – the Temanee cleared his throat huskily and looked at the ceiling – "they are not angry, because they love the Jews very much."

"And we love the Druzes," said the Temanee. "Very much."

The two men embraced and rubbed cheeks, muttering endearments in Arabic. Then they withdrew and the Temanee looked at me with black, burning eyes as the Sheikh continued speaking.

Pinchas continued: "He is explaining to you about the Tomb.... The Druzes originally followed Jethro, the father-in-law of Moses, he says. (Jethro was the priest of Midian, you know, and there is a place not far from here with a name that vaguely resembles Midian.) Anyway, Jethro was the founder of the Druze religion and this is his Tomb and every year the Druzes come to visit it... now give him the toffee."

The toffee was a great success. Coffee was served in the usual tiny cups, the Druzes talked among themselves, and Pinchas and I kept up a desultory conversation about them.

"...and it is *said* that if they die in battle they are immediately reborn as a Druze in China; why China, I don't know, but they believe that there are many Druzes in China."

"Well, I never heard of any when I was there."

"You've been in China? I must tell him. This should be interesting." He leaned over.

The Druzes politely awaited his remarks. I was disappointed in their reaction: they took the news quite calmly, and asked, as they might after my aunt's health, if I had known many Druzes in China. Far be it from me to tell a Druze that China has no Druzes. I said that I had known a Druze in China.

"And what does he do, this Druze?" – via Pinchas.

"What do you mean, what does he do?"

"Does he grow tobacco, or has he olive trees, or what?"

"He has olive trees."

"How many?"

"Many."

"Fifty dunams? A hundred dunams?"

"Two hundred dunams."

At this the conventicle showed genuine interest, and I was forced to plead ignorance of the technical details of the Chinese olive crop. There was more coffee, and there were dates and figs. ("This Druze of whom we have spoken, in China, has he many dunams in dates and figs, and are they as good as these?") Presently, I know not through what graceful Oriental circumlocutions, Pinchas made known that we were leaving.

Would we not care to see the Tomb of Jethro?

We would feel ourselves honored to see the Tomb of Jethro.

The building, as I have said, was small, and lit by dim, hanging oil lamps. The site of the presumable sarcophagus was covered with layers of velvet drapes, which the Guardian turned back for us to admire. One of them was embroidered with a very large, lopsided Star of David. Several minor Druzes who had been outside smoking came in, lifted a corner, bent and reverently kissed the covering, then dropped it negligently and went outside again and resumed their cigarettes.

The Sheikh and Kawasses bade us farewell with benevolent smiles, and for me there was a special word.

"When you are next in China, tell the Druze there, whom you know, that he should try to come to visit the Tomb."

"I will tell him when I see him."

"Because it is the Tomb of Jethro."

And that is all I know about the Druzes. There are very few secrets nowadays.

Introduction to
ON THE HORIZON

THIS TENSE LITTLE STORY IS ABOUT the tensions of the Moroccan Jews. It was published in *Commentary* in January 1953.

Avram's handwritten note on the story provides the introduction: "This was written as well verbatim as my memory allowed, and proved largely prophetic. Not his real last name. AD"

Grania Davidson Davis

ON THE HORIZON

A CITIZEN OF FRANCE
(To Hear Him Tell it)

WHISKEY? NO, DON'T TRY the whiskey here. This is just a small place, there is seldom anyone comes here who would want a good whiskey. A cognac, perhaps. No? Well, I must think. I am sure you have had Calvados: that is the first thing an American does in France: he goes to a bar and orders Calvados. And always he is disappointed, but always.... Ah. I know. Try an *anise pure*. All right? *Deux*, Louis. You see, they know me here. Everyone in Marseilles knows Georgie. And in Nice and Cannes and Antibes. Well, to your good health.

How do you like it? Not bad, is it? No, no, I will pay. Please, no argument. I am always glad to meet an American, and my brother here tells me that you have been very kind.

Well, yes, I like him, too: he is not very clever, but he has a good heart. I am the clever one in the family. I don't boast, it is so. We were seven children, and I am the one who supports the family. The only one who has ever made money. Me, Georgie. Every week I send money, not as much as I wish, because I have now a wife and a little boy of my own. Besides, I am saving money. I save money in American dollars. I am a citizen of France, but there is no money like the American money. Now, how is that, the French are so careful and meager with spending and saving, and the money is worth so little – and the Americans are always making the grand gestures and spending much, and their money is stable? Curious.

Sometimes I cannot believe it is me who has this good suit and shoes and hat, this good apartment and business. I have to take out my passport and reassure myself. Georges Ben Shem Tob. It is really me. Maybe my brother told you something, how we lived in Morocco? – You understand his French? – The nine of us lived in one room where the only running water was what dripped from the walls. My father was paralyzed and couldn't work, so it was very hard. We lived like the poorest Arabs. We would starve only for the Jewish communal office supporting us. Each week they gave us flour and oil and two of those old, big, round silver coins – what are they called? – I forget. Never mind. I have been away a long time. In fact, I have not been back in twenty years. This brother here was a baby when I left. He's a big baby now, what do you say? He can take care of himself, yes; but, ah, all the time in fights. I am glad that he is going now to Palestine.

Excuse me, Israel. *Eress Israel*, I know that. You must excuse me, I am very ignorant. I have never gone to school, only to the *heder* when I was a boy; and to read Hebrew I have forgotten, and to read the Christian languages I haven't learned. Anyway, I am glad that we can go now to our own country. Of course, I am a citizen of France, and it's all right for me, but those others in Morocco – bad, very bad. Because, you know, the people of French Morocco are not by rights citizens of France. No. Spanish Morocco? Well – that's right, yes. Franco has said that the Jews of the old Spanish blood in other countries can become citizens of Spain by just making the oath; I remember when he did that. It was like a bomb to the Moors, a slap in their face. A curious man.

Listen, I'm going to tell you something. You know what's the first thing an Arab does if he doesn't have to spend all his money? He buys his wife a golden bracelet. And the last thing he sells, when he needs money, is that golden bracelet. That's his bank account, on his wife's arm.

Another one? Please, it's nothing. I am very happy. The Americans have always been good for me. I did much business with the Americans; we trust one another. Anything an American wants, I always help him to get it. I have letters – I'll show you. You see? You know Mr. Hopkins from Detroit? I think he must be a very important man there. Admiral Coffey, you know Admiral Coffey? A very gracious man.

To your good health. To Eress Israel.

So... The golden bracelets. Well, what happens now? Who does the Arab buy it from, this bracelet? The Jewish goldsmith. And where does he sell it? Also the Jewish goldsmith. So now I tell you something. The Arabs are not buying bracelets now: they are selling. And why? Only for one thing, to buy rifles. The Arabs in the East do not gain the victory in Israel, the Arabs here are furious. They want the French to go and the Spanish to go. And the old leader, Abd el Krim, he is escaped, you know; he's in Egypt. And the Grand Mufti, he is in Egypt, too. *La-la!* Trouble, trouble. And they do not want to let go the Jews. In this case the French are not at fault, they cannot show favor to the Jews openly, because for every Jew in the French colonies, there are ten – twenty – Moslems, maybe more. And if a Jew in Morocco goes for his passport, who is the clerk? An Arab. He puts away the passport somewhere, and what can be done? Nothing. That's why the Jews must go away at night in the aeroplanes. And in the aeroplanes you can take but a little, and so only some can go.

No, I tell you, only one thing. Someday – maybe not now or to-morrow – but someday – the President of Israel must send to the King, the Sultan, and say to him like this: "See, you are a ruler and I am a ruler, yes? Let us make an agreement. Let go the Jews, like the King of Yemen did. How much do you want?" That's the way to do it. Because it is unpossible – you say "unpossible"? Oh, *im*possible, thank you – it is impossible for the Jews to go on like this. If one has any tiny disagreement with an Arab, quick goes the Arab to the police, to the court – and who is the judge? another Arab – and he says, "This Jew said: '_____ the Sultan!'" Right away they send him to the prison.

Do you know why I save my money? This one here, my brother, even, doesn't know, but I'll tell you. I'm going to buy a car and take it over to Morocco and act like a rich man. I will say that I want to bring my mother and my brothers and sisters – my father is dead – back to France for a visit. Oh, only for a visit. What can they do? I am a citizen of France. The Arabs won't remember me when I was a child, a dirty little child there, before I ran away. They won't dare to put their hands on my head. You know what I mean? No, you don't know. See, the Arabs believe that if one of them can put his hands on a Jew's head the first thing in the day, all that day he has good luck. So one morning, very early, I was helping my father back from the synagogue, because he had a paralysis and it was very hard for him to walk. And an Arab, a drunken Arab – or maybe he'd been smok-ing *teef* – came into the street, and he came over to my father. He brought down his hand on my father's head with all his might, and he yelled, "*Ya Ya-Hood*! My hand on your head!" And my father fell down, and the Arab was so drunk, he fell down, too, and they lay in the street.

When I saw my poor father lying there, trembling, I became like a crazy person. I took out my little knife and I began to stab this Arab, and crying and cursing him. Many times since then I try to think: did I stab him twenty-seven times or thirty-seven times? No use. I don't remember. But I was just a small boy. How did I get the courage? And I even dragged and tumbled the Arab into an alley. This brother here says that I even got my poor father home, too, but I don't remember. Only that I was afraid and ran away. It was a great *scandale*, but they never found out who did it. And I never went back.

But now I'm a citizen of France and I don't care.

To your health. To Eress Israel.

Introduction to
THE ASCALON LIGHT

THIS STORY WAS PUBLISHED IN *Commentary* in January 1957. It is
the last known story that he published in that magazine, and perhaps his
last and best known story of life in Israel. His most famous fantasy story,
The Golem, had been published in 1955, and by the late fifties he became
increasingly involved in fantasy literature.

This is a fully developed story about the Jews of the Diaspora who
have gathered in Israel, and about the social life of dung beetles. It is about
an American Jew in a remote outpost who missed his books and missed the
comforts of the city. Among the things he missed was hot falafel. Here is
Avram's falafel recipe, from his journal dated 1949:

"Sephardic falafel is always the best, and Jerusalem falafel is the
best of the best. How and what? The basic ingredient is a bean which is
ground down to a yellow paste, made into balls and flipped into hot, deep
cooking oil until crisp...Mine host cuts in half a *pita* – a bread flapjack –
the Talmud uses the word – smears it with his own relish (a hot relish, with
peppers) pops in four balls, dribbles on a white sauce, rolls it up, wraps the
roll into an old mandatory gov. tax form. Pickle or green pepper, whatnot,
a garnish. No two places prepare it quite the same. Some have a red sauce
in place of relish; some give cabbage or tomatoes and cucumbers..."

Grania Davidson Davis

THE ASCALON LIGHT

WHEN A PHRASE GROWS TRITE IT IS, I suppose, usual enough that the fact behind the phrase should lose some of its reality. It is impossible for me not to feel for the Athenian who voted against Aristides because he tired of hearing him called "Aristides the Just." I knew that the Israeli pioneers had drained swamps, *had* planted trees in the desert; I knew how wonderful it was, but I had simply heard it too often. I knew also, very well, the realities and difficulties of the *Ingathering of the Exiles* and the Israel melting pot. The return of a million Jews from the Diaspora is one of the wonders of history, truly a great thing, something marvelously real. But it is possible to tire of being so close, constantly, to reality. Although I have always been a heavy reader, in Israel I read more than ever, to escape reality; like my ancestors in the desert, I began to tire of all that manna, and I tried to recapture from books the taste of the fish, the leeks, the cucumbers, and the melons.

My research was interrupted by a request that I leave Haifa and proceed to Jaffa. There, near the old port where the prophet Jonah began his famous voyage (the significance of which is commonly lost in arid arguments over the dietetic capacities of whales), a man named Zvi, whose face I have forgotten, explained my assignment to me.

Near to the ruins of the ancient city of Ascalon were the ruins of the modern village of Jora. At hand to Jora was a non-ruined barracks of British build, and here the Israeli government intended to establish a lighthouse. A group of men were already living there to guard the place and I was now being sent to care for their health. I had found, to my surprise, that my three years in the U.S. Navy Hospital Corps impressed the Israelis far more than it impressed me.

"There are no doctors in the entire area," Zvi said, with much more enthusiasm than I could feel the statement warranted. "The District Medical Officer pro-tem is a pharmacist, and he is five kilometers away."

I reminded him that I had been only a Pharmacist's Mate.

"Never mind," Zvi said serenely.

The Israelis were always saying "Never mind." It was all the English many of them had, and as they continued to say it in answer to my comments, requests, or complaints, I soon learned *not* to mind. Life can be simpler than most of us realize.

128

"Never mind," Zvi said. "You leave in one hour."

I objected. I said that I had things to get.

"What things? Here is your medical chest. It is from Burroughs, Wellcome Company – a British firm – *very* good chest. Sign, please, this chitty."

I recognized the voice of the ex-British army sergeant-major. I signed, not caring to tread on the thin ice of "please."

"Books," I said, signing. "I must have time to get some books." Jora, as far I knew, was in effect as remote as Point Barrow. My Hebrew was not good enough for diversional reading. I would sooner have gone without the chest than without English books. My "medical" experience in Israel had convinced me that "Never mind" could substitute for nine-tenths of the local pharmacopoeia, and that Rish-le-Zion brandy did for the remaining tenth; but for reading matter there was no proxy. I tried to explain this.

"There are books already in Jora," said Zvi, "if you will *wish* to read them. British books. But there is such a beautiful beach there, also fishing, and the Commandant has a shotgun and perhaps will take you hunting for doves. If you are interested in antiquities, there is Ascalon. Many ruins and remains. But *books?*" He smiled, shrugged. "The British left us there an entire library with the barracks. They are such bahstards," he said, fondly, "but at the same time – I must say it – gentlemen. Not only books and barracks they left us, but ports, ships, police stations. How many, many times I have been in those police stations in the old Haganah days! Good beatings they gave me, too. But – if we had had here the French, or the Russians, or even (if you will excuse me) the Americans, I do not know if we would have had so soon our own country and our own police in those stations, with the policemen's wives hanging out the wash to dry in the courtyards."

Zvi then took me and introduced me to the man in charge of the lighthouse detail, a stocky, blue-eyed, fortyish man with grizzled hair: his name was Zvi, too. It is a very common name among Israeli men. So is Ari, Uzi, Uri, Ze'ev; these brisk syllables hold their own despite a fashion for more luxuriant Hebrew names: Avimelech, Yehoyakim, Elchanan. This Zvi looked at his watch and asked if the *Chovesh* was ready. *Chovesh* is, literally, bandager, but English-speaking Israelis generally translate it as dresser or dispenser. I was not so much ready as resigned to leaving unready, so I shook hands with him and followed him into the street.

There was a truck there and attached to it was the light; I realized clearly for the first time that Jora or Ascalon was not going to be the scene of any Captain January type of living. A military anti-aircraft searchlight was what it was, of the kind which nightly pierce the Los Angeles sky, giving notice that a new delicatessen or bowling alley has been opened. The truck, as usual, was overloaded (all Israeli vehicles in the public service were overloaded, and private cars venturing outside the cities with empty seats were apt in those days to be stoned if they refused hitch-hikers); and we were unable to pick up any of the khaki-clad *trampistim* clustered at every crossroad. Now and then Zvi would order a halt to inspect the rope coupling of the light. His grunts of *"Reg' echad!"* (One minute) and *"Sah!"* (Go) punctuated the bumpy trip south.

We entered and left Majdal (anciently Migdal Gad) through gates guarded by military. The paved road gave way to sand, and the abandoned plantations to dunes. The men looked about with more alertness and loaded their weapons.

"Can you use a Czech rifle?" (Years later, when Slansky's neck was cracked upon the garrote I remembered those Czech rides.) I told Zvi I couldn't. I also admitted that I could not use a British rifle either, or a Sten gun or a Bren. I said I thought I might still remember how to use the type of carbine with which corpsmen serving in the Marines were supplied during the Japanese War. Zvi sighed.

"Well, you cannot go unarmed around here," he said. "Last week three men were killed. Two Jews and an Arab. One of our Arabs, I mean."

The truck lurched over another dune and we saw the barracks on the crest of the seashore – "the tideless, dolorous, midland sea" – I felt just like those words then. At some distance to the right and left were small Arab houses, their doors and narrow windows gaping emptily. A dory lay on its side on the strand, waves breaking over it. The barracks itself was a grim, unpainted building. A huge maze of barbed wire was dragged aside just enough to let the truck enter the yard. I unloaded my gear and went inside to look around. On the ground floor was an office and a vast squad room in which were set up a scant dozen wooden trestle beds with thin mattresses. At the back was another room, with an iron bedstead and a chest of drawers. High overhead was a window with a broken pane. This was both my sleeping quarters and the *marpeah*, or sick bay. I suppose it may have been a non-coms' room in British days. Upstairs, besides a few rooms, of nondescript character and indeterminate function, was a kitchen and mess hall, and a recreation room with a warped ping-pong table. There was also an armory and a washroom. An iron ladder led to the flat roof. The brightest color in the place was a dirty gray. Dispirited, I waited for a chance to ask about the library; meanwhile supper was cried by the Iraqi cook, a sallow, thin man with the clever face of a not-so-sad cynic who knows when to keep his mouth shut. We all went in.

It was, now I think of it, a curious supper. Stale bread, pickled olives the color of gunmetal, chunks of halvah, margarine (pale, despite there being no tax on colored – "Never mind"), marmalade, and porridge. All of these were also to appear for breakfast and dinner, often without the removal of what seemed the same dead flies; for dinner we would have soup as well, and fried corned beef hash loaf, a sort of kosher Spam, made in Winnipeg. Some fresh meat had come down from Jaffa, but as there was still a little ice left, the cook intended to save it for another day. There was a chipped black enamel *kumkum* of weak tea and a chipped white enamel one of – of –

"What is *this*?" I asked.

"Coffee surrogate," said Zvi, pouring himself a mug. "Sometimes there is real coffee. Maybe tomorrow. Never mind."

I never learned what the stuff was made of, but it was sweet, and sugar is scarce in Israel (the taste of saccharine clung to my tongue for weeks after I left), so I drank it.

The screens were punctured with bullet holes, and the flies buzzed around unmolested.

"*Chovesh*, you're from America?" asked a plump, blond Teutonic type. "Are they beating the Jews in the streets of America now?"

His name was Bustie; next to him was a redhead called Gingie. There was a Moroccan by the name of Abenshabbat whose eyes did not seem to focus, and who spent most of his time caring for his weapon. There was Menahem, an Irish-looking Turk of Judeo-Spanish descent; Abraham, an Armenian-looking Bulgar of the same stock; Anselm, a thin, preoccupied Algerian; a pock-marked Kurd; a sturdy Rumanian in his thirties (most of the men were in their teens); a Pole whose wife kept a tiny grocery in Jaffa for him while he was away; and a slender, tall sabra, or native son, with a long mustache which he constantly caressed. There were others. I can't remember them.

But Bustie – when I told him that Jews were not being beaten in the streets in America on any large or systematic scale, I knew the next question would be: "Then why did you come here?" and I was tired of explaining – or trying to explain – so merely shrugged. As expected, also: Did I know Moysha the Pole's uncle in Brookleen? The Turk's cousin in Caracas, Venezuela? And: Yes, I'd been in *Holavud*; no, I knew no movie stars. Yes, I'd seen – it seemed a thousand years ago – the film *Tarzan, Baal Ha-Jungle*, currently playing at the Mograbhi, Tel Aviv's leading theater or *kol-noah*, or moving voice. Amid the constant crackle of pumpkin seeds the Israelis had sat, limp with pleasure, their eyes flickering from the main screen to the tiny side screen where the equivalent of "Me Tarzan" appeared in Hebrew script: thus they emancipated themselves from the Talmudic superstitions of their elders.

As the jam was being passed Abenshabbat uttered a wild and fearful shriek and fired his rifle out the window. "*Na!*" he said, in a tone of satisfaction, and "*Riba?*" in a tone of inquiry. Someone passed him the jam. Anselm clicked his tongue once, otherwise no one paid any attention.

"In America," Moysha asked, "how much does a workingman get for 'black labor' for a day, and what does a kilo of meat cost?"

No one was ever sick the entire time I was there. I never had a single request for medications. Each month I drew on Jaffa for a large bottle of brandy, the absence of any pharmaceutical calls on it left me free to drink it slowly and moodily and congratulate myself that the times were past when I was obliged to use brandy for an external antiseptic after the peroxide ran out. As dust gathered on the supply chest, time gathered on my hands. I asked for the library. Zvi asked the sabra, his second-in-command. The sabra meditated. He consulted the Bulgar, who shrugged and murmured something.

"You know," Zvi said, apologetically, "we have not yet any big factory for lavatory paper in Eretz Yisrael."

"The men," explained the sabra, "do not read English."

Two fly leaves and half a title page was all that remained of the library. But one day the sabra, an a state of high excitement, brought me a book.

"Where did you get it?" I asked, after thanking him.

"Never mind."

I unwrapped it from an Arab-language picture paper. It was a copy of *Helpful Farm Hints For Every Day*, published in Milwaukee in 1919. I read it through in twenty minutes, then read it again. And again. How to make headcheese. How to sharpen plow-points. How to spay sows. Two days later the sabra said, "When you have finished that book, I will get you another."

"But where *are* the books?"

"Never mind."

"I am finished with that one, anyway."

"So *soon?*" But he gave me the other, and said he really had no more. The second one was a Penguin edition of *Prince Kropotkin's Mutual Aid*. I rationed myself: one chapter in the morning, one in the afternoon, one at night. Kropotkin wrote about societies, human, animal, insect; those which practiced mutual aid, those which – being "in decay" – did not. Most non-human species were in the first class. The only item I can recall about the second grouping was that certain kinds of falcons stole from one another.

"No one," he wrote, "has ever seen a dung beetle quarreling with his fellow over the balls of dung which they gather." I was not prepared to dispute the statement. I got the point.

Outdoor life? Zvi-of-Jaffa had mentioned hunting and fishing. Zvi-of-Jora did, indeed, take doves with his shotgun. While I did not engage in any spirit-wrestlings with him about this, the fact is I do not hunt. I have nothing against doves, and cannot eat them unless they have been killed according to religious law, and a shotgun is not a valid means to this end. Fishing. There was no fishing tackle around the place, yet I would some-times see the sabra come from the beach with a clutch of fish dangling on a stick. Detonation charges, while illegal, were effective. One day he went to sell his catch in Majdal and I invited myself along. We drove in the jeep ("*ha-jip*") with Abenshabbat and Moysha. There was some concern about the back axle ("*ha-beck-ex*"'), but off we went anyway.

"Listen," I said, as we passed an Arab doing something or other in a wet field with a camel, "do you suppose I could find some English books in Majdal?"

The sabra shrugged. Majdal was a town of one-story buildings made of dirty stone. The last big thing that had happened to it was its occupation by Mehemet Ali. It had, at the time of my visit, about 1,500 Arabs and perhaps half that many Jews. The Jews worked in the nearby abandoned plantations, trying to rehabilitate them. The remaining Arabs were mostly weavers. I could see them at their looms, the workshops open to the hot, dusty streets, or coming from the dye yards – its huge wooden gates half ajar – with skeins of brilliant cotton thread in their hands. A few *fellaheen* rode to or from the fields with wooden implements on their shoulders. While the sabra went to sell his fish and Moysha looked around for some apricots to buy for his grocery, I sat down for a cup of coffee.

The Arab boiled it up in the usual tiny copper pot (by this time I had learned that smuggled coffee and sugar were easily available here be-cause of the nearby border), and his assistant – aged about eight, I would guess – got out the tiny china cup and the beaten-brass lid and the tall tumbler of water and the tray and the crackers or *bisqooeet*. I gazed around the market place. Some old men in baggy pantaloons came out of the mosque, followed by the most memorable figure I ever saw in Majdal. He was a huge Negro, as black as only few are, in a purple robe and the green turban and henna-red beard of the *hadji*; and he fingered his beads and muttered to himself in a voice like distance-muted thunder, his whole person breathing power.

The sabra sold his fish and bought green almonds and roasting ears and cigarettes. Moysha had gotten two crates of apricots for the little grocery in Jaffa.

"The books? The English books?"

We asked all through town and the answer was always the same: the single click of the tongue which is the Arab negative. (Israeli joke: Husband – "Was that Arab here after I warned you?" Wife – "*Tsk!*")

So I went back to the lighthouse where the light didn't work (although it was toiled over the whole day every day), to the sick bay where no one was ever sick. I tried sleeping, but the flies were fierce, they bit, they stung. At night, I discovered, there were mosquitoes.

I began to polish two old bronze coins I'd found in the ruins. I went swimming. The days passed. Elsewhere in the land of Israel, cities were springing up overnight; immigrants from China and Peru and eighty or ninety other countries were being deloused, indoctrinated, and disillusioned; a government decree regulating the shape of bread was discovered to have political overtones and round-loaf partisans battled long-loaf partisans and raided opposition bakeries; tourists went on conducted tours and returned, pronouncing everything ideal; trees were planted and swamps drained; the Prime Minister urged everyone to take as guides the books of Ezra and Nehemiah – and when *"religious zealots"* did so, rather literally, he denounced them with rage; factories were erected and began not only to produce but to export; there was a shortage of small change, and the bus cooperatives printed their own fractional currency which they gave out as change but declined to accept for fares; a *Frenk* murdered and disemboweled his aunt; two new *Messiahs* appeared in Jerusalem and announced conflicting revelations; everywhere, in short, things were happening – except at the Ascalon light.

One day at the table the sabra announced that there was a grapevine report from Gaza: a reward of £125 had been put upon Achmet's head. Achmet was a little swarthy Arab with a shifty grinning mouth studded with gold teeth.

"What has Achmet done?" I asked. The men laughed without much amusement.

"He wants to kill everybody," the sabra said. "He used to go on patrol against marauders and infiltrators from Gaza; but now the Military Governor doesn't let him, because he kills them all."

A squabble broke out between Menahem and the Rumanian.

Menahem's Hebrew grew too rapid, not only for me to follow, but for himself; he broke into Judeo-Spanish.

"Ah, Malta *yok!*" said the Rumanian.

At this, to me, mysterious word, the others laughed, this time light-heartedly. Menahem flushed a bit. I asked for an explanation. The story – said the sabra – was an old, old one, and indeed it must have been. During the days of Turkish imperialism an Ottoman admiral was sent out with a great fleet to invest the island of Malta. The admiral had been appointed for qualities other than proficiency in navigation, and he reappeared after a long absence with no sign of battle joined. To inquiries about Malta he had shrugged and answered, simply, "Malta yok – Malta isn't there." Menahem, as the only Turk, had inherited this crack.

"Malta-*yok*," repeated the Rumanian, snickering.

"Do you know the Haifa bus that goes to Khalissa, where the Rumanians live?" Menahem asked me. I did, I had often taken it to visit a beloved friend.

"Number zero?" I asked, innocently.

"And why is it zero? Because it had a number once, but the Rumanians are all thieves, and they stole it."

The Rumanian had a mug in his hand and he struck Menahem with it above the ear. In another moment Zvi had knocked him down. I expected a riot to break out, but the Rumanian simply put his hand to lip, smeared away a tiny drop of blood, and got up and left. I followed him and said that I would put some ice on it. The cook, with his eternal semi-smile, said there was no ice, and the Rumanian growled that he needed no help. I went back to the table where Zvi was cautioning the men against insulting one another.

"*Yehudim Anachnu* – we are Jews," he ended. But afterwards he said to me that he was beginning to have doubts about "*the Ingathering of the Exile*".

"How hard we fought, how much we suffered, for this one principle, and are they appreciative? Are they willing to work as we worked? Ah, these Orientals."

"But are the Rumanians, then, Orientals?"

"Of course they are!" he was more excited than I had ever before seen him. "Were you ever in Bucharest? No? Then you can't realize. Listen, in *every* city there is vice, but in Bucharest one saw Asiatic vice, not European. It was like Port Said. Tell me, why do the American Jews not come? Ah, you shrug. You are too comfortable there, you have a w.c. in every flat. Wait! In Germany the Jews were comfortable, too." And he smiled that grim smile with which Israelis indicate that they hourly expect news of a pogrom in Indianapolis or Omaha, and would be half-gratified to hear it.

"At least we fix our searchlights there," I said.

We parted without the cordiality that had always been between us. I tried to read Kropotkin. He was talking about the migration of the reindeer; I cannot remember details, but apparently the manner in which reindeers crossed rivers was a bright example of Mutual Aid and a rebuke to mankind. A timid knock on the door, and Anselm came in.

"*Chovesh*, you are not an Ashkenazi?" he asked. I should have liked to discuss with him the theory that the Biblical *Ashkenaz*, which later Jewish geographers located east of the Rhine and north of the Danube, was the same as the classical *Scythia*, but decided that Anselm was not the man for the subject. I said, Oh, but I was an Ashkenazi. "Ah, since you are of French expression, as we North African Jews are, I thought...." The realization that he had very probably learned his French in school just as I did allowed me to swallow the compliment, he sighed. "Tell me, why do the Ashkenazim always mistreat the Sephardim?" I said I didn't think they did, particularly. "What? But look at how the Rumanian gave poor Menahem such a blow!" I pointed out that Zvi, who had promptly defended Menahem by striking an even stronger blow, was an Ashkenazi too; but he refused comfort. The Kurd thrust in his head, murmured an apology, and withdrew. Anselm moved closer to me.

"I am afraid of that one," he whispered. "They are savages, these Kurds; they carry knives, they practice witchcraft. Do you know Algiers, my friend? Ah, what you have missed! A city, Algiers! Well civilized and very beautiful."

"The Kurds," I said, "are they not also Sephardim?"

He got up and looked at me with obvious hurt. "So even you, even you," he said. He left. After a while I finished the chapter and went for some water. On the steps was Moysha, who invited me, in his soft, drawling Yiddish, to sit for a while.

"How much does a watch cost in America?" he asked. "What is the price of a kilo of potatoes? Of oranges? Why do you always say you don't know? If you don't want to tell me, say so. Listen. You know I had a watch? A Swiss watch that cost me five English pounds. Do you know how hard I worked for it? A thief here took it. Some day I'll find who, I'll kill him. Zvi says I lost it. A laughter. A watch loses itself? And how is it Zvi always knows the time and yet he says he has no watch? He's a Russian, and I don't trust him. *Fonya Goniff*, we call the Russ. Cook them sweet, cook them sour: thieves."

After some more of this (the government was bent on destroying the small merchants, the Americans had hearts like stone) he withdrew. I heard a sound from above and decided to climb the ladder to the roof. There I found the sabra smoking a cigarette (not the free issue, which tasted like the scrapings from a refinery furnace, but the most expensive local brand, bought with his fish money) and gazing out to wards Majdal. Somewhere a fire burned and the smell of wood smoke drifted pungently past us and out to sea. In the plantations the jackals yelped and howled.

"What was Moysha saying?" he asked.

"Couldn't you hear?"

"I can't speak Yiddish," he said, scornfully. "The only foreign languages I know are English and Arabic. He was complaining about *me*, wasn't he? Ah, I know. Yes, he was. They are all the same, all these foreign-born, they are all jealous of us, the sabras, because we are the only ones who are free of the ghetto and the taint of the Exile – " and he went on, piling up his complaints. "...and they can't even take orders properly," he concluded, curling up his lip beneath the long mustache, and he leaned over the parapet and spat in the direction of the ravening jackals – the "foxes" of the King James Bible, which Samson had his cruel sport with, before the mill rasped and the temple fell in nearby Gaza.

"Listen," he said, wiping the wings of his mustache; "we've got to get rid of all these sickly European ways that have corrupted this country since the days of the Greeks. Oh, yes, even the Arab is not clean; you know that? Either he squats in his own filth and won't brush away the flies that eat his very eyes, or else he puts perfumed pomade on his hair and starts to talk French."

At the far end of the roof two men climbed off the ladder and sat down, talking in low tones to one another in German. I recognized Bustie and Gingie.

"I know this," Bustie was saying. "I came as soon as I heard the cook call, and when I got there everybody was already sitting down and there was no more meat in the serving bowl, only potatoes. And your plate had a piece of meat on it and you were chewing and I could see by the way you were chewing that it was meat and not potatoes: whose meat could it have been, if not mine? What a low, rotten, thieving trick! How often do we get meat?"

"It's not so, there wasn't enough meat to go around. Never mind what the cook says. I think he sells the meat to the Arabs, anyway."

"Ah, this damned country. In Vienna, in the old days, who would fight about a piece of meat?"

The ululation of the jackals grew louder, then died away. I started to leave.

"We must return to the ways of the ancient *Canaanim*," the sabra was saying. "Then we were really men: before the priests and the prophets corrupted us with their piety."

Breakfast the next morning was spent in silence broken only by Abenshabbat, who grunted and muttered to himself. Afterwards I tried to read more of Kropotkin, but the fierceness of the flies drove me out again, and I walked along the road. My eyes, cast down, focussed on the sandy ground. A troupe of insects passed along whose carapaces wore an odd design in red and black, like a Maori or Papuan ceremonial mask; and, even more baroque, they were joined in pairs, stern to stern, one scrabbling backward as the other went forward. Were we like that? was my thought. But if so, which of us were leading, and which being led? Passing back and forth, much larger than the Siamese twins, were glossy black insects. Here and there along the way, camels had left heaps of dung (dropped with a contemptuous lift of the tail, a lascivious cant of the hips, and an arrogant sway of the neck), quickly dried by the sun. Each heap was a center of the great black beetles. With their forelegs they rolled tiny balls of the strawy droppings, and these they pushed in front of them, rolled along as they walked more or less erect, until they disappeared past the margin of the road.

Camels came in frequent file, bearing sea sand from the beach, led by Arabs; the *zif-zif* was transferred to Jewish trucks and taken away for use in building. There seemed to be a supply of dung ample for all, but as I watched, I saw one beetle approach another and attempt to wrest its cargo from it. The first beetle at once attacked, flipping the second on its back; it struggled, righted itself, returned to the assault, only to be once more capsized. Twice again this was repeated, until finally the marauder gave up and went away. I cheered the victor, who paid no attention, but rolled his ball away.

Then I remembered Kropotkin, and I wondered. Could it be that the European dung beetle, which never "disputed possession," had better social habits than the Israeli dung beetle? I doubted this. It seemed to me that the earnest Prince had created an idealized conception after his own image, that the Cooperative Dung Beetle was to him what the Noble Savage was to Rousseau.

For some reason I felt much better. I looked about me. The sun had never seemed so brilliant, the scent of the sea so fresh and pure. The Arabs passing with their camels smiled and said, *"Marhabaa."* The Jews, waiting

for the *zif-zif*, spat on their hands and picked up their shovels, too busy –
for a wonder – to go through the usual catechistic greeting (Peace be upon
you. From whence comes a Jew? What are you doing here? Married? Parents living? What does your father do? etc.). From the barracks, just over
the next dune, I heard the voice of singing, of men singing. Although the
words did not carry, the tune did, and I recognized it as set to a verse from
the Song of Songs: "*Return, return, O Shulamite,*" they sang. I found them
squatting in a semicircle in the yard. In between verses they ate apricots
and played at seeing who could send the wet pits the farthest by squeezing
them between thumb and forefinger. The Rumanian, his lip a bit swollen,
had just beaten Zvi, and they were laughing together.

"We are going back to Jaffa," they told me. "Tomorrow. All of us.
Ascalon, goodbye!"

I gaped. For a moment I just stood there. Then I thought of Jaffa,
of the tall clock-tower, of King George Boulevard, of cold beer and hot
fellafel, of crowds of people, and fresh-baked bread, and synagogues. I
thought of Tel Aviv: adjacent, of the Brooklyn Ice Cream Bar, and many
book stores; of the dark and beautiful women in the Hatikvah quarter, of
the blind Afghan or Pakistani who played deep music on a strange instrument in Allenby Street. Up and down the people went, to and fro: sabras
and immigrants, Sephardim and Ashkenazim, unbelievers and faithful,
"young men and maidens, elders and striplings." Then I grew a bit angry.

"All this time," I said; "all this effort, all these men: for what? To
guard a light which never worked."

They laughed. Zvi smiled at me. He handed over an apricot.

"Never mind," he said.

"Oh, Avram, Avram, What A Wonder You Were!"

Robert Silverberg

THE
AVRAM DAVIDSON
SYMPOSIUM

Who's Who – by Jack Dann

Avram And God
by Peter S. Beagle

Dinner (Almost) With The Davidsons
by Richard A. Lupoff

Jewish Magic And A Jewish Magician
by Lisa Goldstein

"Love From Bubby, Only Be Well"
by Carol Carr

The Jewish Condition Is The Human Condition

by Barry N. Malzberg

Who's Who
by Jack Dann

The *Oxford English Dictionary*, which is sitting properly on my lap as I write this, weighs approximately 6,000 pounds and contains text that is so small it would make a microdot look like one of the outer planets. This weighty tome defines "symposium" as: "A drinking party; a convivial meeting for drinking, conversation, and intellectual entertainment; properly among the ancient Greeks, hence generally." I think Avram would prefer that to the more staid and boring definition the *OED* provides down the page a-piece; and, indeed, Grania Davis and I invited a convivial group of gifted writers who knew Avram Davidson to tell us whatever they found interesting about him...whatever they wished to reveal; and the results were most rewarding.

Here, Peter S. Beagle will tell you about Avram and the difference between being Jewish and being a Jew; Richard A. Lupoff will recount the problems of a dinner with the Davidsons; Lisa Goldstein discusses Avram's gifts; Carol Carr shows us letters and examines Avram the Jew, poet, and Zen grief counselor; and Barry N. Malzberg describes a serious man of serious purpose.

The *New York Times Book Review* has praised Peter S. Beagle for his "opulence of imagination and mastery of style." He is the author of such beautifully crafted novels as *Tamsin*, *The Last Unicorn*, *A Fine and Private Place*, and *The Innkeeper's Song*. His short story collections include *The Rhinoceros Who Quoted Nietzsche* and *Giant Bones*. He writes nonfiction and screenplays, and forthcoming is the novel *A Dance for Emilia*.

Hugo award winner Richard A. Lupoff is the author of many novels, which include the wildly brilliant *Sacred Locomotive Flies* and *Space War Blues*, and many short stories. He was the West Coast editor of *Crawdaddy*, book editor for *Algol*, and since 1985 has been editor of *Canyon Press*. He has done a number of anthologies including *The Investigations of Avram Davidson* (with – who else? – Grania Davis).

Lisa Goldstein won the coveted American Book Award for her first novel, *The Red Magician*, a haunting, lyrical Jewish fantasy. *The New Yorker* wrote that "She has given us the kind of magic and adventure that once upon a time made us look for secret panels in the walls of wardrobes, or brush our teeth with a book held in front of our eyes, because we couldn't bear to put it down." She has written numerous short stories, which have been short listed for the Hugo, Nebula, and World Fantasy Awards, and her other books include the novels *The Dream Years*; *A Mask for the General*; *Tourists: A Novel*; *Strange Devices of the Sun and Moon*; *Summer King, Winter Fool*; and the collections *Daily Voices* and *Travelers in Magic*.

Carol Carr was born in New York and has lived in the Oakland Hills Fire Zone since 1972. Her work, which she prefers to refer to as her *oeuvrette*, has appeared in Damon Knight's *Orbit* series, *The Magazine of Fantasy & Science Fiction*, and *Omni Magazine*. She was married to the anthologist and writer the late Terry Carr, who said, "Her natural medium is the postcard. She sells everything she writes, but she never writes." True, her oeuvre is an, er, oeuvrette, but look up her story *Look, You Think You've Got Troubles* (You can find it in my anthology *Wandering Stars*.) It's about a nice Jewish girl who marries an alien. If you don't laugh until Tuesday after reading it, I'll eat my yarmulke.

Barry N. Malzberg is perhaps one of the most controversial writers ever to have entered the fields of science fiction and fantasy. He is the author of over seventy novels and over two hundred short stories; some of his short fiction can be found in *Final War and Other Fantasies* (as K. M O'Donnell), *Out From Ganymede*, *The Many Worlds of Barry Malzberg*, *Down Here In the Dream Quarter*, *The Best of Barry Malzberg*, *The Man Who Loved the Midnight Lady*, and in many other collections. He won the Campbell Memorial award for his terrifyingly bleak and humorous postmodern novel *Beyond Apollo*; and he has also written the novels *Herovit's World*, *Guernica Night*, *Galaxies*, and *The Remaking of Sigmund Freud*. His brilliant collection of essays *Engines of the Night* established him as the conscience of the genre.

Avram And G-d
by Peter S. Beagle

In the groundbreaking early '60s revue *Beyond The Fringe*, either Dudley Moore or Jonathan Miller used to say – half-apologetic, half-defiant – "Actually, I'm not a Jew. Just Jew*ish*."

I'm Jewish. Avram Davidson was a Jew. He was the only man I ever knew who spelled the word God with a dash where the O should be. An Orthodox Jew doesn't ever write the full name of God, no more than an orthodox Muslim would portray the human figure. Even so, in all the years that I knew Avram, I never thought of him as orthodox anything. We joked and pondered and quarreled as fellow Jews, of course, inevitably (I used to call him *landsmannito*;) but I remember accompanying him more than once, long ago, to a small, dark San Francisco apartment, where he greeted an elderly Japanese couple, did dignified homage to the household shrine of a religion whose name and tenets I never learned, left a contribution and departed. I don't recall that we talked about it much.

For all that I first came across his work in the Jewish magazine *Commentary*, there aren't a lot of identifiably Jewish themes and currents in Avram's later writing. Leaving *The Golem* out of it, the only two stories that I'm chauvinist enough to think could only have been written by a Jew (as distinguished from the myriad that could only have been written by Avram Davidson) are *Now Let Us Sleep* and *The Certificate*, and I could easily be wrong about those. And yet – and yet...

What on earth can be labeled as "Jewish," after all, in a story? in a style? in a way of looking at the world, and at "whatever brute and blackguard made the world," to quote A.E. Housman, whom Avram loved as much as I? Specific subject matter? A certain distinctive use of language? A certain *rachmones*, the bone-born compassion for all of us born doomed? A characteristic *galgenhumor*, the absurd gallows humor born of forbidden tears? A unique relationship, compounded equally of awe and irritation, with the deity whose name we're not supposed to spell? That would certainly qualify a lot of Jewish writers, but it fits Mark Twain as well, not to mention Gabriel Garcia Marquez, Mikhail Bulgakov, Zora Neale Hurston, and Shakespeare. If I had been introduced to Avram Davidson by way of *The Phoenix And The Mirror* or *The Boss In The Wall*, would I have at once recognized him as my *landsmannito*? I doubt it very much, in all honesty.

And yet.

As I've implied, Avram and I rarely talked about Jewishness, or about religion at all, unless it happened to be a vodka-fueled all-night discussion of *voudun*, Roman Mithraism or the cosmology of the Phoenicians or the Sarmatians. He used to tell me long, ridiculously involved shaggy-dog stories in Yiddish, always assuming (or pretending to assume; who knew with that man?) that my command of the language was vastly more fluent than the handful of words and phrases that it is. But for all the twinkles and nuances that I missed as the jokes tumbled by me, one line, the moral appended by Avram to a particular fable, is with me still, clear and cold and amused as the first time I heard it. *"Don't ever believe that we Jews were chosen by God to be his people. We volunteered."*

And perhaps that's what I mean, or what I'm trying to mean, by describing Avram as an ultimately Jewish writer: a volunteering of the spirit. A willingness to engage – always, no matter how poor, how ill, how alone – with the likely unlikely, with the tale told within the shadows of another tale; with the improbable, unprofitable aliveness of a single paragraph, the twisting journeys of a sentence, of a parenthetical aside, even of one word, wherever it all led him. T's not an accident that Avram's later style became, as his critics have called it, "rambling," "discursive," "distracting," even "bewildering," even "tedious." He was on a kind of quest, I think, in those last years: a voyage past story, past his own astonishing erudition, an odyssey to the heart of language. To the Word, that First Word where all stories begin.

His was the same driven spiritual curiosity that is found in the classic commentaries on the Talmud, in the Midrash, the Zohar, the Kabbala. It's a stretch, perhaps, to conceive of a God whose greatest gift to his people was one that would inevitably lure the most vital – and most genuinely pious – souls among them straight to blasphemy and eventual heresy. Yet it *was* a gift, and Avram Davidson was its beneficiary, and that's why, observant or not, he was truly a Jew, and I'm just Jew*ish*.

Dinner (Almost) With The Davidsons

Richard A. Lupoff

It is not easy to be an observant Jew in a mostly secular society, especially in one where Jews, observant or otherwise, are a minority. Avram and Grania, newlyweds in the early 1960's, were trying it. Pat and I were not-so-newlyweds, self-identified as Jewish but not religiously observant.

Avram and Grania lived on the Upper West Side. Pat and I lived in the East Seventies. It was Friday, and Avram and Grania had an evening appointment to keep on the Lower East Side. If you're a present or former New Yorker, or if you know New York, these geographical distinctions are meaningful. If not, I fear I am speaking in gibberish.

The problem was, How could the Davidsons keep their appointment without breaking the Sabbath Law that forbids working on the Day of Rest?

It seems to me that people who struggle with religious legalisms can stand common sense on its head as well and as maddeningly as those who struggle with, uh, legal legalisms. Thus, it is forbidden to drive an automobile on the Sabbath (work) but it is permitted to walk (not work). But is it not more work to walk ten miles than to drive that same distance? And is it work to ride in a subway car, or in a bus or a taxicab, that somebody else is driving?

At any rate, Avram and Grania arranged to travel by motorized conveyance from their apartment on West 110th Street, to Pat-and-my apartment on East 73rd Street, arriving before the setting of the sun marked the beginning of the Sabbath. They would eat their dinner at our apartment, then proceed the rest of their way on foot. Still, a lengthy trek, but far less of one than if they'd made their entire *hegira* by shank's mare.

Dinner, of course, was another issue. We did not keep Kosher; they did. So Avram and Grania brought their meal with them, in little paper bags. Came dinner time, they sat at one end of the table and ate from their paper bags, using their own implements and paper plates, while we sat at the other end of the table dining on china and using *our* own implements.

After a pleasant if slightly peculiar while had passed, Avram and Grania made ready to leave. They had ridden up to our apartment via motorized elevator. Before Sabbath. Now they would walk down the fire stairs to leave.

But first, Grania wished to check her appearance and to comb her hair before the mirror in the bathroom. Another problem! Darkness had fallen by now, and the bathroom was dark. There were electric lights in the bathroom, which should take care of that situation – but Avram raised another objection: for Grania to turn on the light would be work.

Yes, even operating a light-switch was forbidden.

Pat volunteered to turn on the light for Grania. This seemed to be a solution, but – No, said Avram, if Pat turned on the light for Grania's use, she would be acting as Grania's agent, and thus Grania would still be turning on the light, albeit by proxy, which also would not do.

Clever Patricia! "Suppose," she exclaimed in all innocence, "suppose I go into the bathroom and turn on the light *for my own use*. Suppose, when I finish in there and return, *I leave the light on*. Grania could then go in and have light in the bathroom. You couldn't insist that she turn the light *off* because operating the light-switch would be work!"

Avram considered this proposition for a while, then nodded his assent. I suspected that he did so somewhat reluctantly, as if he'd been snookered but was determined to accept the turn of events in good grace.

Grania was able to leave our apartment with her hair neatly combed.

Jewish Magic And A Jewish Magician
by Lisa Goldstein

In the late seventies I was working at Dark Carnival, a Berkeley, CA bookstore that specialized in fantasy and science fiction. One day a writer who frequented the store, Michael Kurland, brought in a Rabbinical-looking, bearded man with a cane, whom he introduced as Avram Davidson.

We were very proud of our Avram Davidson section. In those days books sat on shelves in warehouses for months, sometimes years unlike today, when books are turned into landfill about six months after they come out. We had called distributors all over the country and ordered every Davidson book still in print, and a few out of it. "We're very proud of our Avram Davidson section," I said.

"As well you should be," Avram said.

"Irascible" was the word used most often to describe Avram.

Nonetheless I liked the guy. We talked about his recent book, *The Enquiries of Doctor Eszterhazy*, which takes place in a mythical Central European country, and it turned out that he had actually heard of the town where my mother was born; the only person outside my immediate family I had ever met who had. "Mukachevo, Czechoslovakia!" he said, pronouncing each syllable with relish. And later I learned that every time he went to Telegraph Avenue, which is where the bookstore was located, he carried a quarter to give to the first person who asked him for money, and still later I found out that he himself was probably as poor as some of the people he gave the quarters to. He took the commandment of *tsedakah*, charity, very seriously.

At that time I had started to write fantasy myself. In the fashion of the time I was writing a very Celtic, or possibly very Nordic, fantasy, full of magic swords and amulets and kings and wizards. The book was going nowhere. Then one day a great many things came together. "What am I *doing*?" I thought. "I'm not Celtic, I have a tradition as fascinating, as magical, behind me, one filled with ghosts and demons and dybbuks and golems. Why aren't I using *that*, instead of playing around with these tired old *tropes*?" And I abandoned that book forever and started work on what became *The Red Magician*.

Recalling this now, it seems to me that I heard Avram in the back of my mind crying out, "Mukachevo, Czechoslovakia!", though this is probably hindsight. What I do know is that it was far easier to write a book using Jewish fantasy when someone as brilliant as Avram had blazed the trail before me. Avram had a gift, unfortunately all too rare in writers, of going his own way, of, as we said at the time, *doing his own thing*. It is not a comfortable gift, and sometimes it can even be seen as a curse: it seldom makes its possessor rich or famous. But it results in stories that are lovingly worked out, stories that the author cares about, and because of this the reader cares about them too. And sometimes this gift, this habit of going off in strange directions, of deliberately turning one's back on the rest of the world, can make its possessor seem, well, a little irascible.

"Love From Bubby, Only Be Well"
by Carol Carr

In 1964, only a few years after I met Avram, I asked him for a favor. He was not grumpy yet, in those days, which was a good thing, for like all my people I am thin-skinned and will carry a grudge to the grave, on my back. I asked Avram if he would mind translating a letter I'd received. It had been sent to me in the hope that I could read Yiddish. As if. I sent him a copy of the letter and waited, and pretty soon I received his reply:

"I gamely put aside my two longoverdue [*sic*] novuels [*sic*]," he wrote [notice the deft synthesis of guilt-tripping and innovative spelling]... "and produced the following:

Dear Carol great peace. I have your letter received.
And it has me very happied to hear from you. Thee
terribly helping with all possibles. But illegible how
thus you be now in Amerika. Israel."

It goes on. So does Avram, and he apologizes for not finishing the translation and not doing a better job of it, and ends with: "Please excuse me a million times; go into a kosher butcher's and buy a pound of meat and ask him to translate for you. Are there no ivory towers anymore?" And then he adds, inexplicably: "I'm not even cooking this week, peanut butter and eggs." Looking at his letters, almost thirty years later, I see uncanny similarities between Avram's prose and Phil Dick's – their off-the-wall humor, temperament, and eccentric brilliance.

Yes. What can I possibly say about Avram that he didn't say better himself, if only he could read his handwriting. Now and then I'd have the honor of proofreading Avram's stories, for publication in one of Terry's Carr's anthologies (Avram bought Terry's first story for *F&SF*; later, Terry bought Avram's). It was a terrifying experience. With most authors, proofreading was a piece of cake – you leave something alone or you change it. Before starting a story of Avram's, I'd call my therapist back from vacation, take a long hot bath, and sign up for a linguistics course. I'd read one word at a time and then take a nap in order to be refreshed for the next word. You just couldn't be too careful. What looked like a common typo could be, and most likely was, the long-dead future perfect tense of the irregular verb "to fall to one's knees in a cold sweat." And it should not – *must* not – be disturbed.

Avram and I had little relationship to speak of outside of occasional letters, social-type visits, and random meetings at conventions. But we had great flavor together. He often started his letters to me: "Dear Teeny-tiny, eentsy-weentsy, itsy-bitsy, Carolkin," (whomp! that should do wonders for his bearded, dignified image). Since I was none of those things, I adored it. And here is a typical closing:

> *I cannot write more right now, as my every move is*
> *being watched by secret agents from Birobidjan,*
> *who are also spreading rumors that I am paranoid.*
> *When merely being noid is bad enough. Love, from*
> *bubby, only be well.*

See what I mean about Phil Dick?

Once Avram visited us with a very young Ethan. They sat very close to each other on the couch and spoke in an unknown language that was probably a subdialect used by fathers and sons in Ancient Sumeria. I had no idea what they were saying, but I could tell it was rich, complex, and lit with love.

Years passed. We were in California, he was everywhere. In 1980 he wrote:

*Last week I bought some office supplies and slightly
overpaid. Today I returned and a person handed me
an envelope saying the change was inside. I didn't
examine the envelope till I got home, and found that
on the envelope, in a corner, as an aide-memoire
evidently, someone had penciled, "Little old man
with cane." I tottered off to bed at once.*

In 1983 my mother died. Avram:

*For your pain and sorrow, I am painfully sorry.
There is, however, I have noticed, usually, a certain
measure of relief. And for whatever relief you feel,
feel therein neither pain nor sorrow. Flow with it.
Resume the voyage, float, float; and whenever
crocodiles appear, whack them on the snout with
the paddle.*

A Jew, a poet, a Zen grief counselor.

In 1989 Avram wrote ("Dear eentsy-weentsy," etc., still) to
ask me if I could find, among Terry's papers, a certain manuscript
he'd lost track of. "Now, Carol, it is highly desired that I should have
this in order to have something else to neglect."

And he ended one of his last letters to me with this fillip of
brazen insouciance: "Well, time to cover the parrot."

Indeed. Sleep good, Avram, and don't forget to whack those
crocodiles.

The Jewish Condition Is The Human Condition
by Barry N. Malzberg

The central if not necessarily greatest of Davidson's great stories is *no fire burns* which appeared in *playboy* in the mid-sixties; I haven't read it in thirty-five years, inexplicably it appears in none of his collections, but it remains indelible in memory.

Joe Clock (how could one forget a name like this?) is an ordinary guy living a seemingly ordinary suburban life: some kind of blue-collar occupation, wife, kids, lawn, the usual financial troubles, bowling team on Thursdays...there's only this one thing about Joe Clock which we discover about halfway through: he's one of a gang of psychopaths recruited by some unknown organization (crime syndicate? the government?) to kill people whose names and address are supplied. Joe and his pals pick up their assignment sheets the way that they pick up bowling shoes, go to the directed address, do their job...Joe is no more interested in motive or culpability than he is concerned about the fate of Chinese peasants; it's just another job for him, moonlighting, a way to grab a few extra dollars. Joe is in every other way indistinguishable from his friends and neighbors; he performs his tasks with no more compunction than he cheats a little on his bowling score. Joe is delineated, fairly described, not judged; he is neither exciting nor excited. He simply *is*; he drifts in and out of the population and you're as likely as not to pass his barbecue party on the Fourth of July. You might even be invited. Just don't ask what or who is being barbecued.

Parable of the good German? Well, sure, although this trivializes the story; it's a parable of humanity or maybe humanity as it will devolve through a time when technology makes possible the utter separation of motive from consequence.

And under that, of course, what we might call the *shtetl mentality*, that avatistic understanding at the heart of every Jew (I generalize, but I do so in full awareness) that at any given moment regardless of your circumstance or possibility, the Cossacks are as likely as not to come into the village, burn, sack and plunder and carry you off... and the Cossacks will do this as calmly, in as detached a fashion as God himself placed Jonah under that gourd, and left him stricken in the sun as a lesson in good manners.

Well, Avram understood this pretty well and perhaps better than any fantasist or science fiction writer conveyed that insight with casual skill; "fantasist or science fiction writer" is also trivializing; the man's litany, shrug and tear and scream places him with Kafka, Mandelstam, Singer, Malamud, the great writers of our steaming and distraught condition. The skill which evoked *Joe Clock* beyond pity and terror also enabled him to be perhaps the greatest comic writer of his generation, author of the funniest story ever published in a science fiction magazine *Selectra Six-Ten* and the funniest and darkest story ever published in a science fiction original anthology *Goslin Day*. Of course he struggled, often cheerfully, in penury and anonymity through most of the decades of his life; that was precisely the point of all of this.

Avram was in and out of Orthodoxy; there was a period in his life when he appeared in full Chasidic garb, longer periods when he marginalized religious belief or practice; his disbelief was, I propose, merely another facet of his overall belief; the most fanatical observer, after all, trembles on the edge of renunciation. But he went far beyond gesture; Davidson quit an agent who, in the face of his passionate and uncompromising policy, sold his work to a German publisher, refused to sign the contracts. (I know this to be true; I was an employee of the agent at the time.) Avram, in that regard, wrote the agent the greatest quit letter of all time, subsequently refusing to sign a contract for a domestic paperback sale: "I hate you so much that I cheerfully give up my ninety percent so that I can deny you your ten percent."

This was a serious man of most serious purpose indeed. In sum then, his perception, the perception of all the sages: the Jewish condition is the human condition. My boyfriend is a Golem; my boyfriend's name is Jello. Me is Jello. Recognition of this writer's achievement is still in the earliest stage. *Thank G-d*, as Avram would say.

Introduction to
GOSLIN DAY

(Story first published in Orbit 6, 1970)

KABBALISTIC MAGIC; divination; angels; demons; dybbuks; golems; beatific visions (ah, Ezekiel's vision of the chariot in the heavens and the *Ma'asch Merkavah*, the mysteries of the chariot); the mystical contemplation of the shimmery, slippery alternate worlds such as Yetzirah, where the ten orders of angels dwell...and the dead, dark dangerous worlds, which are the very sources of evil: all these labyrinthine realms and spinning manifestations of the fantastic are a vital part of Jewish thought and fiction. Judaism is a cathedral of rationality built deep into the bedrock of mathematical magic and numinous mystery.

Which brings me to those dark Yiddishe demons called goslins that swim through mirrors when the universe of everything-that-was tilts and shifts and allows the terrible monsters of the id to dance.

Goslins...

Goslin Day is one of Avram's most stylish (in the true literary sense), slyest, and discomforting creations. I'll bet you'll enjoy the story as you read it...but afterward, ah, afterward, perhaps weeks later, *that* is when the goslins will swim out of your unconscious.

When that happens, you might offer up a prayer to Avram for this magical creation that continues to go bump in the night. But before you begin, you should know that *gozlin* (as opposed to Avram's own *goslin*) is a thief...a swindler.

Perhaps gozlins only take – or swindle – souls.

Have a good (goslin) day!

Jack Dann

GOSLIN DAY

IT WAS A GOSLIN DAY, NO DOUBT about it, of course it can happen that goslin things can occur, say, once a day for many days. But *this* day was a *goslin* day. From the hour when, properly speaking, the ass brays in his stall, but here instead the kat kvells on the rooftop – to the hour when the cock crows on his roost, but here instead the garbageman bangs on his can – even that early, Faroly realized that it was going to be a goslin day (night? let be night: *It was evening and* [after that] *it was morning: one day.* Yes or no?) in the warbled agony of the shriekscream Faroly had recognized an element present which was more than the usual ketzelkat expression of its painpleasure syndrome. In the agglutinative obscenities which interrupted the bang-crashes of the yuckels emptying eggshells orangerinds coffeegrounds there was (this morning, different from all other mornings) something unlike their mere usual brute pleasure in waking the dead. Faroly sighed. His wife and child were still asleep. He saw the dimlight already creeping in, sat up, reached for the glass and saucer and poured water over his nails, began to whisper his preliminary prayers, already concentrating on his Intention in the name *Unity*: but aware, aware, aware, the hotsticky feeling in the air, the swimmy looks in the dusty corners of windows, mirrors; something a tension, here a twitch and there a twitch. Notgood notgood.

In short: a goslin day.

Faroly decided to seek an expert opinion, went to Crown Heights to consult the kabbalist, Kaplanovics.

Rabbaness Kaplanovics was at the stove, schauming off the soup with an enormous spoon, gestured with a free elbow toward an inner room. There sat the sage, the sharp one, the teacher of our teachers, on his head his beaver hat neatly brushed, on his feet and legs his boots brightly polished, in between his garments well and clean without a fleck or stain as befits a disciple of the wise. He and Faroly shook hands, greeted, blessed the Name. Kaplanovics pushed across several sheets of paper covered with an exquisitely neat calligraphy.

"Already there," the kabbalist said. "I have been through everything three times, twice. The *NY Times, the Morgen Dzshornal,* I. F. Stone, Dow-Jones, the *Daph-Yomi,* your name-Text, the weather report, Psalm of the Day. Everything is worked out, by numerology, analogy, gematria, noutricon, anagrams, allegory, procession and precession. So.

"Of course today as any everyday we must await the coming of the Messiah: 'await' – *expect*? *today*? not today. Today he wouldn't come. Considerations for atmospheric changes, or changes for atmospheric considerations, *not-bad. Not-bad.* Someone gives you an offer for a good airconditioner, cheap, you could think about it. Read seven capitals of psalms between afternoon and evening prayers. One sequence is enough. The day is favorable for decisions on growth stocks, but avoid closed-end mutual funds. On the corner by the beygal store is an old woman with a pyshka, collecting dowries for orphan girls in Jerusalem: the money, she never sends, this is *her* sin, it's no concern of yours: give her eighteen cents, a very auspicious number: merit, cheaply bought (she has sugar diabetes and the daughter last week gave birth to a weak-headed child by a schwartzer), what else?" They examined the columns of characters.

"Ahah. Ohoh. If you get a chance to buy your house, don't buy it, the Regime will condemn it for a freeway, where are they all *going* so fast? – every titan who has two legs thinks he needs three automobiles – besides – where did I write it? oh yes. There. The neighborhood is going to change very soon and if you stay you will be killed in three years and two months, or three months and two years, depending on which system of gematria is used in calculating. You have to warn your brother-in-law his sons should each commence bethinking a marriagematch. Otherwise they will be going to cinemas and watching televisions and putting arms around girls, won't have the proper intentions for their nighttime prayers, won't even read the protective psalms selected by the great grandson of the *Baalshemtov*: and with what results, my dear man? Nocturnal emissions and perhaps worse; is it for nothing that The Chapters of the Principles caution us, 'At age eighteen to the marriage canopy and the performance of good deeds,' hm?"

Faroly cleared his throat. "Something else is on your mind," said the kabbalist. "Speak. Speak." Faroly confessed his concern about goslins. Kaplanovics exclaimed, struck the table. "Goslins! you wanted to talk about goslins? It's already gone past the hour to say the Shema, and I certainly didn't have in mind when I said it to commence constructing a kamea." He clicked his tongue in annoyance. "Am I omniscient?" he demanded. "Why didn't you let me know you were coming? Man walks in off the street, expects to find – "

But it did not take long to soothe and smooth him – Who is strong? He who can control his own passion.

And now to first things first, or, in this case, last things first, for it was the most recent manifestation of goslinness which Faroly wished to talk about. The kabbalist listened politely but did not seem in agreement with nor impressed by his guest's recitation of the signs by which a goslin day might make itself known. "'Show simonim,'" he murmured, with a polite nod. "This one loses an object, that one finds it, let the claimant come and 'show simonim,' let him cite the signs by which his knowledge is demonstrated, and, hence, his ownership..." but this was mere polite fumfutting, and Faroly knew that the other knew that both knew it.

On Lexington a blackavised goslin slipped out from a nexus of cracked minors reflecting dust at each other in a disused nightclub, snatched a purse from a young woman emerging from a ribs joint; in Bay Ridge another, palepink and blond, snatched a purse from an *old* woman right in front of Suomi Evangelical Lutheran. Both goslins flickersnickered and were sharply gone. In Tottenville, a third one materialized in the bedroom of an honest young woman still half asleep in bed just a second before her husband came back from the nightshift in Elizabeth, New Jersey, uttered a goslin cry and jumped out the window holding his shirt. Naturally the husband never believed her – would *you*? Two more slipped in and out of a crucial street corner on the troubled bordermarches of Italian Harlem, pausing only just long enough to exchange curses and goslin looks out of the corners of their goslin eyes. Goslin cabdrivers curseshouted at hotsticky pregnant women dumb enough to try and cross at pedestrian crossings. The foul air grew fouler, thicker, hotter, tenser, muggier, murkier: and the goslins, smelling it from afar, came leapsniffing through the vimveil to nimblesnitch, torment, buffet, burden, uglylook, poke, makestumble, maltreat, and quickshmiggy back again to gezzle guzzle goslinland.

The kabbalist had grown warm in discussion, eagerly inscribed circles in the air with downhooked thumb apart from fist, "'...they have the forms of men and also they have the lusts of men,'" he quoted.

"You are telling me what every schoolchild knows," protested Faroly. "But from *which* of the other three of the four worlds of Emanation, Creation, Formation, and Effectation – from *which* do they come? And why more often, and more and more often, and more amid more and more often, and – "

Face wrinkled to emphasize the gesture of waving these words away, Kaplanovics said, "If Yesod goes, how can Hod remain? If there is no Malchuth, how can there be Quether? Thus one throws away with the hand the entire configuration of Adam Qadmon, the Tree of Life, the Ancient of Days. Men tamper with the very vessels themselves, as if they don't know what happened with the Bursting of the Vessels before, as though the Husks, the Shards, even a single shattered Cortex, doesn't still plague and vex and afflict us to this day. They look down into the Abyss, and they say, "This is high," and they look up to an Eminence and they say, "This is low."... And not thus alone! And not thus alone! Not just with complex deenim, as, for example, those concerning the fluxes of women – no! no! but the simplest of the simple of the Six hundred and Thirteen Commandments: to place a parapet around a roof to keep someone from falling off and be killed. What can be simpler? What can be more obvious? What can be easier?

" – but do they do it? What, was it only three weeks ago, or four? a Puertorican boy didn't fall off the roof of an apartment house near here? Dead, perished. Go talk to the wall. Men don't want to know. Talk to them *Ethics*, talk to them *Brotherhood*, talk to them *Ecumenical Dialogue*, talk to them any kind of nonsenseness: they'll listen. But talk to them, It's written, textually, in the Torah, to build a parapet around your rooftop to prevent blood being shed – no: to this they won't listen. They would neither hear nor understand. They don't know *Torah*, don't know *Text*, don't know *parapet, roof* – this they never heard of either – "

He paused. "Come tomorrow and I'll have prepared for you a kamea against goslins." He seemed suddenly weary.

Faroly got up. Sighed. "And tomorrow will you also have prepared a kamea against goslins for everyone else?"

Kaplanovics didn't raise his eyes. "Don't blame the rat," he said. "Blame the rat-hole."

Downstairs Faroly noticed a boy in a green and white skullcap, knotted crispadin coming up from inside under his shirt to dangle over his pants. "Let me try a sortilegy," he thought to himself. "Perhaps it will give me some remez, or hint ..." Aloud, he asked, "Youngling, tell me, what text did you learn today in school?"

The boy stopped twisting one of his stroobley earlocks, and turned up his phlegm-green eyes. "'Three things take a man out of this world,'" he yawned. "'Drinking in the morning, napping in the noon, and putting a girl on a wine-barrel to find out if she's a virgin.'"

Faroly clicked his tongue, fumbled for a handkerchief to wipe his heatprickled face. "You are mixing up the texts," he said.

The boy raised his eyebrows, pursed his lips, stuck out his lower jaw. "Oh indeed. You ask me a question, then you give me an answer. How do you know I'm mixing up the texts? Maybe I cited a text which you never heard before. What are you, the Vilna Gaon?"

"Brazen face – look, look, how you've gotten your crispadin all snarled," Faroly said, slightly amused, fingering the cinctures passed through one belt-loop – then, feeling his own horrified amazement and, somehow, *knowing... knowing...* as one *knows* the refrigerator is going to stop humming one half second before it does stop, yet – "What is this? What is this? The cords of your crispadin are tied in *pairs*?"

The filthgreen eyes slid to their corners, still holding Faroly's. "Hear, O Israel," chanted the child; "the Lord our God, the Lord is Two."

The man's voice came out agonyshrill. "Dualist. Heresiarch. Sectary. Ah. Ah ah *ah – goslin!*"

"Take ya hands outa my pants!" shrieked the pseudochild, and, with a cry of almost totally authentic fear, fled. Faroly, seeing people stop, faces changing, flung up his arms and ran for his life. The goslin-child, wailing and slobbering, trampled up steps into an empty hallway where the prismatic edge of a broken windowpane caught the sunlight and winkyflashed rainbow changes. The goslin stretched thin as a shadow and vanished into the bright edge of the shard.

Exhausted, all but prostrated by the heat, overcome with humiliation, shame, tormented with fear and confusion, Faroly stumbled through the door of his home. His wife stood there, looking at him. He held to the doorpost, too weary even to raise his hand to kiss the mezuzah, waiting for her to exclaim at his appearance. But she said nothing. He opened his mouth, heard his voice click in his throat.

"Solomon," his wife said. He moved slowly into the room.

"Solomon," she said.

"Listen – "

"Solomon, we were in the park, and at first it was so hot, then we sat under a tree and it was so *cool – *"

"Listen."

"...I think I must have fallen asleep... Solomon, you're so quiet... Now you're home, I can give the Heshy his bath. Look at him, Solomon! Look, look!"

Already things were beginning to get better. "*And the High Priest shall pray for the peace of himself and his house.* Tanya Rabbanan: – and his house. This means, his wife. He who has no wife, has no home." Small sighs, stifled sobs, little breaks of breath, Faroly moved forward into the apartment. Windows and minors were still, dark, quiet. The goslin day was almost over. She had the baby ready for the bath. Faroly moved his eyes, squinting against the last sunlight, to look at the flesh of his first-born, unique son, his Kaddish. What child was this, sallow, squinting back, scrannel, preternaturally sly – ? Faroly heard his own voice screaming screaming changeling! changeling!

– Goslin!

Introduction to
Dr. Morris Goldpepper Returns

THIS STORY WAS PUBLISHED IN *Galaxy Magazine* in 1962. It is the sequel to one of Avram's most famous stories, *Help! I Am Dr. Morris Goldpepper*. In the first story, Doctor of Dental Surgery Morris Goldpepper, widower, father of a grown daughter, and loyal member of the American Dental Association, is abducted by wizened aliens with blue gums. These elderly appearing and toothless extraterrestrials want Dr. Goldpepper to fit them with false teeth, so they can sneak into the United States and collect Social Security. As the first story closes, the American Dental Association vows to rescue brave Doctor Goldpepper, famed inventor of the Goldpepper Bridge and the Goldpepper Crown. The story, *Help! I Am Dr. Morris Goldpepper* can now be found in the book, *The Avram Davidson Treasury* (Tor, 1998).

In this sequel, Dr. Goldpepper has been rescued from the alien planet, and is now recovering from his ordeal at the ranch of a friend in Texas. But the aliens haven't forgotten Morry Goldpepper, and neither will you.

Grania Davidson Davis

DR. MORRIS GOLDPEPPER RETURNS

JAMES E. (FOR ELPHONSUS) DANDY paced the floor of the office of his ranch at Tishomingo, the showplace of the State of Texas (and hence not to be confused with any ranch which might be located in or at Tishomingo, Oklahoma), in a manner which can only be described as restless. From time to time he sought, like Boethius, the consolations of philosophy – using this word in its former interpretation as meaning "science" – from his bookshelf. But for once, the writings of Crowe, Holwager, Barrett, Shields and Williams – not to mention Oliver – for once the writings of these great scientific pioneers failed to either to console or absorb him. His burden was heavy. His need was great. His pace was restless.

Some distance away, exactly how much is unnecessary to state in terms of exact precision, all things (as the great Einstein has taught us) being relative: what counts as a long way in the State of Rhode Island and Providence Plantations is a mere jaunt in Texas... some distance away, to continue, a pretty and personable young person of the female persuasion was weeping bitterly. Great tears rolled from her large eyes and down her soft cheeks.

"But Daddy, Daddy, Daddy!" she pled and implored. "None of that is Little Jimmy's fault. Why can't we get married, Daddy, Daddy, please?"

Her name was Mary Jane Crawford. The man whom she addressed in terms of filial allegiance was her father, Dr. Clement (or "Clem") Crawford, a landowner and husbandman; in other words, a rancher; besides holding the *eclat* of a degree in Dental Medicine.

The question instantly and quite properly arises, why was this last fact not mentioned first, and the answer is that Dr. "Clem" Crawford – or "Doc," a familiarity and diminutive which would give justified offense in large centers of populous habitation such as cities, but which in rural areas may be, and often is, used without offense – Doc Clem Crawford had for some years given over and retired from active practice of this highly important profession, and had since devoted his time to agriculture and its allied crafts.

"Mary Jane," he said, somewhat testily, "I wish you'd quit all that bawling. I didn't say you couldn't marry Little Jimmy, I only said you couldn't marry him *now*. It's not his fault that 'Big Jimmy' got himself into this pickle. But all he's got in this world is his share of whatever his daddy's got, and it looks like there's a powerful big chance his daddy might *lose* whatever he's got. I just couldn't hardly bear to think of my little girl having to rough it, cooped up in some little old ten-room house. 'Course, you could go right on living *here* and Little Jimmy could work for *me*. But no. He's just as bullheaded as his daddy."

Mary Jane went off, disconsolate and unhappy. Her father continued to sit in his chair, as if brooding over his daughter's Affairs, but the fact is that he had unwelcome worries of his own.

In the vast kitchen of the Crawford ranch-house a comely woman of middle age was engaged in baking pies of fruits and other delicious comestibles. This was Mrs. Doothit, the housekeeper, a widow-woman, as the local vernacular idiom has it. There had been a time when she felt that she had reason to believe an interest in her existed on the part of her employer, Dr. Clement (Clem) Crawford – who was a widower – which was separate and apart from such considerations as her flaky and juicy pies, her toothsome steaks, her savory coffee, and delicious roasts... though by no means diminished by them.

During this time she thought she was aware of a certain look in her employer's eye, and a certain tone in his voice. But that time had passed, and with it had passed much of Mrs. Doothit's interest in her work. She had even been considering taking a position as housemother in an establishment for underprivileged girls that was maintained in a suburb of Dallas by the Southern Baptist Convention.

But she put off making this decision from day to day.

Upstairs, in the spacious suite of rooms generously put at his disposal by his host, Clement (Clem) Crawford, *DDM* (Ret.), was yet another of the *dramatis personae*, or cast of characters, of the narration which we now peruse, namely and videlicet one Morris Goldpepper, Doctor of Dental Surgery, inventor of the Goldpepper Bridge and the Goldpepper Crown, and perfector of the Semi-Retractable Clasp which bears his name. He is as it were, the Livy, Macrobius or Gibbon of this annal. (Modesty, epitomized by my automatic shrinking from the spotlight, obliges me – with this one exception-to cleave to the Third Person previously and henceforth.)

The suite of rooms was a veritable apartment of its own, consisting of a sleeping chamber, a lounge, an office, a kitchen, a bar (which Dr. Goldpepper's well-known temperate habits rendered about as useful as certain mammalian appurtenances on a boar), a games-room and what had previously been another sleeping chamber but which had been converted at no small cost and effort into a laboratory for the fabrication and synthesis of dental prosthetic devices.

All this had been done out of pure generosity, affection and respect by Dr. Crawford on behalf of his old Navy Dental Corps "buddy," Dr. Goldpepper.

It is not to be thought that Dr. Goldpepper had surrendered occupancy of his bachelor apartment in the Hotel Davenport, nor yet of his laboratory on Broadway in the Upper West 70s, in order to live the life of a country squire in the sylvan or (considering the sparseness of trees) semi-sylvan fastnesses of John C. Calhoun County, Texas. The facts of the matter, not altogether pleasant, are that he was undergoing the long and delicate process of recuperation intendant upon the aftermaths of his rescue from the grasp and clutches of the malevolent inhabitants of a distant planet in another part of the Galaxy, the captivation and captivity whereon has already been recorded in these pages; anent which, enough – no point in chewing a twice-told tale.

At any rate, Dr. Goldpepper rested in his luxuriously appointed guest quarters. He took long walks around the ranch, delighted in the verdant greenery of its crops and the rolling undulation of its hills. And, for the first time since his boyhood, he recommenced the gentle piscatorial craft or pastime of angling.

The M Bar L Ranch (named after the Honorable Mirabeau Bonaparte Lamar, sometime President of the Republic of Texas, and a boyhood idol of Doc Clem) was located on the Little Comanche River. To those used to the Majestic Hudson and the navigable East, the application "river" to what others might well deem a mere creek is at first difficult. However that may be, the waters of the Little Comanche teemed with trout, bass and other edible species of fish. Dr. Goldpepper considered himself too impatient to undertake mastery of dry – or even wet – fly fishing, but his efficient host kept his bait box supplied with worms of a most surprising stature or length, and, thus aided, the guest seldom failed to come home with something in his creel besides air.

It was on the day on which our story opened that Dr. Goldpepper returned from a circumambulation of the scenery and was told by his host that someone was waiting to see him.

"Waiting to see *me*?" was his surprised rejoinder. "*Who*?"

"*I* don't know, Morry," said Doctor Clem. "Some little old man."

Put completely off guard by his awareness of the Texan habit of placing the words *little* and *old* before almost any odd noun – a "little old baby," "a little old elephant" or "brontosauras" – Dr. Goldpepper was therefore astonished to see that the personage waiting for him was literally little and – to all outward presages – old.

But in another fraction of a second he recognized the typical blue gums in the individual's mouth, open in a fawning sort of false, deceitful smile, and recognized himself to be in the presence of a member of the hideous and alien race whose unwilling captive he had been on far-off Upsilon Centauri (as he had with wry humor denominated it to himself, to avoid becoming embittered).

Startled, Dr. Goldpepper uttered a cry of surprise. Inadvertently he stepped behind Doc Crawford, who inquired, "Morry, what in the Hell is the matter?"

Goldpepper lashed out fearlessly at the invader with his fishing-rod, but the diminutive alien evaded the blow and groveled on the floor, crying, "Have kindness, Merciful Goldpepper!" and attempted to place his head beneath Goldpepper's foot.

Once it was realized that this was a sign of submission, indeed of homage or obeisance, and not some sort of wrestling hold, the latter at once became calm.

"What is the meaning of this outrageous intrusion?" Dr. Goldpepper demanded, sternly and outraged. "Is it your intention to abduct me yet another time, as if I hadn't had enough *tsuris* already?"

"Assist, assist, Benevolent Goldpepper!" the alien wailed as he writhed on a floor-rug made from the pelts of fifty-four coyotes shot by the owner of the M Bar L. "Forgive, Great Dentist of the Ages!"

Seizing the unwelcome one by the scruff of his collar while he was still attempting his act of vassalage, Dr. Crawford inquired, in some amazement, "Do you mean to tell me, Morry, that this little old thing was one of the gang that kidnapped you?"

"It was not by violence, but by subterfuge," said the erstwhile victim, wearily. "And I don't care to dwell on the subject. Ask him to leave."

"*Ask* him?!" Dr. Crawford exclaimed with an oath, opening the door and flinging the intruder out with some measure of violence. He then summoned one of his employees, a tall, dark and ugly man with only one eye, known as Ojito Gonzales, and on whose head there was declared to be in the State of Chihuahua (or it might be Sonora) an unofficial reward of ten thousand pesos. He enjoined the Mexican not to allow the extraterrestrial upon the premises again under pain of severe displeasure.

Much shaken by these events, Dr. Goldpepper allowed himself to be persuaded to take a small glass of Bourbon whiskey, and Mrs. Doothit made him some strong coffee.

While the agitation produced by these untoward events had yet to die down, a sound of an automobile was heard outside in the driveway. Looking out the window, those inside perceived the well-known palomino Cadillac of James E. (for Elphonsus) "Big Jimmy" Dandy. Seated with him was his son Little Jimmy, a perfect example of hyperbole, or exaggeration not intended to deceive, for it was obvious to the naked eye that Little Jimmy was at least six feet six inches tall, and had an open and pleasant face. It was a source of sorrow to Dr. Morris Goldpepper that circumstances beyond his control were providing impediments to the marriage of this young man to Mary Jane Crawford, of whom he was very fond (in an avuncular way, she referring to him as "Uncle Morry").

The young man waved to them and then walked off with his fiancee, who had run out to meet him. His father looked at them, shook his head and walked slowly into the house.

"Howdy, Clem," he said, in greeting. "Howdy, Doc" – referring to guest, not host.

"Anything new, Jimmy?" Dr. Crawford inquired. As Mr. Dandy slowly shook his head, Dr. Crawford pressed his lips together. Then he rose. "I've got to tend to some business down at the south forty," he said. "You and Morry entertain one another, now. Jimmy, you and your boy stay for dinner, now, hear?" And he disappeared. Plainly, he did not desire an occasion to arise for him and his friend to be alone together, doubtless for fear the subject of the postponed nuptials would be broached.

Doing his best to make conversation, Dr. Goldpepper inquired, "I wonder why people always talk about the *south* forty. How is it that a person seldom if ever hears mention of the *north* forty?"

But Mr. Dandy didn't rise to this intriguing ethnoecological problem. He merely shook his head in a bemused fashion and said, "damn if *I* know, Doc." And then he sighed.

He was a typical Texas-type rancher: tall, reddened face, boots, Stetson.

He sighed again, looking at a mounted portion of a white-tailed deer which Dr. Crawford had, in rather questionable humor, placed over the mantel of the giant fireplace.

"Mr. Dandy – "

"Jimmy, Doc."

"Jimmy – forgive me for intruding on your own personal emotional difficulties, but if you won't mind – after all, although not a physician in the common sense of the word – let alone a psychiatrist, psychologist or psychoanalyst (whether Freudianly oriented or otherwise), still, in the long years of professional duty before I commenced the more solitary work of dental prosthesis, in my civilian practice as well as the United States Navy Dental Corps, I have had patients confide in me all manner of difficulties, and – "

Mr. Dandy groaned aloud. "Doc," he said, "do you know anybody who wants to buy fifteen million earthworms?"

There was a silence.

Dr. Morris Goldpepper was convinced that the man's mind had snapped, thus causing a mental aberration of no mean proportion.

"How do you mean, fifteen million earthworms?" he inquired, cautiously. Delusions of the most multifarious kinds he had met with before, but this was something new.

"It's all the fault of that damn Federal Government," said Mr. Dandy. "If it wasn't for Them, I'd never of gotten in this here predicament. The least they could do is buy 'm off me. They buy surplus wheat, don't they? Butter? Cotton? Goober peas? Why, do you know that last year the Federal Government spent over eight million tax-dollars to keep up the price of lard?"

"What!" exclaimed Dr. Goldpepper, stung to the quick. "With my money?"

Mr. Big Jimmy Dandy smacked his right fist into his left palm. "Yes, sir, with your money! And with my money! But can I get some of it back when I need it? No, sir. Them and their damn flood control! Why, when I think of it – "

Wistfully, Dr. Morris Goldpepper thought of the perfectly equipped laboratory upstairs, with its neat array of wires of teeth, shellac trays, plaster, dental stone, denture trays, casting ovens and machines, Baldor lathes and Bunsen burners. Here he could have been at work on his favorite project, developing the Goldpepper Cap, instead of listening to the disjointing babblings of some backwoods anti-Federalist. He sighed.

"What is the precise or even approximate connection," he inquired, "between governmental projects for flood control, and the sale or purchase of earthworms?"

The rawboned, rugged rancher looked at him ruefully. "That's right," he said. "You're not from around here. You wouldn't know. Well, Doc, the Federal Government was supposed to start this here flood control project of building dams along the Little Comanche, Big Comanche, Middle Comanche, Muddy Tom, Clear Tom and Bullhead River Valleys, which would provide twenty-seven new lakes. Now, you know, Doc, lakes are pretty scarce in this part of Texas. I don't suppose there's more than one or two a man couldn't, us, spit across, with a favorable wind behind him.

"So you can imagine what twenty-seven new lakes would mean. *Twenty-seven lakes!*"

"Hmm," said Dr. Morris Goldpepper thoughtfully.

Every fisherman in Texas, Mr. Big Jimmy declared enthusiastically, would flock to the new Lakes Area, to say nothing of multitudes from other states. It would be the biggest thing since the discovery of oil. "So naturally," he said, "I looked to increase my stock."

"Your stock?"

"Yes. On my ranch."

Dr. Goldpepper, who had been thinking in terms of mutual funds, common and preferred, a subject about which he knew little or nothing, not being a speculator by nature, chuckled gently. "I see," he said. "Black Angus? Santa Gertrudis? Brahmas?" – terms he had acquired from his host, Clement (Clem) Crawford, *DDM* (Ret.). "You planned to sell meat to these visiting tourists? Barbecue? Hamburgers?"

Mr. Dandy cast a most peculiar look upon him. "Do you mean to say, Doc," he inquired, "that you don't know what kind of critters I raise on my ranch?" In the embarrassed silence which followed they could hear the two young people who were walking by outside. Mary Jane was sobbing all over Little Jimmy's silk shirt and had soaked it to a transparency. He was patting her shoulders with his huge hands and saying, "Now, Honey. Now, Honey."

"Er – *what* kind?"

"In Texas, Doc, when they say Jim Dandy, they mean earthworms. And when they say earthworms, they mean Jim Dandy. Simultaneous terms, sir. Simultaneous terms. I started out with one worm tub twenty-five years ago and now I've got the largest worm ranch in the State of Texas! And that means in the world. One square mile of worm pits, Doc – think of that. One square mile of worm sheds, worm tanks and worm boxes." He gazed into the far distances, a proud and dreamy look on his seamed face. "Earl B. Shields – you've heard of Earl B. Shields, everybody's heard of Earl B. Shields – Earl B. Shields devotes two whole chapters to me in *Commercial Earthworm Raising*. George H. Holwager's *Bigger and Better Red Worms* has fifteen illustrations of my ranch. Calls me 'a model for all progressive worm ranchers to follow!' What do you think of *that*? Barrett, Oliver, Crowe, Williams and the others, they all refer to me, yes, sir."

Then the look of exaltation vanished from his rugged features.

"But I raised my sights too far," he said. "It was the mere thought of them twenty-seven lakes and the folks flocking to all of 'm that set me off. What a market for bait worms! And me setting right here in the middle of it, astride the main highway! I advertised, took whole pages in the *Na-*

tional Worm Rancher, offered top prices – eight dollars per five hundred for Giants, five dollars per five hundred for Mediums and four dollars per five hundred for Run-of-the-Pits. Offered purchase agreement guarantees for three years ahead...”

In order to house his new stock, the enthusiastic rancher had erected new buildings. In order to pay for them, he had borrowed.

Alas for the vanity of human wishes! (As Samuel Johnson, Ll.D. (Oxon.) called it.) Alas for ambition!

The Federal Government, in the name of Economy, had canceled the flood control project for the area including the Little Comanche, Big Comanche, Middle Comanche, Muddy Tom, Clear Tom and Bullhead riverine regions – thus leaving “Big Jimmy” Dandy of the Jim Dandy Earthworm Ranch holding, as it were, the bag.

What right (he demanded) had the Federal Government to come messing things up in Texas with Economy? If Texans had wanted Economy (he declared) they'd have stayed a Republic.

“And so here I am,” he asseverated, “with fifteen million worms in my pits, and my regular markets can't take no more than a million of 'm. Doc, you see before you a ruined man. My hopes are blasted, my lands are mortgaged and it looks as if Little Jimmy and Mary Jane won't be able to get married for years and years, because I just know my boy wouldn't break his daddy's heart by taking on the responsibility and expense of a wife before his daddy's debts were paid off down to the last copper penny. I'd blow my brains out if I thought otherwise, and he knows it; yes, he does.

“Just the thought of all them hungry beauties crawling and wiggling in my worm pits, and no market a-tall for 'm, makes me feel raw and miserable in the pit of my stomach. I wonder if Miz Doothit baked any sweet potato pie lately. Though I'll take rhubarb-pecan if she hasn't.”

Doctor Morris Goldpepper declined an invitation to join the rancher in the kitchen, and, on the terminologically inexact plea of a headache, withdrew to take another long walk in the country.

With one part of his mind Dr. Goldpepper mused upon the problem of the Goldpepper Cap, for so many long years his perpetual Work In Progress – should it be, for example, reticulated or non-reticulated? – while simultaneously with another part of his mind he brooded over the question of Big Jimmy, Little Jimmy and Mary Jane.

Almost before he realized it he found himself upon a sort of a high mound or hillock, from whence he had a view of much of the property belonging to his friend Dr. Crawford. Everywhere the green verdure grew-except on the hillock, which was dusty and arid and nourished (if that is not too strong a word) only a handful of sickly weeds.

A scrabbling sort of noise caught his attention, and he turned to observe the identical alien from Upsilon Centauri who had earlier been ejected from the property, in the current act of kneeling and pouring handfuls of dust on his head with both hands.

"Abject I am, Great Goldpepper," he whined. "Abasing myself before you in humility I am. On behalf of my people apology offering, I am. Forgive, forgive, Compassionate Goldpepper!"

At first Doctor Morris Goldpepper resolved to sell his life dearly. But the thought occurred to him that this creature from another galactic quadrant might just conceivably be telling the truth. Furthermore, his curiosity was piqued.

"What are you doing here?" he inquired. "On the terms of the peace treaty signed between your planet, the American Dental Association and the Waterfront Works Union (acting through their representative, Mr. Albert Annapollo, and the Longshoremen's Dental Health Plan – who acted as our shock troops – I was to be released from the captivity wherein I toiled making false teeth to enable your naturally toothless race to pose as Earthmen; and those of you on this planet were to leave *istanta*, on pain of having your planet's water fluoridated without mercy! Therefore I must beg to inquire what you think you are doing here?"

"The slightest trace of fluorine to us instant death is, Life-loving Goldpepper," the alien sniveled. "Have Ruth!"

Touched despite himself, Dr. Goldpepper magnanimously directed him to speak without fear. This the nonterrestrian lifeform (his race had two hearts, and six distinct and articulate digits on each hand and foot) proceeded to do so.

"Since you from us taken were, great calamity upon us has come, Auspicious Goldpepper," he moaned. "Assist, assist!"

"What seems to be the trouble?"

"Overpopulation."

Somewhat stiffly, Dr. Goldpepper pointed out that he was not Margaret Sanger.

"Malnutrition! The soil of our home world for cycles, sickening has been. Woe, woe, woe! Our stricken planet aid, Scientific Goldpepper!"

In a *precis*, or nutshell, the story he told was that, as a result of some curious condition of their planet's soil itself, the slith crop, source of their staple gelatinous food, had failed by forty percent, and was still failing. Purts, the prime source of gruel, had dropped to a mere twenty percent of normal; and as for sneet, kutch and zooky, the nutritive elements of which were scantier, it was doubtful if the crops would reach maturity. The

172

soil chemists of Upsilon Centauri, who were as advanced, probably, as our own, had pronounced themselves baffled. Large areas had been sprayed with Kz. Pf. Kz. to no avail, and larger ones irrigated with snurg without the slightest results.

"Once our whole planet like *that* looked," the spokesman wailed. "Now, like *this* it is." He gestured from the greenery on all sides to the sterility of the hill, or undulation, on which they stood; and he stooped to cast more dust on his head.

As Doctor Goldpepper followed his gestures, he observed one of the ranch-hands coming their way, and indicated, by waving his hand, that he desired this man to come up.

"Doc, seens you're here," the man said, coming up to him, "I got thishyere tush that's been givin me Hell, my face is all swoll up, and I been livin mostly on beans an beer. See?" And he obtruded a dusty finger into his mouth to indicate the offending canine.

"Come to the ranch-house when you can, where I have my instruments, and I'll take a look at it," said Dr. Goldpepper. "Meanwhile, if you will pardon my curiosity, why is this particular hill so desolate, compared to what I might call the lushness of the rest of the ranch?"

The man withdrew his finger, sucked meditatively on the tooth and then said, "Why, how the land looks hyere, that's how *all* thishyear land use ta look, twell we got in them Jim Dandy Giant Golden-Red Hybrids. Now, evva othuh bit a land hyere is green an growin. We keeps thishyear little old hill seprut jus fer showin whut it oe'ul use ta look like; will it hurt much, Doc?"

And in this wise was Dr. Morris Goldpepper reminded of the singular and curious ability of the common earthworm – let alone the Jim Dandy Giant Golden-Red Hybrid earthworm – to rejuvenate a piece of ground by moving through it, and by moving *it* through *them*. "Disgusting subject," some might say, but to Dental Science nothing natural is disgusting; thus cogitating, he returned to the ranch-house, followed by the Upsilon Centurian, just in time to catch Big Jimmy.

America's leading worm rancher was loath to believe that the alien was from another planet, but, upon being assured and reassured that he was not, at any rate, from the Soviet Union, he professed his complete willingness to do business. After all, it is not every day in the week that one finds a customer for fifteen million earthworms.

However, the term "customer" implies not only sale, but purchase as well. Purchase may be by cash, goods or service. Cash, it was obvious, the Upsilonians did not have. The only service of which they were possessed which was at all likely to be of use was that of teleportation (matterproting, according to another usage); and it was agreed that this was something for which the world was not yet prepared. Which left "goods".

The Upsilonian offered, when the crops of his native world should be restored to their former yield, to pay for the worms, pound for pound, in slith, purts, sneet, kutch and/or zooky. But on being informed by Doctor Morris Goldpepper (who had lived on these substances and their derivatives for months) that the best of them tasted like old library paste, Mr. Dandy declined. He also eructated.

"Pardon me, folks," he said, abashed and discomfited. "It's a sort of nervous indigestion, which I get every now and... What in thee Hell are *these*?"

"These" were a number of objects in a small box offered by the alien Upsilonian, apparently the same bulk as a five-grain aspirin tablet, but shaped rather like tiny pretzels.

"Minor medications of my planet, they are," he said. "For ailments of stomach, colon, freest and grunk, good they are. Take, take, Worm-Raising Dandy."

He took, and while he was swallowing, Doctor Crawford asked, "They good for anything else?"

The Upsilonian reflected. "Arthritis," he said, after cogitating thoughtfully. Doctor Clem avowed himself an irregular victim to what he thought might be arthritis, in his left knee, and swallowed one of the pillular pretzels before his colleague could point out to him that this was all a non-scientific approach to a highly scientific problem.

It was at this point that Little Jimmy came in and reminded his father that they had fifteen million worms to take care of and hence for that reason couldn't stay there all day and all night, much as he (Little Jimmy) would personally prefer to do. The muffled sound of Mary Jane sobbing outside was audibly heard when he paused, reluctantly.

His father rose. "Boy's right," he posited. "Well, I guess I'll have to come back tomorrow and continue the discussion. I sure do hope we can think of something. Bye." And they drove off in the palomino Cadillac, and then Doctor Goldpepper had to treat the ranch-hand with the infected tooth. It was a root-canal job, but, with the able if reluctant assistance of his colleague, was successfully accomplished.

Everyone retired to bed rather early, including the Upsilonian. "I believe I'll take another one of those doohickeys," the host observed, as he prepared to go upstairs.

"Has your arthritis been bothering you?" Dr. Goldpepper inquired solicitously.

"No; but why take chances?" was the rejoinder. "Night, Morry. Night, Mary Jane. Night, um."

Mary Jane sniffled.

The next morning found Doctor Morris Goldpepper sipping his pink grapefruit juice (from which fruit Texas should be more famous than it is) with only Mary Jane for company; and she had nothing to say except an occasional semi-stifled sob.

Before he had finished the job, the Dandys drove up, Mr. Dandy, Senior, bounding into the breakfast-nook (it was as big as the Grand Ballroom at the Hotel Davenport) with his red face full of beaming joy. "It worked!" he cried – a noise which produced the Upsilonian on the scene. Big Jimmy picked him from his feet and danced around the room with him. "It worked! Settled my stomach like it never was settled before! It's just got to be good for arthritis, too! I figure half the population of the *U*nited States has got nervous stomachs, and the other half has arthritis! Mr. Upsilonian (say, are you Armenian? I've known some real fine Armenians!), I'll take seven and a half million white ones, and seven and a half million pink ones, a worm for a pill. A deal?'

The alien was too startled to do more than nod.

Dr. Crawford came down at that moment. "Mary Jane, honey," he observed, "you trot right out and give your sweetheart a real big good-morning kiss, hear? And tell him that the wedding is *on*!"

The delighted girl rushed, squealing merrily, from the room, and her father, in a lowered tone of voice, winked and dug the other Earthmen in the ribs with his elbows, as he observed, "I found something *else* that those pills are good for! Why, good *morning*, Lilybelle!"

Doctor Goldpepper, on the point of asking *what* else, looked up to see who Lilybelle might be, and lo and behold, it was no other one but the comely housekeeper, whom he had never heard Clem address other than as "Mrs. Doothit, ma'am," before. She blushed, and her eyes, before she cast them down, were seen to sparkle.

"Hmm," observed Big Jimmy, adding, "Well, I guess now we know what *freest* means. Or maybe it's *grunk*. Mr. Upsilonian, make that five million white ones, five million pink ones and five million green ones. Tell them factories to start gearing for increased production! Yippay!"

"Ee-Yih-Hoo!" cried Doctor Crawford.

The alien said nothing, but genuflected and kissed the cuffs of Doctor Goldpepper's trousers.

How Upsilon Centauri was saved from soil sickness and famine, how the Jim Dandy Ethical Drug Company of Texas, Inc., moved with the speed of light into the ranks of the great corporations along with its sister-syndicate, the Jim Dandy Giant Golden-Red Hybrid Earthworm Company; how James E. (for Elophonsus) Dandy, Jr., married Mary Jane Crawford at the same double ceremony which united her father in matrimony to Mrs. Lilybelle Doothit, are matters too profuse in content to be recorded here by Doctor Morris Goldpepper, now restored once again to health and duty; who, desiring only the good and welfare of the American Dental profession and the human race, is glad to go down to posterity merely as the inventor of the Goldpepper Bridge and the Goldpepper Crown, and perfector of the Semi-Retractable Clasp which bears his name.

Introduction to

THE IRREGULAR UNION OF MENDEL AND ESTHER SLONIM

IN THE MID-1960s, AVRAM DAVIDSON began a series of long stories titled *Dear Annie Vandergale*, which he hoped to collect into a book. The stories were linked by the letters that people wrote to an advice columnist, about their personal problems. The stories and the book were never published, and Avram eventually abandoned the project.

Why weren't the stories published? Of course we will never know, but my guess is that they just didn't fit into any of the genre niches that were publishing Davidson's work at that time. They aren't fantasy or science fiction or mysteries. They are simply *stories* about diverse people and their varied problems. In this story the people and the problems are Jewish, so at last one of the stories has found its publishing niche.

Grania Davidson Davis

THE IRREGULAR UNION OF MENDEL AND ESTHER SLONIM

SAM AND SANDRA SLONIM were married for it must have been close to ten years before she discovered the truth about his family background. You can image how she felt. Right away she confronted Sam with the facts. He went right on drinking his coffee and reading his newspaper. Just as though she was talking to the wall. Naturally she was furious.

"What are you, a graven image or something?" the poor woman demanded of him. "You can't answer me when I'm talking to you? I asked you a question. Did you. Or did you. *Not*. Know this about your parents?"

Sam slowly looked up from the paper and slowly put down his coffee, only not all the way down. Looked at the bowl with the sour cream and vegetables in it. "Mmm," he said. As though he was thinking. "Yeah..." he said, after a minute, as though maybe he had found the answer in the bowl along with the chopped cucumbers and green peppers. "Yeah... I guess I knew it..." And with that, just as calmly as you please, he asked if there was more coffee.

She could have died.

"What do you mean, Is there more coffee. Never mind coffee. I'm *talk*ing to you, Sam," she cried in her despair. "At least allow me the courtesy to look at me when I'm talking to you."

So he did her a big favor and he looked at her, but with that expression on his face that made you want to plotz, as though she were a little child and he was doing her a favor and being very, very patient – "What do you mean, you *guess* you knew it? Either you knew it or you didn't know it." Wasn't that only reasonable?

"Okay. So I knew it. What are you getting all excited about for; they raised seven kids and we're all still alive and in good health and none of us were ever in jail. So it was a common law marriage. So what?"

Sandra was at such a loss for words at this callous and stupid rejoinder that she had all she could do to keep herself from screaming. She clenched her fists and her eyes rolled up and her breath hissed. Finally she was able to speak. "Are you out of your *mind*? *Sam* – "

Something funny occurred to him. Can you *imagine*? – he *smiled*! "You're laughing? I feel like I'm coming apart, and you – "

But he had to have his cheap, common joke, had to put in his rotten two cents' worth. "What's the matter, you don't recognize a common law marriage? You know what that makes *me*, don't you? So you married a bastard. Shouldn't surprise you," he said, guffawing. "What's the matter, you didn't tell me often enough that's what I am?"

Wait, thought Sandra to herself. Just wait, that you don't even have the common decency to treat me with respect and seriousness in this matter, that you laugh at me... But she didn't say a word, she didn't open her mouth, and she forced herself to seem calm, cool, and collected: no easy task, under the circumstances, you may rest assured So she just said to him, very dignified, "Very funny," that was all, that was enough, no more, just so he'd know how reproachful his conduct must appear to decent, civilized human beings.

"Now, Sam," she said, "let's discuss this in a very calm manner – "

"*I*'m calm."

" – without getting agitated – "

"I'm not agitated."

"– and without loosing sight for a minute of what the really basic considerations are. *All right*?"

He craned his neck. "Any more coffee?"

That's what she had to put up with.

Well, it's a true saying that one person doesn't know what another person's heartbreaks are. Anyone observing Sandra Slonim going about her daily tasks in her usual efficient manner would in all probability merely admire such details as the crispness of her attitude and how immaculate her children were, what beautiful manners, how well-raised; such a person would never in her life imagine that Sandra's heart was breaking, that she was actually burning up with fear lest someone should whisper or give a sly glance, some schoolchild utter an ugly taunt which would scar her children's emotional life forever. To say nothing of how she herself, would feel. How could she *stand* it? What could she do about it? There must be *something* she could do about it.

What she would have *liked* to have done about it, if her rotten husband and his rotten parents – but what was the use of talking? Wouldn't you think, after finding out that she knew all about it, after learning how she *felt* about it, after she had made it perfectly clear, that he would have the decency, that Sam would have the common decency, to go to his parents and speak to them frankly, mince no words...

But what was the use of talking.

Plenty of people would envy her. Plenty of people probably *did*, not that this gave or had ever given Sandra any satisfaction because she wasn't that kind of person, absolutely not. Nevertheless it was a fact, it was a simple fact, that certain people who had just been so damned snotty to her when she was a child because her father was a fruit-and-vegetable peddler who still went around in a horse and wagon just as though automobiles hadn't been invented and there were no such things as *stores* to be rented – the Feigenbaums, just to give you one example; thought they were an aristocracy or something, just because the parents were born over here and had a wholesale drygoods business and went to the Temple; how they used to look at her if she so much as *dared* come near their front lawn when she was bouncing her ball – and now look at them: the son Wilbur, in and out of the mental institution, in and out, in and out, in and out: and *Evelyn*, their precious *Evelyn*, with her ruffled dresses and her French lessons and her violin lessons and her dancing lessons and her stuck-up ways: and what had *Evelyn* come to in the end, despite all these so-called advantages? What was *Evelyn*? – a bum, a tramp, a real no-good, with her face all haggard and her hair starting to get grey; you heard of men picking her up in bars and she was involved in one scandal after another, and now that high-class, hotsy-totsy-American-born old Feigenbaum couple had lost their business and they lived on who-knows-what in a tiny two room apartment and when Sandra went by with her two beautiful and immaculate children you could see that it just killed the fancy Mr. and Mrs. Henry Howard Feigenbaum just to *look* at them, – some people in the old days would have been afraid of an *Eyin Hurra*, an Evil Eye, from the envy and the jealousy of such people; but Mrs. Sandra Slonim had never been in the least bit superstitious at any time, and so you can imagine how such people as these Feigenbaums would have *loved* to, how they would have just loved to hold up their noses and laugh and sneer to hear that Sandra Oshinsky had married the son of a couple who not only were not married at that time but had never even *gotten* married! Can you *imagine*? What would she *say*? What would she *do*? Where would she *look*?

So that was the tragedy of it. Here she was, still a young woman, who had waited and worked and slaved and saved until she and Sam were able to see their way clear and had bought a house and had two children and so naturally she had given up her job and devoted herself entirely to their welfare, Jeffrey, aged eight, and Sherri, aged six, her pride and her joy, the sun rose and set for her in the expression on her children's faces. You try to set an example, work your fingers to the bone, nobody should ever be able to find fault, nobody should ever be able to say they saw a single speck in your house or a spot on your children's clothes, and then this is what happens. This is your reward.

The prevailing note in the older Slonim's kitchen was enamel. Plastics, Formica, Teflon, and sundry other modern inventions to ease the lot of the housewife: were simply not there. The table (never covered with a cloth) was enamel, the sink-cover was enamel, the pots and pans were mostly enamel, too, although a few were cast iron. And on the enamel-topped stove stood an old-fashioned enamel coffee-pot. To be sure, all of this whitework had suffered through the years by the assaults of seven vigorous Slonim children banging one item – or, often, each other – upon another item, as well as the superabundant housecleaning of Esther Slonim herself. At the moment she was at rest. A Turkish cigaret smoldered in a dish. An old Russian novel with yellowed pages and crumbling edges was propped against the sugar-bowl. Her husband sat across the table reading the shadchonis ads in the Yiddish newspapers, elbow planted precisely between two sunburst-shaped fractures which had chipped off the white surface of the enamel and exposed the dark-blue beneath. Her hair was white and in its usual Einsteinian disorder or profusion: take your pick. His was a short yellowish-grey, his eyes were blue-green, hers were jet black.

"*Lady lawyer, owns mink coat,*" Mendel read aloud. "A question: do her clients own mink coats? A question." His comments were made in a low mumble seemingly not addressed to anyone in particular. Ut-tut-ut, listen here: *Young widow seeks widower to manage very good delicatessen store, or will sell cheap.* An authentic American tragedy, husband works himself to death – " He lifted his eyes without lifting his head, observed his wife had done the same. They observed each other a moment in perfect understanding and perfect contentment. Then the sound of an automobile drew their attention.

"Sam's car."

"But Sam's not in it." Unhurriedly but without dallying, Mr. Mendel Slonim got up, folded his paper, put it under his arm, and headed for the back door.

His wife viewed this with less than total pleasure. "What will she say, you always vanish as soon as she comes?"

He waved his hand. "*Sie is tsufrieden, Un ikh bin oykhit tsufrieden.* I'll pick her a flower." The bell rang and with a final wave of his hand, he went out.

Esther let her daughter-in-law in, greeted her with, "It's nice you came now, I was just going to make coffee."

"Sure, sure, you're always 'just going to make coffee' whenever I come," said Sandra, undeceived but undissatisfied. She put down her coat on the living-room sofa, followed her mother-in-law on into the kitchen. "Pop's not home?"

"In the garden." Esther measured coffee. "Thirty years it was only the backyard, then he buys half-a-dozen second-hand rose bushes and right away it becomes the garden." She chuckled.

Sandra said nothing. She didn't actually dislike her father-in-law, but there was something in his gaze...too high a trace of humor perhaps... or perhaps too keen an air of appraisal...which made her a bit uneasy. He very seldom spoke to her in words but had a way of catching her eye and then commencing a series of little nods of his head which seemed to constitute a sort of answer to a question she hadn't asked and which seemed as well to make them both sardonically privy to the follies of mankind. If he wished to be in his garden she was content to leave him there.

Now she wrinkled her nose at the strong, curious reek of the funny cigarets from the flat box with the funny pictures on it. And she looked around the old-fashioned kitchen and her gaze had a sort of wonder in it. Then her head snapped back. Her mouth, which had fallen into a sort of childish uncertainty, formed itself into something almost grim. "Mom, I want to tell you – I want to ask you something."

"All right."

"But I don't want you to be angry with me. All right?"

"All right."

The old woman's equaniminity was almost unnerving, she didn't seem to have any notion of how to play the conversational games which had to be played. She was always so calm, always so brief. For just a moment it occurred to Sandra that, this being so, why beat around the bush? Mom, please you and Pop get married because I'm afraid that somehow it might be bad for my children otherwise... Why not just say that? Sandra opened her mouth. And didn't say it. And waited for the old lady to help her out, play the next step of the conversational game by saying, *So ask –* or something like that. But the old lady didn't. And wouldn't. Sandra felt resentment rising in herself again. Trouble, trouble, trouble, what did she need it for, why should she have to suffer for it.

"I'll just make two cups, if we want more, I'll make more."

Sandra shook her head, impatiently. Why was it all left for her to do? Wouldn't you think Sam would have at least *told* his mother – ? And maybe he did. Maybe she knew. If she knew, how could she just stand there, watching the stove, looking out the windows, smoking her cigaret? Why didn't she say something about something? What kind of a hostess did you call that, to just sit there and not say anything? Sandra moved restlessly, issuing small sighs, teenytiny grunts and groans, hoping to provoke at least *one* comment, *one* question, to serve as a peg or a fulcrum. Finally her mother-in-law turned to her with a smile and Sandra, knowing that the old lady was going to say something at last, grew tense and nervous and looked away.

"Mary is pregnant," Esther Slonim said.

Mary was another daughter-in-law; Arnold's wife; Arnold was next after Sam... Well, that wasn't anything like what Sandra expected her to hear, but it was something at least; in agitation, her mind scurried and thought and sought how to use this: she could say, oh, mmm, Isn't it lucky they're married – No, for Heaven's sake! No, of course she couldn't! What kind of a thing was that to say? They'd think she was crazy. 'A good thing they were married,' who *wasn't* married and lived together and had children? Answer: Esther and Mendel Slonim, her in-laws, that's who. Her in-common-laws... Sandra winced. And – Mary – it just wasn't usual for Jewish women to be named Mary. Miriam, Marion, Marcia, yes. "What is this, the third?" she heard herself asking. "The fourth?"

"The third. The only one who has more than three is Betty."

Yes, of course. Naturally. Betty, the next to the youngest. Betty the bohemian. Sandra could never get it straight what it was exactly that Betty's husband made, but he made it in a kiln or a foundry in a ramshackle old house and he wore a beard and they played folk-music and wore old clothes even when they came *visiting* and they had a million kids, and do you think that Betty would at least go in the *bathroom* when she nursed them, if she had to nurse them, she couldn't use a *bottle*, for God's sake?

Better forget about Betty.

"Here is sugar, milk... Oh, you use the fresh not the canned – "

"Mom, don't get up, I take it black now and I have saccharine."

The old lady didn't bother even to nod, to comment, ask a few sociable questions. But she understood all right. And after a while she said, "I was always a skinny one like you see me now. In those days even if you were slender people would say, '*Nebbich, ah dahrer! Famished*!' But a girl who had a figure like a barrel, with her face as round as the moon, then they would smile and approve: '*Oy, vie sheyn*!'...In those days."

And that did it. Almost as though she were hearing another person's voice Sandra heard herself saying, "In those days did they approve of marriage?" And felt herself grow hot and cold and she clenched her hands. So maybe she shouldn't have said it. But how long could you keep still and just bundle it all up inside of you? Now it would come out, there would be a real battle –

Only there wasn't. That was the worst of these Slonims, you could never, never depend on them. *They had no shame.*

"Well..." The old lady considered. "Depends on what you mean by 'they.' Some did, most did, just like the world was the same world it used to be, no change. Others thought that everything was going to change overnight and all the old ideas were going to be thrown out in the morning like the garbage: Bang. Smash. *Varf es aveck.* Marriage? A relic of the past. Like private property. Religion. The family. The state... The state will wither away and so will the family. Man wouldn't have to toil to feed his children, woman wouldn't have to stay home like a slave to the washtub and the stove, children would be the common responsibility of society, *ai yai yai yai!* – what beautiful dreams we had then," and the old lady rocked her head from side to side.

And Sandra thought, *You call them "beautiful"* – but she kept her mouth shut.

'Buhhhht... So things didn't change over night. A woman still liked to know who was the father of her children. She still liked to have her own home. The other way was maybe very nice," Esther said, raising her eyebrows and nodding, "for these lustful young men, they wanted a different girl every night, and no responsibilities, and so they persuaded themselves it was all political, social, economic, but mostly, really, it was all sex. And for the girls it came to be realized so it wasn't quite so nice. The state didn't wither away, and, to tell you the plain simple truth, neither did common sense. You'd like more coffee?"

Sandra hadn't even remembered drinking hers. "Uh? Oh. No, no, don't go to the trouble." But the old lady went right on making more coffee. Well, at least the old lady was still calm. She saw which way the wind was blowing, and she wasn't angry. All right, then, take the bull by the horns –

"– So then you and Pop were never married –?"

For a minute the old lady didn't move. Then all of a sudden she whirled around and one look at her face Sandra thought Oh Boy! Is she angry now!...but she wasn't. At least not with Sandra. And she had the funniest expression on her face, like she was just so astonished. Although what –

And then she sat down, the old lady sat down and she pressed her hands to the sides of her head, her fingers stirring up the foaming cataract of her hair. "*Gevalt,*" she said in a low voice. "*Gottinyu.*" Sandra was frightened that...who knows what? Then the old lady took away the hands and shook her head and she got up and took the coffee pot and poured out the two fresh cups and after she drank some of hers she said, "What a shock. Can you imagine... When you said that...thought to myself, No, what is she talking about? *Darft mn zyne meshuga*, 'we weren't married,' what does she mean? And all the time I was thinking this, my mind was looking and looking and remembering backwards and suddenly I realized what I was trying to remember, I was trying to remember the *chuppa...when* it was, *where* it was, *how* it was...

"And thehhhhn: like a *frahsk in oonim*: I remembered: There was nothing to remember, it never happened, there was no *chuppa*, so how could I remember it? Tsk tsk tsk, what a funny thing the memory is." She sighed, finished her coffee. Sandra said nothing. Funny it might be to Mrs. Esther Slonim, but to Mrs. Sandra Slonim it was very, very far from being funny.

The old lady got up again, washed and dried the dishes and set them in the china closet, a polished cabinet with curtains inside its glass windows. Then she lit herself another of her oriental cigarets and, with a sigh, sat down. "So the answer to your question? It was a marriage by common consent. Common? Mutual? And still is."

And so what could Sandra say? Nothing. She took her leave after thanking the old lady for the coffee and while she was getting in the car the old man came along the side of the driveway and he gave her some roses (for which she thanked him, though in a somewhat subdued manner) and his usual peculiar nods and smiles in which it seemed to her that there was more than a mere trace of mockery.

So now she knew for sure. But of course, was she the only one who knew? Of course not. Of course not.

What to do?

What to do?

Dear Annie Vandergale,

My parents-in-law are a very fine old couple now living in retirement on union benefits and social security in addition to the rent from the other half of their house. My own marriage is a very fine one and I have a fine husband and two beautiful children, aged eight and six. I have always been very happy that there was no breath of scandal attached to any of us particularly for my children's future, so you can imagine my shock and horror on discovering that my husband's parents were never formally married. I live in constant dread that this irregular union will be exposed to public attention. My husband says that he can't think of anything which will persuade his parents to regularize this situation. I am at my wits' end, for how can I inculcate my two children into religious and moral principles when they may find out any day now that their grandparents have been defying these religious and moral principles all these years?

Wits' End.

Obviously, if religious and moral principles such as you very properly instruct your children haven't persuaded your in-laws all these years it isn't likely at this time that an appeal based upon them will carry much weight. Yours isn't the only such problem. Have your husband inform your father that unless he does the right thing even at this late date, his widow will not be legally a widow at all and won't be eligible for social security benefits. Spell it out like that and I think you will find that Uncle Sam will become "Marryin' Sam" as well!

Well the old couple took it well enough. They even consented to apply for the marriage license out of town where Betty lived, and gave her address so that nothing would appear in their own home-town newspaper. And naturally enough, instead of the regular Rabbi there, they got in somebody from the City. But do you think they got in somebody who didn't know anybody? – oh, no; no such thing – who did they get but this old Rabbi who was a boyhood friend from the old country and the old days in the tenements:

"So you're getting married?" he asked. "What's your hurry?"

Can you imagine?

Furthermore, and despite all of Sandra's hints to the contrary, no matter how much she winked, clicked her tongue, shook her head, mentioned objections in a low voice and nudged her husband – did it help? Like cupping helps a corpse – they had a big celebration and they made a regular song and dance about it. And the old Rabbi, who you'd think he would have known better, he had to make a whole speech: he said that since neither of them had been married to anyone else and since they had lived together openly as man and wife all these years, so they had actually *been* married in the Eyes of God and the Jewish Religion and they couldn't even have gotten married to anyone else without a religious divorce, did you ever *hear* of such a thing? – instead of maybe telling them a thing or two in a subtle manner – no. He has to tell them that they were married all along according to the Law of Moses. And his little old wife in her disgusting wig, as though at her age any man was going to be attracted to her because she showed her own hair, she stood there as the matron of honor with a big smile on her face: Sandra didn't know which way to look, thought she'd fall through the floor. And then they were all drinking afterwards and singing and dancing and this one dance in particular when the Rabbi holds one end of a handkerchief and the bride (in this case, Esther (Mrs. Mendel) Slonim) holds the other – well it was just too much for Sandra. She said to Sam, "I'll be waiting in the car!" and she gave him *one look*...but it was no use, so, after waiting and waiting she went back in the house just to get a drink of water, and they made her eat something, because, after all, there was that long drive home afterwards.

Well, after getting over the aggravation from this particular incident, Sandra continued with her plans for introducing her mother-in-law into middle class western civilization. She herself had been a member of the Eastern Star for years, being the sister of a master mason, and since Jack Slonim, the old lady's oldest son, was also one, so they got her into the chapter too. Well, let it be admitted that who knows everything about what the ritual means, and for that matter, who cares? The masons tell you that at least their ritual comes down from King Solomon's Temple in Jerusalem, and as for the Eastern Star's ritual, who has time to look into such things and who is interested. The point is that it's a very good organization and not just anyone can get in.

Well, there was a certain amount of congratulations directed towards Sandra for actually inspiring the old lady at her age, not everyone would go to so much trouble for a mother-in-law, and it was a very well-attended meeting. *Unfortunately.* Because what happened? Everybody was being perfectly quiet and the beautiful and inspiring ceremony was proceeding as usual when they got to the place where it says, *We have seen His star in the East and we have come to worship Him;* and with that, the old lady gets up and just walks out. Yes! Did you ever *hear* of such a thing? Sandra went after her, thinking, well, maybe she didn't feel well or something, and she found her putting on her hat and coat, ready to go.

"Mom, what's the matter?" she asked.

And the old lady, without even bothering to look up, pulled on her coat and said, "So if I've got to be religious in my old age, then let it be my own religion."

"What are you talking about?"

And her mother-in-law just gave two or three nods of her head and pulled on her gloves and she said, "If I've got to be religious in my old age, so let it be my own religion!" And with that, she went home. Well! You can imagine! *What* a scandal there was about *that*! – As though the whole Chapter wasn't Jewish...

That was how it all started. The next thing, old Mrs. Slonim says, just like that, she's going to keep a kosher home.

Sandra could have dropped dead.

In this day and age!

Well, of course, the old Rabbi had said – he did say to them at the wedding, "I hope you'll keep a kosher home," but any sensible person would have assumed that this was one of his so-called jokes, like, "What's your hurry?" in getting married. Besides, every Rabbi says that at every wedding, like they always say, "I hope you'll give your children a good Jewish education" and other such things which are none of their business.

Sandra went right over and sure enough – *new dishes*! And her dear mother-in-law was heating her cast-iron pots and pans red hot to kosher them, but the enamel ones she was getting rid of because they were all chipped and if something is chipped you can't make it kosher because, well, who knows why because, and what difference does it make anyway. So Sandra stood there absolutely dumb-founded at this spectacle and at first the thought entered her poor bewildered mind that perhaps Mrs. Esther Slonim was becoming senile in her old age, – as though she (Sandra) needed any more difficulties, she didn't have enough. New dishes! Complete sets of new dishes! Because, the old lady said, earthenware you can't make kosher if it was ever something else – but – listen – can *you imagine*! – what that *meant*? *New dishes*? Enough to feed...because, all right, she had this crazy idea like a bee in her bonnet, so why she couldn't simply have gone out and bought at the five-and-ten just enough for herself and her husband...but no: absolutely not...enough to serve *all* her children and *all* her grandchildren and not just one such set, oh no, nothing of the sort, maybe you don't know what it means to keep a kosher home. Listen. *One,* set for *milchig. One* set for *fleishig.* And two entire sets, milchig and fleishig, for Passover!

Oh, Sandra thought she would die! What a crime, what a criminal thing, to throw away the old man's hard-earned money like that, instead of wouldn't you think they would want to leave at least a little something to their grandchildren when they passed on? Or if they had it to spare, so why couldn't they do something for their grandchildren right here and now – ?

Old Mrs. Slonim, as though she couldn't read what was passing over her daughter-in-law's face, or probably she just didn't want to, she looked up and said, "Don't make any arrangements for Passover this year, we want the whole family to come here for the Seder... It will be nice," she said, "to have the whole family here for the Seder?" Well, Sandra thought to herself, Yes, nice for Who? – don't think that you're going to rope me in for singing chickens and skimming soup and grating horseradish or getting messed-up to the elbows making matzoh balls: oh no. But she didn't say a word.

Then the old man caught her eye and she couldn't help asking, "And what do you think of all this, Pop?"

But it seemed like the senility was catching because he only gave a little shrug and a little smile and some little nods of his head and he opened his mouth and he sang

"Chad gad-yawwwwww,
Chad-gad-yaw..."

– some song from the Seder. "Only one kid, One little goatling," he said.

"You see?" asked his nutty old wife. "He didn't forget, all these years?"

"Who forgets?" he said, in a soft voice.

Sandra pointed something out to him. "You know what this means? It means no more bacon for your breakfast."

He just kept on his nods. "To tell you the truth," he said, "I never was crazy about it." Nod, nod, nod, nod, nod.

Well, what's done is done, they had their Seder, and, as though once wasn't enough, the next night they had another Seder! Noise? – don't ask such silly questions! Of course the children all enjoyed it, what do they know, each one got his or her chance to ask The Four Questions; then this business of trying to steal the broken matzoh that the father hides – this is some fine way of inculcating ethics into young children – and all that wine-sipping. To say nothing of Grandpa Slonim trying to sneak in some kind of political message when he wasn't muttering or singing in Hebrew, I'm telling you, some people never learn: Bondage, slavery, freedom, liberty – she didn't want her children hearing all that kind of stuff, suppose they would say something outside and people might start to talk.

Well. Anyway.

Then there was the incident of the High Holy Days. Sandra would just as soon her children stayed in school, all this talk about religion doesn't mean a thing if you don't have an education, but what with *Grandma says this* and *Grandma says that* and a lot of people who you'd think they would know better were keeping their children out of school – So she drove the

189

two of them down to this little shabby old shul where her dear in-laws had decided to value with their presence and she sent them inside to be with their grandparents and not have them underfoot the entire time because they weren't in school. And what happens. Just as she was getting ready to drive back for them they turn up at her front door, they had actually walked the whole way back, it must have been over a mile, a six-year-old and an eight-year-old child! and Jeffrey was still wearing this little yarmulka that someone had stuck on his head, who knows where it had come from or what diseases it might have carried, but he had *walked the whole way home with it on*! – there isn't enough Antisemitism in the world already! And he didn't want to take it off and he wanted to keep on wearing it, like some four-year-old child with a security blanket or something, until finally his mother was forced to get rid of it on the Q.T. And didn't he carry on.

"You better speak to your parents," she told her husband.

Talk to the wall.

Hardly had *this* incident passed over when out of nowhere up came another Holy Day, such as Sandra had hardly even so much as heard of since she was a child herself, and there in the side yard of her parents-in-law's home they built this succah, as they call it, this – this *hut* – out of old doors and bedsheets with mere branches of trees for a roof and they decorated it and they ate in it and you would see people stopping to look at it from the sidewalk, and they kept this up for *eight days*! And Mrs. Thompson, a very refined person whom Sandra barely knew to exchange the time of day with, Mrs. Thompson actually stopped her on the street with another person and asked her about it!

"Is this intended to represent the tabernacle of the Children of Israel in the Wilderness?" and "Oh, I think it just so interesting!" and so on and so on; Sandra didn't know where to *look*, she was so embarrassed, she assured them that she had nothing to do with it, knew nothing about it, but no wonder they gave her funny looks. She was just burning up inside.

And as for talking to the old people about it, hinting that they could at least be a little discreet, for Heaven's sake, don't you think that this occurred to her? Don't you think she didn't go over to see them with just such an idea in mind? And what did she find but *another* Gentile lady sitting there in the living-room and listening with bated breath, as it were, while the old lady babbled on and on – this was Mrs. Marcy, *the* Mrs. William Wilson Marcy who you read about in the local paper as being connected with this good cause and that prominent event, and she had actually been so taken aback or something on seeing this succah that she had come and asked if she could go in and look at it, and afterwards they came back into the house – do you have such luck or do I have such luck? – no, but Mrs. Esther Slonim has such luck, and what does she do with it, does she even give a thought to other members of her family, what difference does it make if by marriage or not by marriage? No. No, she doesn't, and no she didn't.

Instead, she was telling Mrs. W. Wilson Marcy all about her father and how he was such-and-such a number of years in the Russian Army under the Czar of Russia and how he refused to bow to the ikons and how he refused to eat pork and what he had to go through and what he didn't have to go through: Sandra could have fallen through the floor.

And meanwhile Mrs. W. Wilson Marcy, though she's not so much to look at close up, they must print old pictures of her, just as though she didn't have all these charity concerts and benefit flower shows to take care of, just sat there and sat there, saying "My word!" and "My goodness!" and "Oh, how *awful!*" while the old lady poisoned the atmosphere with these weird oriental cigarettes and her hair looking as usual like last year's bird's nest.

"To think that after all these years you have returned to the faith of your fathers, how wonderful," Mrs. Marcy said. And then they talked about women's suffrage and sweatshops and settlement houses until finally the fancy society lady got up to go and as she went out she actually vouchsafed Mrs. Sandra Slonim a gracious little smile and nod and that was that and Sandra supposes she was lucky to get that much. So, seeing that mere words would be useless, she went away, too.

The last blow, the straw that broke the so-called camel's back, was when the Theater Group was organized. Mildred Silberthing, Evelyn Greenwurm, Fanny Kaye, and others, they organized it: once a month they all went down to the City and had lunch and saw a matinee at a reduced price and did a little window-shopping and then they came back to resume their household duties. Naturally Sandra was tickled pink to join and to have this opportunity, only what to do with the children was her only problem. She asked their grandmother, this Mrs. Esther Slonin whom we have been hearing about, if she would be so good as to take care of her grandchildren on the theater Saturday from the late morning till the early evening, and lo and behold she agreed, thank you very much. So at least *this* was off Sandra's mind.

Well, naturally, Sandra is not one of these mothers who merely takes everything for granted, not where her children are concerned. And it wasn't even the third, well, maybe it was the third, it was only the third time after coming back from her little well-deserved outing that she inquired about how her children had passed the day. Maybe she had some suspicions about this old lady and her crazy notions. At first, she was listening, and it all seemed harmless enough, Grandma made lemonade and Grandpa taught them how to play chess and they all went for a walk down to the lake and picture books and a couple of other cousins came over and they played together: Fine. Perfectly fine. But after all one of the most important questions hadn't been answered, so Sandra had to ask them point-blank: *What did you have to eat?*

"We had chicken and salad and kugel and Grandma put chocolate syrup in the glasses and we squirted in seltzer and made chocolate soda."

Well, it was just as though something made her ask, and Sandra enquired, "And what about soup?" No soup. And one thing led to another, and what kind of chicken did they have to eat, they had cold chicken! Did you ever hear of such a thing? Late Fall and almost winter, she gives them a cold meal! Sandra was furious. Oh, she was just *furious*! She just almost *flew* at the old lady, after all she had taken from her she was in just no mood.

"What's the matter, is it too much trouble for you to give your grandchildren one single hot meal one day a month?"

And the crazy old lady, *Mrs.* Esther Slonim, so do you know what her reply was? "*Shabbas*, I don't cook." That was her total reply. It's against her religion to cook on the Sabbath, can you imagine. Well, Sandra put that in its right place immediately.

"Where children's health is concerned," she said, "there is no such thing as a Shabbas – you couldn't at least heat up a meal for them, Mrs. Frumkeit? If you're supposed to be so religious – "

Would you believe it, the old lady had the nerve to be *annoyed* at her? "So suppose I could," she said, "and so suppose I don't? Do they get sick at my house? They don't eat a cold meal the times your Bridge Club or your Mahjong Group meets at your own house? And does it hurt them?"

Oh, it's no use talking. When people make such ridiculous comparisons there is no use *talking* to them. Sandra could see that this was just going to go on and on forever, one scandalous incident after another, just one humiliation after another humiliation. But she bottled it all up inside of herself because that is the kind of person she is, she didn't say a *word*. But one thing you can depend on: Should she ever, should she *ever* discover that her in-law's marriage was for any reason or in any way, shape or form not valid and should be performed over again, you can bet your life that *she* will never say a word to anyone about it, not if her *life* depended on it. And meanwhile the outside world imagines she is so fortunate and happy, because, believe me, it is a true saying that one person doesn't know what another person's heartache is. Believe *me*.

AVRAM DAVIDSON

Introduction to
WHO IS ETHEL SCHNURR

AVRAM DAVIDSON RETURNED TO the pages of *Jewish Life* in 1970 with this story, about a plain young woman who found happiness by learning elocution.

By 1970, Avram Davidson had won awards in the science fiction, fantasy, and mystery fields. He had published a number of his classic novels, and had edited *The Magazine of Fantasy and Science Fiction*. In this story he returned to his roots in a New York bakery, with a *hamish* fantasy.

Grania Davidson Davis

WHO IS ETHEL SCHNURR?

THERE WERE THREE SISTERS. The first was Mrs. Goldbeater, she looked like a cow. Bessie Goldbeater was her daughter, you've heard of Bessie Goldbeater? Everybody's heard of Bessie Goldbeater, she went to live in Brazil, and the next sister was old Mrs. Katz who was married to Katz-the-Painter and there was this big scandal about her in her old age. And the third sister was the Old Lady Schnurr.

They were nothing like each other. Old Mrs. Goldbeater nobody ever saw, she was as big as a house and had swollen ankles and never went outside of her kitchen. Mrs. Katz you know about already. And the Schnurrs have this little bakery on Oak Street in the old Jewish neighborhood. Not Frenkel's, that's the big bakery in the next block, and not Popkin's, that's more of what you might call a dairy restaurant although they do have cakes and things that you can buy to take out. But not bread and not rolls. Schnurr's is in the next block, you know where I mean? On the corner is Fisher's Hardware Store, then comes old Shlemon in the second-hand place, he's not Jewish, and next to that is where Drabin had the live poultry market before he got rich and moved to Louisiana, did you ever hear of such a thing? Florida wasn't good enough for him. It's been empty for years. And then there's the candy store and next to that, is Schnurr-the-baker. So now you know.

I'll tell you what they look like. The Old Man Schnurr is a little bit of a man, he's got a kind of a long nose, and he's on the dark side, but not too dark. And the Old Lady Schnurr is also a little bit of a woman – you know the old joke, "*Eyn oyg felt eym un fin onder nut*"? – yeah. Well, it's not so bad as all that, it's just that it always reminds me. She's a little bit cross-eyed in one eye and she has a palsy, not much, her head always shakes a little, but only the head. And he, as far back as I can remember, he had white hair. So that's the Schnurrs, the old people, I mean.

What do you mean, So who is Ethel Schnurr? That's what I'm telling you, if you'll have a little patience. Ethel Schnurr is the daughter. The father is little, the mother is little, even the aunt, Old Mrs. Katz, isn't very big, but the daughter must take after the other aunt, the one that's – Mrs. Goldbeater. Only not that I mean she's fat, the daughter, only tall.

Not hefty and not skinny, just tall, kind of dark like the father, a long nose, and that's all. To begin with they're very ignorant people. The Old Lady I'm not even sure can read. There was a Mr. Krimbein who lived in the house, you wouldn't know him, he didn't mingle much. So every night he used to read out loud the *roman* from the Jewish paper, and she would go up and listen to it. The serial, you know. A *roman*, they called it. And that was her entertainment.

They were no business people. What I mean is they used to keep the bakery closed Shabbas. They thought they were still in Europe. On Friday night if you wanted a challah, it should be *freylach* on the table, they were already closed. And on Saturday night, when people were out buying, he first opened up the store and started baking, and what did they have to sell? Only the stale stuff from the day before. So naturally, Frenkel's got all the business, and who came to Shnurr's on Saturday night but all the Shvartsas and the Polacks, because the stale stuff they sold cheaper, and some of it they even gave away if you'd tell them a hard luck story. So naturally they were no business people. But they made a living.

In those days there was a Mrs. Bodenheim, a very refined woman, her husband was Dr. Bodenheim the Dentist, and she had no children, she had a maid, and she didn't know what to do with herself the whole day long, so she gave elocution lessons. Nowadays they call it dramatic readings, they call it speech therapy, and it's a different sort of thing altogether; but in those days they called it elocution and it was a different sort of thing altogether. You know what I mean?

Anyway, this Mrs. Bodenheim had various pupils, there was no Jewish Community Center in those days where they have classes in everything for the children, and so different people, if the children weren't taking violin lessons or going to Hebrew School, they gave them elocution lessons with Mrs. Bodenheim. So what was meant by elocution? First of all, they had these vowel exercises to develop the tone and the voice in speaking. That was very important, but that was just the training. Most of all, she taught them to recite poetry. Famous speeches, too, but the poetry was more popular. She taught them, like "The Song Of The Shirt," and "Trees," and "In Flanders Field The Poppies Grow," and in fact she taught them poems I haven't heard of in years – "A Frenchman, Once, So Runs A Certain Ditty," and there was a patriotic one about "When Freedom From Her Mountain Height," and "She's Somebody's Mother, Boys, You Know," and humorous ones such as "Darius Green And His Flying Machine," and, oh, what was that one called, "It's Nothing To Laugh At, As I Can See, If You Were Stung By A Bumble-Bee."

But she said, I mean Mrs. Bodenheim, that it wasn't just memorization. Anybody can be taught to memorize, she said. Even a parrot can be instructed in how to memorize. What she placed her greatest emphasis on was expression. The pains she took with those children you wouldn't believe.

She didn't just give them a book and say, go, learn. She used to have everything typed out and then she would put these marks on the words to show where to put the expression and the emphasis. It was very well thought of by everyone, including the schools, and once a year she used to have her pupils give a recital. So, naturally everyone was surprised when Ethel Schnurr started going.

I mean, they just weren't the type. They worked all day long and the Old Man went to his shul and the Old Lady went to listen to her *roman*, and that was all they knew. Elocution, they never heard of it. In fact, they never heard of anything. You want to hear a story? Believe it or not. Someone once said to the Old Lady, it was after the election or the inauguration or something, I forget which, and somebody said to her, "Well, we've got a new president now." And the Old Lady looked at him, and she looked at him, and her face got real sad and she said, "Uncle Sam isn't there no more?" Believe it or not. She thought Uncle Sam was the president's name. This is an American citizen for you. So how she came to elocution was a mystery.

Anyway, to make a long story short, the daughter, Ethel Schnurr, wanted to take elocution lessons. After all – pretty, she wasn't – I forget how old she was then, just a girl, but pretty she certainly wasn't and inasmuch as certain of the other girls were going to these lessons, so she wanted to go, too. So she went. And she went and she went and she went. Sixteen years old and she was still going. People didn't know whether to laugh or to cry. She didn't even finish high school. She never read a book. She just worked in the bakery and helped her mother around the house and studied elocution and every year she got up to recite at these annual recitals that Mrs. Bodenheim used to give. I mean, this child was six years old, this one was seven years old, the other one was ten years old – it was cute, you know what I mean? It was cute. But then up comes Ethel Schnurr and she's what you call a young lady already, and she stands up to recite these dramatic and sentimental poems with all the expression and the gestures, and believe me, it was something to see. Boys? Boys didn't care about her and she didn't care about boys. And the Old Lady Schnurr was always on hand in the audience and she was so proud of her daughter that she was all ready to cry from happiness, she was so proud.

Well, what could you do? You couldn't tell her, "Mrs. Schnurr, excuse me, your daughter is making a public idiot out of herself," could you? Let alone the Old Man, let alone Ethel herself. And to talk to Mrs. Bodenheim was equally impossible – how would you do it? Anyway, it was taken out of everybody's hands when Mrs. Bodenheim's brother died out in Toledo, Ohio, and he left a hotel and he left a factory and this piece of property and that piece of property, and he was an old buck, as the expression goes, he never got married, and so who inherited all the property and everything else? Mrs. Bodenheim is who. The rich get richer and the poor get children, believe me. So they moved out to Toledo, Ohio, and insofar as I know, they were never heard from again.

So – meanwhile, what of Ethel Schnurr? She went on working in the bakery and helping her mother in the house, and she didn't get any younger and she didn't get any prettier, but she always had a smile for you, and that was that. Now comes the beginning of the story. Enter Manny Rothman. Rothman from the cigar store, not Rothman from Adams Street who married the *shicksa* and she drank him out of house and home, his own kind wasn't good enough for him; the other Rothman, Manny Rothman. From the cigar store. You know the one I mean? A *macher, a koch-lefel*, always running something. The Masons, the War Veterans, the Oddfellows, the Merchants Association, the B'nai B'rith, that's Manny Rothman. So once a year the War Veterans used to give a party for the Orphanage, and, they did a very good thing. And who would run it? Manny Rothman.

What they used to do was to hire that old movie down on Oak Street, the Rialto was the name of it, it was only open at night, so the War Veterans would hire it for the afternoon and give a party for the Orphanage. They showed them movies, Our Gang Comedies, and cowboy pictures and each one was given a bag of candy, and the mayor would address them, and they had soda in dixie cups and after all this there was a sort of vaudeville and then the bus would come and take them back to the Orphanage.

So, one afternoon Ethel was in the bakery and Manny Rothman came rushing and he told her she had to come right away and recite for the Orphanage. One of the vaudeville acts didn't show up and the party wasn't supposed to be over until the chartered bus came back for the children. He said they were supposed to pay the vaudeville act fifteen dollars, and why shouldn't she get it instead, and besides, she'd be doing everybody a favor and it would be a mitzvah, too, entertaining these poor Orphanage children. So she took off her apron and left the Old Lady in charge of the store and off she went.

Well, when people heard about it, they were furious. "What do you mean, allowing that girl to make a public spectacle of herself like that?" She could do as she pleased, she was happy, the kids were happy and the War Veterans were happy and so whose business was it, anyway?

You can't faze that one; he always has an answer for everybody.

And Ethel Schnurr told everyone who came into the bakery that she'd made fifteen dollars from her elocution and of course she got congratulations right and left, some of them didn't know any better and some of them were just being tactful, and some of them figured – listen; fifteen dollars is fifteen dollars. You know what I mean? Well, they say nothing succeeds like success. Don't you think, from time to time different people didn't come into the bakery and say that there was going to be a children's party for one purpose or another and the question of entertainment was not as yet settled? And Ethel Schnurr would smile and look down and the Old Lady Schnurr would say, "She would recite for you," and these different individuals would say, well, they couldn't afford to pay. And the Old Lady would say, "She wouldn't need to take any money" and she'd call the Old Man in from the back and she'd say, "They want Ethel to recite for them." And the Old Man wouldn't say a word, he was always on the shy side, but he would look at you and smile and look at Ethel and the Old Lady and you could see that they were all very proud.

And this went on over a good many years.

It's a funny thing, and this is just a guess on my part, because I'm no mindreader. But I am convinced, I am absolutely convinced, that Ethel Schnurr in her own mind regarded herself as a member of the professional entertainers. Just from her attitude and various little things she said. Even though all she got was that little bit of money once a year for a few years from the War Veterans, and the rest of the time she seemed to think she was doing people a favor by reciting these poems at the children's parties. "I don't mind," she'd say. "I don't mind a bit. Glad to do it." And if you gave her half a chance she'd talk your ear off about using expression and how important the right gestures were, and what a pity nobody was teaching elocution around here anymore.

And that was all she had to talk about, and what she cooked for supper and how she cooked it, and how she made her father's eggs in the morning, until you were glad to get out of there and get away. I mean, it was just a little hole-in-the-wall bakery, with fixtures from the Year of One and the walls were painted brown fifty years ago and the walls are still painted brown. You couldn't get anything fancy there, either, I mean, if you wanted something like an ice-cream cake you could want it forever. Just bread and rolls and sponge-cake and honey-cake and *shtrudel* and *mandelbrote* and old-fashioned things like that. Still, they made a living.

So – one day, in came Manny he said, "Ethel, I am going to put you on the stage." And he had a telephone number for her to call. Yes – Ethel Schnurr. That's what I'm telling you. What was it all about, you remember Stein-the-butcher? Well, Stein-the-butcher has this son, George Stein, Craig Stone he calls himself, I don't know him myself and if I met him on the street I wouldn't know him from Adam. But be that as it may, he was sick when he was a boy, the virus was then in its infancy and there was no such thing as penicillin. So he stayed in bed and he started reading books about the stage and he kept on with it when he was better – this all came out later, in the stories in the newspaper – and instead of going to college he went to New York and got into the stage.

No, not an actor. He was a scenic designer and a choreographer as they call it and he directed and he did this and that and the other thing. So one day they were casting a play and he was reading it and there was a part there about a girl who was always reciting poems from her elocution class. And he said to himself, "Didn't there used to be a woman back in my home town who used to do that?"

And he said, "*Yes.*" He wasn't sure what her name was, but he knew that Manny Rothman knew her, so he called up Manny Rothman. And that's how it all happened. She went down to New York and she tried out for the part, and lo and behold, she got it. Did you ever hear of such a thing? Ethel Schnurr! Whoever heard of such a thing!

Lilly Feffer, you know Lilly Feffer, don't you? Well, Lilly Feffer is an aunt by marriage to this George Stein or Craig Stone, and according to her, they called Ethel Schnurr down originally to show this actress, the one who originally had the part, how to do it – recite, you know, with the expression and the gestures – although why they had to call in Ethel Schnurr, for Heaven's sake, to teach them their own business, is beyond me, and I don't put much stock in that story. So, what happened, if somebody got taken sick and they shifted the cast around or if this actress just didn't want the part, I forget. But Ethel Schnurr got it, all right.

The play was called "Anybody Round My Base Is 'It.'" Did you ever hear of such a title? Well, the play was just as crazy as the title was. To this day I can't make heads or tails of it, as the saying goes. But it was all about this family way back in the Twenties or maybe even longer ago, they never told you when, exactly, but everybody was wearing old-fashioned clothes, so it must have been a long time ago. What a crazy family! The mother was always being thrown in jail for Woman's Suffrage and the father kept trying to invent a perpetual motion machine and they had a houseful of kids and everybody was always screaming and yelling. The oldest daughter was in love with a boy from down the block, his name was Rodney, and to tell you the truth I think she was really having an affair with him. He was a goodlooking boy, but I don't know what he saw in her, she had no figure whatsoever.

So anyway. There was this girl named Sadie and she lived next door but she kept coming over to the Mason family's house because the acoustics were better, and who was Sadie but Ethel Schnurr. The clothes she had on were a scream. Everybody would be screaming and yelling and then the telephone would ring or something and everybody would become quiet and then you'd hear Ethel Schnurr reciting one of these poems. And everybody would laugh their heads off, everybody in the audience, I mean. What was so funny was more than I could see. Here she was, making a fool of herself as usual and everybody laughed. I felt so embarrassed, I didn't know where to look. And that was all she did, all through the play.

Of course the Old Man and the Old Lady Schnurr were there. Believe me, where ignorance is bliss. I almost fell out of my seat when I saw them. The Old Man looked like someone who came to fix the plumbing. And the Old Lady was wearing a fur coat that if I say it was thirty years out of style I'm not exaggerating. I understand it was the only one she ever owned. The Old Man gave it to her for their anniversary and she kept it in cold storage and this was maybe the third time in her life she ever wore it. And I saw them talking to this man in the intermission and he got up with them and they went back-stage. Listen to me – "back-stage" – you'd think I was familiar with all these terms!

Well, to make a long story short, they say that the critics can either make you or break you. You've heard that saying. The play opened on a Wednesday and it closed on a Wednesday. The same Wednesday. It lasted exactly one performance, which was one too many if you ask me. Did they pan it! I've got the clippings somewhere around here. But one of them, there was one sentence in it which I will never forget as long as I live. It said, "The ins and outs and whys and wherefores of 'Anyone Round My Base Is "It"' are beyond your poor reviewer. The only redeeming feature of this raucous comedy was the performance of newcomer Ethel Schnurr as Sadie, her humorous and nostalgic version of old-time elocution brightened an otherwise wasted evening."

Can you imagine?

But wait, wait. That was nothing. Remember I said I saw the Old Man and the Old Lady Schnurr talking to this man during the intermission? Well, who was it but the man who supplied the costumes for the play. I forget how many thousands of dollars they cost him, and of course he can kiss his money goodbye, you know what I mean? Opened on Wednesday and closed on Wednesday. He got into conversation with the old couple and he met Ethel and after the play was pronounced a failure and closed its doors he came up here and he went to the bakery and told them his tale of woe and he talked and talked and he stayed for supper. And that was the beginning of Mr. E. Mandell. That's his business, he's a theatrical outfitter or whatever they call it, and either he makes a lot of money or he loses a lot of money.

He said that the Old Lady Schnurr reminded him of his own mother and she was a very religious woman and after she died, his sister kept house for him and then she passed away, too. Of course, the nature of his business was such that he had to meet with all kinds of people and to eat what they eat, but he was always used to a kosher home. He had no use for most of these young actresses, they were mostly bums and tramps, he said, and all he wanted was to marry a decent Jewish girl like his mother and sister, they should rest in peace; and beauty was only skin deep and he was tired of clever women. Anyway, that's what Sandra Millman, she used to be a Katz, in other words the old lady's niece, said she was told. And the long and short of it is, he proposed to Ethel Schnurr and she accepted him and they were married a month later.

So that's the whole story, and after that she had a baby. Did you ever hear of such a thing, a woman forty-five years old gets married for the first time in her life and right away she has a baby. It was a boy and they named him Nathaniel, after the grandfather on the father's side. They live out on Long Island in this huge and expensive house and she has every modern convenience and she has a maid and she has a second maid and she doesn't have to put her hand in cold water and all she has to do is take care of the baby and cook for her husband when he's home. And all these prominent theatrical personalities come out to their place and she cooks for them, too, and they're just crazy about her, Sandra Millman says. And she's in her element. She talks to them about expression and gestures and they talk to her about expression and gestures. And the bakery is only open five days a week now. It's closed on Sundays, too, and every Sunday morning the chauffeur comes from Long Island in this great big automobile and the old couple come out loaded down with bread and rolls and cake, as if the son-in-law hasn't got the money to buy it, and they drive out to Long Island and spend the whole day there and then the chauffeur drives them back. So that's the whole story and you go figure it out and if you can figure it out then you're better than I am, because when you come right down to it, who is Ethel Schnurr? You know what I mean?

Introduction to
On The Right Is Michael

SOME OF MY EARLIEST MEMORIES ARE of Avram teaching me the Hebrew prayers.

There were, of course, the blessings over the bread, and the wine, and the Chanukah candles. But one in particular stuck in my mind. As he tucked me in, he would say the prayer of the Archangels, which is alluded to in the title of this story. I don't remember exactly which angels went where, but the prayer said basically, "Gabriel in front of you, Rafael in back of you, Uriel to the left of you, and Michael to the right of you."

It was very comforting for me to go to sleep surrounded by Angels.

As a child, I listened to Avram's stories about his time in Israel, in the military and on a Kibbutz. Avram tried to teach me Hebrew, but gave up because I was such a resistant student. But when I was twelve, and living with my mother in Hawaii, he moved there for several months in order to tutor me for my Bar Mitzvah, and I was able to learn at least a few basic prayers.

Later in life, Avram did study other spiritual traditions. But he never lost touch with his Jewish roots. I read a note he wrote giving specific instructions on what he wanted done with his body after he died. It included the request that a marker be put in a military cemetery, with a Star of David on it.

This story was found among his papers after his death. We do not know when it was written.

Ethan Davidson

ETHAN DAVIDSON is the son of Avram Davidson and Grania Davis. He grew up in Sausalito, California, lived in Hawaii, Belize, Tennessee, Japan, and Texas before settling in San Francisco, where he feeds the homeless. He has studied creative writing, social work, and public health. He has had short stories, poems, and essays published and has had a play produced.

ON THE RIGHT
IS MICHAEL

THE BUILDING HAD ONCE BEEN a moving-picture star's mansion. Stars no longer wanted houses like that, the last of them had long since left the neighborhood, gone to Beverly Hills, Brentwood, Malibu. But the house suited the needs of its present owner perfectly. The Reverend Doctor Mordecai Blum (rhymes with *plum*, not pl*ume*) was its present owner. Or, to be more exact, it belonged to an incorporated religious body with which the Reverend Doctor Mordecai Blum held a life contract. Officially its name was the Congregation Adath Achim, the Band of Brothers, but it was known now universally as The Temple In The Hills. From its grounds on a clear day all of Hollywood could be seen.

Clad in a robe of white nylon and with a white satin biretta on his head, Rabbi Blum had his place at a lectern next to the elaborately-carved 17th-century Holy Ark which had been brought, some years before, from Italy, at no small expense: the gift of a sportswear manufacturer in memory of his mother. The Rabbi prefaced each Holy Day service by explaining something of the Temple's religious philosophy to the congregation.

"This is not an Orthodox service. This is not a Conservative service. This is not a Reform service." He paused. "This is a *Jewish* service."

Heads nodded in approval. "You will find the best-known and best-loved of those wonderful prayers and songs which make up so important a part of the heritage of American Jewry. We will, however, omit a number of lengthy pages which have not stood the test of time so well. And we will read together quite often in English so that the service will be more meaningful to those of you who do not have an intimate knowledge of the Hebrew. Sometimes we will read responsively. From time to time I may explain the historical background of various sections of our glorious liturgy. I will always be announcing the pages so that everyone can follow. Please refrain from conversation and give your complete attention to our very fine young cantor, Harold Handlin."

Young Cantor Handlin had succeeded old Cantor Greenberg, whom he had assisted the previous year. Greenberg was getting on in years and could not be convinced that his voice no longer had the same strength or range. And he was apt to forget the direction he had been given, and to go off into lengthy repetitions and falsetto variations. This year Cantor Greenberg was to be found singing for overflow services held by another congregation in a theater on Beverly Boulevard, while its regular cantor sang in the synagogue proper. Many theaters were rented for this purpose, because few synagogues could hold the crowds of worshippers who attended the High Holy Day services; and the few which could stood largely empty the rest of the year round. The Temple In The Hills did not have this problem because only High Holy Day services were held there. However, it was far from remaining unused at other times, because it was in regular use for weddings, Bar Mitzvah celebrations, and dances and luncheons and dinners and different kinds of meetings and gatherings. Some of the smaller rooms were still just the right size for a Ladies' Benevolent card-party. But of course Yom Kippur was the best day. And it was on a Yom Kippur that a very disturbing thing happened.

"The *Aleynu* prayer," Doctor Blum had explained, "is one of the most ancient. In fact, Tradition formerly ascribed it to the authorship of none other than Joshua, the successor of Moses. During the days of the persecution of the Spanish Inquisition, it was solemnly chanted by the martyrs at the stake as the flames of the Auto-da-Fe rose about them. It was formerly the custom – and some of us may remember our dear parents and grandparents doing so – at the line, 'we bow down and prostrate ourselves before the Supreme King of Kings, the Holy One blessed be He' – at this line the people would actually and literally bow down, in the fulness of their devotional feelings, please give your complete attention to the Cantor and kindly refrain from conversation as he chants the *Aleynu*."

The Cantor began the slow solemn notes. "*Aleynu le-shabeyach la-adon ha-kol*....It is our duty to praise the Lord of All." The four-man choir chanted with him, and some of the congregation as well. It was a familiar tune, or at least, familiar to those who had even a slight knowledge of the liturgy. He recited the opening lines, coming to the passage the Rabbi had mentioned. Then he sank to his knees as he sang the words, and bowed down. He was silent. The Rabbi announced that the congregation would read the rest of the prayer aloud, responsively, in English. As they began to do so the Cantor rose to his feet, leaned his head on his hand.

At the conclusion, Rabbi Blum directed the congregation to read the next page of the prayerbook in silence. He caught the Cantor's eye and summoned him. "You misunderstood me, Harold," he said, in a low voice. "I didn't mean that you should kneel – I would have told you – "

The young man nodded rapidly. "I know, I know.... I had this impulse."

Dr. Blum clicked his tongue. "I'm not paying you to have impulses," he said. "Greenberg had impulses, too."

The Cantor gave him a friendly, crooked grin, struck the left side of his bosom with his clenched right fist. "*I have sinned, I have trespassed....*" He stopped. The grin faded.

"All right, I'm not angry," the Rabbi said. "Not *yet*. Go back, and no tricks."

The service proceeded. The Rabbi was in complete touch with the congregation. He knew when it was bored, when it was merely tired, when it was quiet but inattentive; he knew the time for silent reading and the time for communal singing and the time for him to read aloud and the time for the Cantor to sing alone (the choir, of course, could be called on only for the parts it had rehearsed) and the time for a few words of explanation. The service for the Day of Atonement was a long one, and the fact that The Temple In The Hills used an abridged prayerbook did not make it any shorter because the time saved was taken up with reading aloud in English – which meant reading slowly – things would have been quickly run through in Hebrew. And so, finally, which they came to the middle of the Afternoon Service.

By this time the men who had wandered out to talk to old friends had all wandered in again. The women had sufficiently admired one another's new outfits. All the grandchildren had trotted in to be kissed and had trotted out again. The Reverend Dr. Mordecai Blum decided it was time for him to read aloud. "This very beautiful liturgical passage is not in your prayer books," he said; "so you will have to give me your very close attention." He nodded to the Cantor.

"*Michael mi-yamin mehallel*
U-Gavriel mi-s'mol memallel
Ba-shamayim ayn ka-el
U-va'arets mi k'amcha Yisrael"

the Cantor intoned slowly. The Rabbi swept his eyes over the congregation. He recited the first lines without looking in the volume on the lectern.

"On the right is Michael praising, and on the left is Gabriel declaring, that in Heaven there is none like thee, Oh God! And on the earth....

"For His chariot is in the Heavens, and His
strength is in the skies,
His mighty arm is in His dwelling, and His
holiness in His habitation,
His dread is in thick darkness, and His
fear in the Heaven of Heavens,

His bow is in Heaven, and His voice
is upon the waters,
His habitation is on high, and He
looketh attentively below,"

read Dr. Blum. He saw that his Cantor was again resting his head on his
hand, but he could not catch his eye. Anyway, why shouldn't he rest a
minute? He'd been on his feet all day.

"He is hallowed above, and He is
blessed below, From the waters he
receives glory, from the rivers the voice
of praise,
From the earth, singing, from the trees,
rejoicing, From the mountains, leaping,
from the Valleys, song From every
creature, strength, from every head,
bowing,
From every eye, submission, from every
mouth, thanksgiving,
Praise from every tongue and heart,
meditation from every part,
From every knee, bending, from every
height, prostration,"

Dr. Blum pressed a finger to close one ear: it was all right, his voice was
still resonant, he could go on without a rest. Once more his eye rested on
the Cantor, but the young man hadn't moved.

"From the old, glory, from the men and women, song,
From youths and maidens, praise, from the
babies and sucklings, strength,
"From generation to generation, might, and
from eternity to eternity, blessing, for
Thou hast created them all...."

The Cantor was looking directly at him now – no, he was looking *past* him,
as if he didn't see him. The young man's face was pale and there were
circles under his eyes. All at once a sudden thought came to the Rabbi,
which such force that his head snapped back. As if he had seen the slight
movement, the Cantor sighed, looked down at his book.

"They call on each other, and answer each
other, and say to each other: 'Draw near,
assemble, hasten, and let us reverence
the King of Glory, the God Who is
reverenced and hallowed in holiness.'"

He paused. The Cantor gave a short nod, the choir chanted, the congregation followed, the Cantor repeated:

"Holy, Holy, Holy, is the Lord of Hosts,
the whole earth is full of His glory."

As soon as he had finished, the Cantor left his place and went out. The Rabbi announced another page of silent reading, and followed him. The young man was sitting at the table in the ante-room, with his face in his hands.

"What's the matter, Harold? Do you feel all right?" Blum asked.

"No."

Blum pulled away the hands and put his own under the Cantor's chin. His suspicions confirmed, he said, sharply, "You've been *fasting*, you foolish kid? On Yom *Kippur*?"

There was an exclamation from the door. A thin, dark-haired woman entered; she was Mrs. Handlin, the Cantor's mother, and she had evidently heard.

"How do you like that?" she asked, in a suppressed voice. "On Yom Kippur, when he needs all his strength! Are you trying to kill yourself?"

Blum breathed out, heavily, through his nose. He considered for moment, then turned to Mrs. Handlin, who looked at him, nervously eager, her tongue caught between compressed lips. "Go upstairs to my apartment – here's the key – in the icebox – my wife will show you where it is – there's some cold coffee – and – milk."

The truth, however, was more complex than either of the older people had guessed. It was not hunger and not fatigue and not thirst which had troubled Harold...or, at any rate, not the physical things alone. He had been singing in synagogue and temple choirs since he was ten, and had been acting, on and off, as a lay cantor since he was eighteen. Today, and just a short while ago today, an absolutely shocking thought had come to his mind: These hymns, these prayers, these declarations of belief in the might and power of God, the King of the Universe and of the Day of Judgement – *what if they should all be true?*

This possibility had never before occurred to him.

SHEMIRAS SHABBOS

They do not on the Sabbath ride.
Nor arch their necks in wilful pride;
But humbly, fitly, do they talk
Of one who did on Sinai walk,
And hearken well unto the Law
Whose ringing summons down he bore
From that most holy mount.

"If on this Day thou dost restrain
And from all vanities refrain,
Nor speak of them, then, by My grace,
Thou thy very loot shall place
On Earth's high summits, and, indeed,
On Jacob's heritage shall feed,
By My most holy Word."

Introduction to
THE CROWN JEWELS OF JERUSALEM
OR THE TELL-TALE HEAD

THE ADVENTURES OF DR. ENGELBERT ESZTERHAZY, Imperial Wizard, Doctor of Philosophy, Science, Music, Literature, Laws, Engineering, etc. are regarded by many critics and fans as Avram Davidson's finest work. The Dr. Eszterhazy stories enhanced his reputation as "prose laureate of the old country" with their Eastern European steam-era setting. The first series, including *The Crown Jewels of Jerusalem*, was published in the mid-1970s, and collected in a slim paperback called *The Enquiries of Doctor Eszterhazy*, which won the prestigious *World Fantasy Award* for the best story collection of 1975.

Avram described how Dr. Eszterhazy's magical world came into his mind: "Gradually it came to me that there had been an empire in Eastern Europe which had been so completely destroyed that we no longer even remembered it...that being an empire, it had an emperor; that the emperor had a wizard; the wizard drove about the streets of Bella (BELgrade/ViennA) in a steam runabout;...that the emperor's name was Ignats Louis; and that the wizard's name was...was...was Engelbert Eszterhazy...I sat down at the typewriter, and in six weeks wrote all eight stories of the first series. No rewrites were ever even suggested...Everything came so clear to me, the bulging eyes and bifurcated beard of Ignats Louis the fatherly King-Emperor, the teeming streets of the South Ward of Bella...and all the rest of it – came so clear to me – that now I recognize that I did not at all "make them up," that Sythia-Pannonia-Transbalkania *did* exist!"

The above quote, and the further tales of Dr. Eszterhazy were collected in the handsome book *The Adventures of Doctor Eszterhazy*, published by Owlswick Press in 1990. If you are something of a wizard, perhaps you or your bookseller can locate a copy. Another Dr. Eszterhazy story, *Polly Charms*, can be found in *The Avram Davidson Treasury* (Tor).

Grania Davidson Davis

THE CROWN JEWELS OF JERUSALEM

OR

THE TELL-TALE HEAD

THE SPA AT GROSS-KROPLETS is not one of the fashionable watering places of the Triune Monarchy, else Eszterhazy would scarcely have been found there. Nor, as he did not practice the curiously fashionable habit of abusing his liver for forty-nine weeks of the year, did he ever feel the need of medicating it with the waters of mineral springs for the remaining three.

It was entirely for the purpose of making a scientific analysis of those waters – or, specifically, those at Gross-Kroplets – which had brought him from his house in Bella, Imperial Capital of Scythia-Pannonia-Transbalkania, to the comparatively small resort high in the Rhiphaean Alps. Two moderately large and three moderately small (four, if one counts the House of the Triple-Eagle) hotels served to provide room and board for visitors to the spa; and although all were privately owned, the Spring itself had been the property of the Royal and Imperial House of Hohenschtupfen since the Capitulations of 1593 and was under the management of the Ministry of the Privy Purse.

Anyone, therefore, not in a condition of gross drunkenness or equally gross nakedness is free to drink the waters (the waters may actually be drunk free in the original, or Old, Pump Room in what is now the First Floor or Basement, but few except the truly indigent care to avail themselves of the privilege; most visitors prefer to employ the drinking facilities in the First, Second, or Third Class Sections of the New or Grand Pump Room reached from the Terrace, where a schedule of fees is in operation); and anyone is, accordingly, free to walk about the pleasantly – if not splendidly – landscaped grounds.

Eszterhazy, therefore, neither said nor did anything when he became aware that someone was not only closely observing him but in effect closely following him. When, of a morning, he walked with his equipment from the small, old-fashioned inn called The House of the Triple-Eagle, someone presently appeared behind his back and plodded after him. When he set up his equipment next to the basin of rough-worked stone whence the Spring welled up and bubbled on its way upstairs and down, someone stood outside the doorless chamber and looked in. When he returned with his samples to the Inn, someone followed after him and vanished before he reached the sprawling old building.

In the afternoons, the whole thing was repeated.

In the evenings, when what passed at Gross-Kroplets for A High Fashionable Occasion was at its most, Eszterhazy stayed in his sitting room, making entries in his *Day-Book*, after which he read, first, from some technical work, and, next, from some nontechnical one. He was particularly fond of the light novels of an English writer named G.A. Henty, although he more than once complimented the stories of G. de Maupassant, Dr. A. Tchechoff, and H. George Wells.

It was the morning of the fourth day of his visit, as he was on his knees commencing a check of comparative sedimentation with the aid of a pipette, when someone came to the doorway of the Spring Room and, after coughing, said, "Are you not Engelbert Eszterhazy, Doctor of Medicine?"

Since Eszterhazy felt several simultaneous emotions, none of them amiable, he was for a moment incapable of elegance. Why, for example, was the cough considered a sound worthy of announcing a supposedly polite address? Why not a gasp, an eructation, a hiccough, or a flatulency? But all he first said was, "You have caused me to contaminate the pipette."

The questioner paid as much attention to this as he might have to, say, "Brekekekex koax koax." With his eyebrows raised, he merely made an inquiring sound of "*Mmm*?" Which moved his previous question. He was an inordinately ordinary-looking man, in a short jacket, baggy trousers and string tie, with a moustache which straggled too long on the right side, and pinch-nose spectacles; and had the look of a drummer for a firm of jobbers in odd lots of oilcloth. A writing-master in a fifth-rate provincial gymnasium. Or, even, the owner by inheritance of two "courts" in one of the proliferating jerry-built suburbs of Bella, whose rents relieved him of the need to be anything much in particular. And, with only another wiggle of the raised eyebrows, this person again repeated his "*Mmm*?" And this time on a note of higher urgency or pressure.

"Yes, sir, I am Engelbert Eszterhazy, Doctor of Medicine," the scientist said, irritably. "I am also Engelbert Eszterhazy, Doctor of Jurisprudence; Engelbert Eszterhazy, Doctor of Philosophy; Engelbert

Eszterhazy, Doctor of Science; and Engelbert Eszterhazy, Doctor of Literature. And I do not know why any of this should entitle you to burst in upon my quietness and research."

The other man, as he heard all this, looked all around him, as though inviting spectators (of whom there were none) to witness it; then he said, "I must depart from my invariable incognito to inform you, sir, that *I* am King of Jerusalem and that you have unfortunately just prevented yourself from the reception of a *very* important appointment at my court!"

Eszterhazy looked down into the bubbling waters and heaved a silent sigh of self-reproach at himself for allowing himself to be irritated by a noddy. When he looked up, a moment later, prepared to offer a soft and noncommittal rejoinder, the man had gone.

During the rest of his stay in Gross-Kroplets, he did not see any more of the man; and his single enquiry met with no information at all.

He recollected the incident next, some months later, at the Linguistic Congress, during the middle of an interesting discussion on the Eastern and the Western Aramaic, with the Most Reverend Salomon Isaac Tsedek, Grand Rabbi of Bella – who – with his perceptive mind and eye, and observing that a different idea had occurred to Eszterhazy – paused inquiringly. " – Your pardon, Worthy Grand Rabbi. Who is King of Jerusalem?"

"Almighty God, King of Heaven and Earth, in a theological sense. In a secular sense, I suppose, the Sultan of Turkey." He did not offend against good manners by adding, "Why do you ask?" as he – as all sensible men and women should – recognized that if Eszterhazy wished to say why he asked, he would say why he asked. And they returned to their discussion of the construct case, and of the genitive.

Some weeks after the Linguistic Congress, Eszterhazy, passing peacefully through the Pearl Market, where he had been pricing some Russko chalcedonies, observed his friend Karrol-Francos Lobats, Commissioner of the Detective Police, deeply engaged in conversation with De Hooft, the President of the Jewelers' Association. De Hooft, usually reserved to the point of being phlegmatic, was shaking his head excitedly, and even took the Commissioner by the coat lapels. Lobats did notice Eszterhazy, who was going on by, and made as if to disengage himself; after a moment he fell back, as though it had not happened. And Eszterhazy continued on his way.

The visit to the Pearl Market, where gems of all sorts, plus ivory and amber, had been bought, sold, appraised, and bartered for centuries, was a mere brief amusement. Eszterhazy had an overflowing schedule. For one thing, he wished to prepare the final draft of his report on the therapeutic qualities (or otherwise) of medicinal spring water for the *Journal of the Iberian Academy of Medicine*. For another, he had already begun another study, an enquiry into the practice of clay-eating among the so-called Ten Mountain Tribes of Tsiganes (in which Herrekk, his manservant, was of course of invaluable assistance). Eszterhazy liked to have one enquiry overlapping another, in order to avoid the letdown, the lethargy, which otherwise often accompanied the conclusion of an enquiry.

And in addition, the end of the Quarterly Court of Criminal Processes was approaching. Eszterhazy wished few men ill; he was by no means a Mallet of Malefactors; but the chance – which the conclusion of every quarter furnished him – of examining from the viewpoint of phrenology the freshly shaven heads of anywhere from fifty-odd to two-hundred or so newly convicted criminals was one which could not be passed up. Indeed, a few of the regular recidivists looked forward to the examination with an enthusiasm which the fact that Eszterhazy always gave each one a chitty payable in chocolate or tobacco at the canteen in the Western Royal and Imperial Penitentiary Fortress alone could not explain.

"See, this noggin o' mine goes down into history for the third time," one professional thief announced triumphantly to the guard, after Eszterhazy had completed the reading of his remarkably unlovely head.

"The rest of youse has already gone down into history five or six times on the Bertillon System," the guard said.

"Ahah, youse is just jealous, har har! Thanks, Purfessor, for the baccy chit!" And he swaggered off, prepared to spend three to five years under circumstances which no farmer would provide for his dogs or oxen. However, interventions on the part of Eszterhazy had already worked to the abolishment of the so-called Water Cure punishment and of the infamous Pig Pen.

The docket of Doctor Eszterhazy was rather full.

And so he made no much – about the tiny article, almost a filler, in the *Evening Gazette of Bella*:

> The Honorable Police can give no substance to rumors
> about alleged thefts of certain antique jewelry, it was
> learned today by our correspondents.

And he passed on to the lead *feuilleton* of the issue, entitled, by a most curious coincidence, *The Romance of Old Jewelry*. Liebfrow, the editor of the *Evening Gazette*, was in many ways an old nannykins, but not in so many ways that he was unable to get a point across with a delicacy envied by other editors.

Skimming through the article, noticing references to the Iron Crown of the Lombards, the Cyprus Regalia, and the Crown of St. Stephan (the *feuilleton* seemed somewhat heavy on regalia), Eszterhazy observed some word which triggered a small mechanism deep in his mind. He had not quite registered it on the upper level, and was about to go over the article, column by column, when Herrekk silently set upon the table a dish of cheese dumplings. Although the master of the premises at Number 33, Turkling Street, could have endured it very well if cheese dumplings were to be abolished by joint resolution of both Houses of the Imperial Diet, he knew that his housekeeper, Frou Widow Orgats, prided herself on her cheese dumplings – indeed, she regarded it as though an article of faith established by the Council of Trent that her master was deliriously fond of her cheese dumplings – speaking of them in high praise to the Faculties of Law and Medicine, and praising their remarkable lightness and sweetness to the Gentry and Nobility; in fact (Eszterhazy knew damned well from experience) she was certainly even now behind the dining-room door, waiting expectantly.

So he performed.

"Ah, Herrekk, Herrekk!"

"Lord," said Herrekk, a Tsigane of few words.

"Ah, these cheese dumplings of Frou Widow Orgats!"

"Lord."

"How delightfully sweet, how incredibly light!"

"Lord."

"Herrekk, be sure and see she gives you some. Let me know, should she overlook doing so."

"Lord."

Next Eszterhazy made a series of sounds indicating his being reduced to wordless ecstasy by the mere mastication of the cheese dumplings. And then he felt free to continue the rest of his dinner. Should he overlook having done all this, Frou Widow Orgats – an after all truly firstrate cook and housekeeper, otherwise would clump back into her kitchen a prey to injury and grudge, slam about the tinned-copper cookpots, and burn the coffee.

By the time this comedy of manners was completed, Eszterhazy had clean forgotten what it was that he wanted to do about the newspaper piece on the Romance of Jewels. So he set it aside to be boxed for later perusal.

It was over the coffee and the triple-distilled liqueur of plum that the message arrived at the hands of Emmerman the night porter. The message consisted of some words scribbled over, as it happened, a copy of the same *feuilleton*.

"What's this, Emmerman?"

"Someone give it me, Lord Doctor."

"What someone?"

"Dunno, Lord Doctor. He run off." Emmerman, bowing, departed to take up his post of duty from Lemkotch, the day porter.

"Well, Eszterhazy," said himself to himself, "you train your servants to be brief, you must not complain if they are not prolix."

"*See Sludge*", said the message, in its entirety. The handwriting tended toward the script favored in the official Avar-language schools of Pannonia, which brought it down to only seven million or so possible people. Still, that was a start of sorts. As for *Sludge*. The word was an epithet for any of the three and one half to four million Slovatchko-speaking subjects of the Triune Monarchy, and for their language. Its use was rather a delicate matter. "Who you shoving, Sludge?" was, for example, grounds for blows. Yet. Yet the same person who violently objected to the word might easily say, "Speak Sludge" – meaning, talk sense. Or: "What, three beers 'much to drink'? Who you talking to? You talking to a Sludge!" On reflection, and considering that the message had been scribbled on a newspaper....

There had always been a kind of genteel pretense in the office of the *Evening Gazette* that the premises constituted a sort of extension of the College of Letters. No such notion had ever obtained in the raucous chambers of the *Morning Report*, where sometimes the spit hit the spittoon, and sometimes it did not, and nobody cared or commented, as long as the details of the interview with the Bereaveds of the latest butcher-shop brawl got set down in full, rich description. Whereas the *Gazette* (if it mentioned the distasteful matters at all) might say, "The deceased was almost decapitated by the fatal blow. One of his employees was taken into custody;" the *Report* would be giving its readers something to the effect that "Blood was all over the bedroom of the Masterbutcher Helmuth Oberschlager whose head was pretty nearly all chopped off by the frenzied blows supposedly delivered in an enraged love-quarrel over the affections of Frou Masterbutcher Helga Oberschlager, third wife of the elderly Masterbutcher Helmuth Oberschlager. The corpse lay almost upside-down propped against the bloodstained bed and the scant undergarment of Journeymanbutcher," etc.

That was the way they did things at the *Report*.

As the editor of the Report had been born in the Glagolitic Alps, the very heartland of the Slovatchko, he was not eligible to become President of the United States. So, instead, he had accomplished something almost as difficult, namely, becoming editor of the largest-circulation Gothic-language newspaper in the Imperial (and officially Gothic-speaking) Capital where he disarmed all insults in advance by using the nickname of "Sludge" almost to the entire exclusion of his real name.

There would be little point in making references to someone's illegitimacy if he chose to answer his telephone with "Bastard speaking, yeah?"

So.

"Hello, Sludge."

"Hel-lo. Hel-lo! Doctor Eszterhazy! What an honor! Clear out of that chair, you illiterate son of a vixen" – this, to his star reporter, who had in fact already stood up and was offering the chair – "and let the learned doctor sit down."

"Thank you, Swarts."

Sludge, a squat, muscular man with a muddy complexion and prominent green eyes, looked at his visitor with keen appraisal. "I suppose you haven't really come to give us a story to the effect that Spa water is as good for the bowels as an Epsom salts physic, and no Goddam good whatsoever for consumption, rheumatism, liver complaint, kidney trouble, and all the rest of it, eh?"

Eszterhazy did not ask him how he had put two and two together. They looked at each other with understanding. "You may perhaps be interested in a forthcoming article in the *Journal of the Iberian Academy of Medicine.*"

The editor, who had eagerly picked up a pencil, flung his head to one side and put the pencil down again. "Oh, why, certainly, I'll have Our Special Correspondent in Madrid..." His voice trailed away; the pencil was taken back, a note made. "I would ask what you would advise about it, eh, Doctor?"

What the doctor would advise about it was that the *Report* wait until an abstract had appeared in the French medical journal, which would be excerpted in the British *Lancet*. After that, an article in a Swiss scientific publication of immense standing was inevitable. And the subject would by then be provided with all sorts of guarantees and precedents, and ready to be sprung upon the population of Bella without risk of Sludge spending perhaps thirty days in jail for, say, Libel of the National Patrimony (to wit, its medicinal spas).

"Yeah. Yeah." Sludge scribbled away. "But not me, never, no. Not even thirty days. Not even thirty minutes."

He arose without a word of warning, and, at the top of his lungs, screamed something absolutely incomprehensible, and waited. From somewhere far off, above the clatter of the typewriting machines, the pounding of the steam presses, a voice called up words equally obscure. Sludge smiled and sat down. He looked at his caller again, waiting.

Who was not yet quite ready.

"Why not?" asked Eszterhazy. "You are the Responsible Editor of the *Report*. What?" Sludge rapidly shook his head. The star reporter smiled. "But.., it says so, on the masthead. 'L. Methodios Hozzenko, Responsible Editor.'"

Sludge smiled. The star reporter laughed out loud.

"That's my Uncle Louie," Sludge said. "The world's worst loafer, bar none. *I* am down on the payroll as L. M. Hozzenko, Nephew, Municipal Editor, see? Trouble comes up, who goes down to the courthouse? Uncle Louie. Who goes to jail? Uncle Louie. We bring him cheap cigars and beer in a bucket and sandwiches and hot-sausage-and-crout, and he plays cards with the cops.... *He* don't care! And what really brings *you* here, Doctor E.?"

Eszterhazy said that the Romance of Old Jewelry brought him there. The star reporter choked on a snort. Sludge threw his head back and his arms out.

Eszterhazy said, "Details. Details. Details."

"This won't get out? All right, excuse me, Doctor, of course you won't – Not until our first morning edition gets out. After that – 'Details?' Well, what is it that you don't know? Obviously you do know that the Crown Jewels of Jerusalem have been stolen, and that – "

A multitude of thoughts rushed headlong through Eszterhazy's mind. "*The Cyprus Regalia!*" he exclaimed.

Sludge shrugged, indulgently. "That's for you educated folks," he said, without malice. "Us Glagolitski, we never even heard of the Cyprus Regalia. Never even heard of *Cyprus*! But – the Crown Jewels of Jerusalem? Oh, boy, did we ever hear of *them*! Say, one day, down at the little old farmstead, Grandpa rushes up, waving his stick, 'Who let the dogs knock over the barrow of pigturd, was it you?'

'Oh, no, Bobbo! It wasn't me! I swear it, I swear it, by the Crown Jewels of Jerusalem, I swear it!' See?"

And the star reporter said it was just the same among the Avars. "Suppose two old peasants have agreed on a deal for the rent of the orchards for the next plum harvest. They join hands and repeat the terms and then each one says in turn, 'I swear to keep this word and I swear it by the Holy Cross and the Avenging Angel and the Crown Jewels of Jerusalem....'

You talk to any of them about the Cyprus Regalia and he's likely to think he's being insulted and to hit you with his pig-stick."

Eszterhazy slowly, slowly nodded, and looked around the disorderly office, observing with only a sense of the familiar the photograph of The Presence. He observed with mild surprise the photograph of the American President, A. Lincoln. "Yes... I could sit here and, without having to send out for research materials, write an entire book to be titled... say... *The Cyprus Regalia or Crown Jewels of Jerusalem in Law, Legend, and History in the Triune Monarchy....*"

Said Sludge, "And also. *With Added Details As To Their Theft From the Crypt of Saint Sophie... Yeah...*"

From an article, "The Romance of Old Jewelry," published in the *Evening Gazette* newspaper, Bella, April 7th, 190 –

> Among the other items of jewelry pertaining to our beloved Monarchy are those sometimes called The Cyprus Regalia, or the Crown Jewels of Jerusalem. These consist of a crown with pendants, an orb with cross, and a sceptre, which, in turn, bears a miniature orb and cross. The popular history of these items derives, ultimately, from the *Glagolitic Chronicle*, composed for the most part by the Monk Mazzimilianos. According to this document of the later Anti-Turkish Resistance Period, these items formed the Crown Jewels of the Christian Kings of Jerusalem during the Crusades. Most modern historians tend not to accept this account. Some, such as Prince Proszt and Proszt, concede that The Regalia did form part of the Crown Jewelry of the Lusignan Kings who reigned over Cyprus prior to the rule of Venice - though only a part - and who were indeed crowned in two ceremonies: one, as Kings of Cyprus, and, two, as Kings of Jerusalem. The learned Prince, however, denies that these same Regalia were ever actually used during the earlier, or Jerusalem period at all. Other modern historical scholars, of whom it may suffice to mention only Dr. Barghardt and Professor Sz. Szneider, do not agree even to this account. The learned Dr. Barghardt goes to so far as to state: "The Turks could not have found them in the vaults of Famagusta when they captured Cyprus, for the very good reason that they (that is, the Jewels) never were in Cyprus at all." And Prof. Sz. Szneider suggests that The Regalia were probably made for the use of

one of the many late medieval Christian princes of the Balkania whose brave defiance of the Turks, alas...

Eszterhazy sighed, ran his finger farther down the column, grunted, stopped the finger in its tracks.

> But popular opinion prefers to accept the traditional account that these were indeed the very Crown Jewels of Jerusalem, that they were in very truth captured from Prince Murad in single combat by the great and noble Grandduke Gustave Hohenschtupfen, direct ancestor of our beloved Monarch. Popular opinion makes a very definite connection between the possession of these Regalia by the Royal and Imperial House and the August Titles of our beloved Ruling Family: which, as every schoolchild knows, commence with "Holy Roman Emperor of Scythia, Apostolic King of Pannonia, and Truly Christian King of Jerusalem, Joppa, Tripoli, and Edessa," and...

Popular opinion, to be sure, was taking the whole thing very, very seriously indeed. Already reports were coming in from the wilder regions of Transbalkania that some of the peasantry were claiming that, with the loss of the Holy Crown Jewels of Holy Jerusalem, the Imperial and Royal power had passed in effect into abeyance, that Satan was now let loose to wage war upon the Saints, and that it was accordingly no longer necessary to pay the salt tax and the excise on distilled spirits.

All things religious were always touchy in the wilder regions of Transbalkania, but even closer to home – in fact, two blocks away – Eszterhazy had heard a drayman shouting to a troika driver, "Did you hear what them damned Turks have done, the dogs?"

"Yes, the dirty dogs," the troikanik had howled, "they stole back the Holy Jewels, we ought to send our gun-boats down the Black Sea and bombard Consta' until they give them back, the dogs!"

The drayman had a caveat.

"We haven't *got* no gunboats on the Black Sea, damn it!"

"Well, we better *get* some there, then, blood of a vixen, the dirty dogs, *shove*!" And he cracked his whip over the backs of his horses, as though Mi Pasha, Murad the Midget, and Abdul Hamid themselves were all in the traces.

And now a voice called from the staircase, "Berty art home?"

Not many people addressed Engelbert Eszterhazy in the *thou*-form. Even fewer called him "Berty."

"To thee, Kristy!" he called back.

Visits from his first cousin once-removed Count Kristian-Kristofr Eszterhazy-Eszterhazy were rare. When he was not acting in his official capacity as Imperial Equerry the Count preferred, in his purely personal capacities, to visit places much more amusing than the house at 33 Turkling Street. No merely familial duty or memories of boyhood spent much together had brought him here now, his moustache unwaxed, his figure for once unassisted by the usual corset, and smelling rather strongly of Cognac, cologne, and extreme agitation. Without pause or further greetings, he made rapidly for the champagne bucket in the corner and, with a hand which trembled slightly, poured himself a drink from the bottle, tossed half of it off, and –

"No," said Dr. Eszterhazy, "it is not champagne. It is a mixture of geneva with an Italian wine which has been steeped in a profusion of herbs. Courtesy of the American Minister. He calls it 'martini.' I don't know why."

Count Kristy downed the other half and sighed. "Listen, Berty, up, up, and into the saddle. Bobbo has gone round the bend."

It was one of His Royal and Imperial Highness's amiable little habits, which endeared him much to his Slovatchko subjects, that he liked to refer to himself in the third person... at *certain times*...dialects, by the term which meant, varying slightly in the Glagolitic Grandfather, Godfather, Foreman, Headman, Father-in-law, or – somewhat mysteriously – a boar with either three tusks or three testicles. "What!" he would exclaim, to a delegation from the Hither Provinces. "What! No rain this year? What! Crops bad? What! Want your land rates reduced? Ah, my children, you did right to come to Bobbo! Bobbo will take care of it! Pray for Bobbo! Bobbo is your *friend*!" And so the Dissolution of the Triune Monarchy would be postponed for another five years. At times the intelligentsia and the underground felt certain that Ignats Louis was a stupid old fool. At other times, they were not so sure.

"What? Like poor old Mazzy?"

"Well... not quite so bad as that. Doesn't ride his white horse up and down the stairs hunting for Bonaparte. What he does do... he blubbers, flops on his knees every other minute and prays, shouts, storms, curses, weeps, smacks his riding crop on his desk, and – It's these damned Cyprus Regalia things. (Wouldn't be surprised if they aren't actually *glass*, myself.) Poor old Bobbo, he has the notion that until and unless the Holy Jewels are found, his Crowns, his real crowns, I mean, are in peril."

Eszterhazy, whose devotion to the Person of the Imperial Presence was based on a deep-seated preference for King Log over King (or President, or Comrade) Stork, winced and shook his head.

"This is not quite reasonable," he said.

"When you are seventy-five years old, and an Emperor," Count Kristy pointed out, "you don't have to be quite reasonable. The Old Un is really in a *state*, I tell you! Won't review the Household Troops. Won't read the Budget. Won't sign the Appointments or the Decrees. Won't listen to *Madame* play the harpsichord – "

"Oh! Oh!" If Ignats Louis would not listen to the twice-daily harpsichord performance of Madame de Mouliere, whose position as *maitresse en titre* had, presumably, for many years been so purely titular indeed that it rested chiefly on the remembrance of things past and on the twice-daily performance upon the harpsichord, then, then, things were very bad indeed.

"Weeps, prays, storms, stamps," Count Kristy recapitulated. "Reminds everyone that it is still part of the Imperial Prerogative to flay his servants up to and including the rank of Minister – Well. And speaking of which. The Prime – "

"The Prime Minister had ordered extra guards around the Turkish Legation, yes. What else?"

"Aunt Tillie asked me to mention that she is also very disturbed."

The Grandduchess Matilda was the wife of The Heir. And where was The Heir? "Where would he be? If he isn't murdering grouse, stags, and boars, he's on maneuvers. Right now – *fortunately*! – he is on maneuvers just about as far as he can be, in Little Byzantia, with no posts, no telegraphs, and the heliograph limited to matters purely military."

Little Byzantia was, in fact, one of the kernels in the nut. Little Byzantia was, nominally, still a *pashalik*, although the Triune Monarchy had administered it for forty-two years. During all that time, its eventual annexation to the Triple Crowns had been anticipated. And now, though very *sub rosa*, final negotiations with the Sublime Porte were underway. The Sublime Porte did not very much care at all. The Byzantian underground nationalists cared very much. Negotiations were very delicate. Anti-Turkish riots were not desired. Or – and this was another kernel in the nut – they were not desired now. The nut, of course, had many kernels. The temper of The Heir, always largely under control when at home and surrounded by ceremony, tended to become less and less under control the farther away from home it got.

There was a very possible and very undesirable order of progression. It went like this: First, Anti-Turkish riots in Bella... or, for that matter, in Transbalkania, where a minority of several score thousand Turks still slept away their days over their hookahs and their prayer beads. Following such riots: A Reaction, any kind of a Reaction, on the part of Turkey. Following *that*, and assuming The Heir to find out (and find out he must, sooner or later), precipitate action on the part of The Heir. Following *that*: Protests by France, Austria-Hungary, Russia, and Roumania. And, following that: A stroke, a heart attack, or any of the other disasters lying in wait for an excited old man of seventy-five. And, *following that* –

The Heir had many lovable qualities. One loved The Heir. One wished him many more long years... as Heir.

Slowly, Eszterhazy said, "In fact, Kristy I am working on it now. But I will need time. And I will need help."

Count Eszterhazy-Eszterhazy said, "I can't do a damned thing about time. But as for help, well – "He fished something out of his equerry's pouch. "Bobbo ordered me to give you... this."

"Jesus Christ!"

"This" was a piece of parchment, deeply imprinted with the Triple Crowns at the top. In the middle, a hand (and Doctor Eszterhazy well knew Whose) had scrawled the one word ASSIST. Underneath the ASSIST, the same Hand had drawn the initials

I   L
I   R

And, at the bottom (more or less), in wax, the Seal Imperial. And, in each corner, another initial, forming together the **I N R I**.

"I've never even held one in my *hand* before!"

The Count said, somewhat gloomily, "Neither has anyone else now alive, hardly. – One more glass of that American wine – St. Martin's, you call it? – then I must go."

The old King-Emperor's mind had, under stress and woe, evidently (at least in this one matter) gone back clear sixty-odd years, when the *Provot* (as it was commonly called) had last been used: and that was to harry the horse thieves of the Lower Ister. (Quite successfully, as a matter of fact.) Usually worn out in the course of their commissions, only a few survived to be seen in even museums. But everyone had seen pictures of them, in newspapers, magazines, even almanacs. Theater bills and posters. They were a staple feature of the popular melodrama.

"Baron Bluegrotz, will nothing stay you from your mad determination to throw me and my aged wife out of our cottage into the snow because we will not allow you to take our promised-in-marriage-daughter into your castle?"

"Nothing [with a sneer]! Nothing, nothing will stay me!"

A commotion, the door is flung open.

"*This* will stay you!" The *This* being, of course, the Provot which the hero holds up in his hand. – At which the evil baron and all his henchfellows fall upon their knees and bare their heads and cross themselves and hope they will be merely hanged and not flayed or impaled, and the audience jumps to its feet and shouts and stamps and claps and cheers.

Perhaps the aged mind of Ignats Louis had buckled under the strain. Thinking that this relic of the Middle Ages and the Early Turkish Wars was appropriate in the era of the telephone, telegraph, and police force. However. Ignats Louis (**I L**) had, indeed, issued it. He was, indeed, *Imperator* and *Rex* (**I R**). And it took not much to see clearly the association in his ancient and pious mind between the supposed Crown Jewels of Jerusalem and the letters, traditionally placed around the corners of the parchment, initials of the words *Iesus Nazarenus, Rex Iudaeorum....*

"Well," said Doctor Eszterhazy, crisply, "it is not for me to bandy words with my sovereign. He issues, I accept. Make His Imperial Majesty an appropriate reply."

"And what," asked Count Kristy, putting his uniform cap back on, and, with a rather weary shrug, preparing to depart, "what is 'an appropriate reply'?"

A moment's pause. "Tell him," said Doctor Eszterhazy, "tell him I said, '*Adsum...*'"

"Lemkotch, I am not at home to anyone."

He had known now for some time that the key word in the *Gazette* article, and the one which had tripped the flare in his mind – he had known now for some time that the word was **Jerusalem**.

"*Are you not Engelbert Eszterhazy, Doctor of Medicine?*

"I must depart from my invariable incognito to inform you, sir, that *I am King of Jerusalem....*"

Over and over again, head resting in his hands, in the silence and solitude of his study, he went over the odd scene in the old Spring Room at the mountain spa. Was there, now that he deliberately tried to think that there might be, was there something else in his memory, besides that single scene, connecting himself with the man behind that totally unmemorable face? Or was this delusion?

After a while he sat up, took a pad and drawing pencil, and, as best he could, made a sketch of the man as he remembered him. The clothing, he somehow felt, the clothing was nothing. The *face* – He discarded the first drawing and sketched, and larger, the face alone. With the pinch-nose eyeglasses. And the absurd moustache, trimmed shorter on one side. And the hair... The hair, now... Well, the man had worn a hat, a hat like millions. Take off the hat, then, and draw the face without it. Did he part his hair in the middle? Perhaps. Trim it close, like a Prussian officer? Unlikely. Or was he, perhaps, bald? On the whole, and although he could not say why he thought so, Eszterhazy rather thought that the man *was* bald. He finished the sketch. And stared. Still nothing. Or, rather... something...

Take off the eyeglasses.

Take off the moustache, too.

After another while, he got up and, fixing the latest sketch to a drawing-board, set this one up on an easel. Turned the gaslights down very low. Turned the shade of the electric lamp so that it acted like a spotlight. Sat back in his chair. Allowed all the rest of the world to fall away... except for The Face ...

Had he seen it before?

He *had* seen it before.

Question and answer.

Where had he seen it before?

Question – but no answer.

The stillness grew. There seemed to be no one passing in the street. There seemed to be no carriages in the city. The cathedral bells did not ring. The last voice in the world spoke, many, many blocks away. Then all fell silent.

But if the sense of sound vanished, other senses remained. There was a smell, and a rather bad smell it was. He could not exactly say what the smell was. Familiar, though. Damnably familiar. That face. Face. Where had he seen –

Without even being able to recall the steps in between, Eszterhazy was in the kitchen. His housekeeper stared at him, her mouth all agape and askew.

"What did you say?" he was asking her, urgently, urgently.

"Why, High-born – "

"What did you say, what did you *say* – " He forced himself to speak in a softer voice. "Goodwoman, now, do not be afraid. But it is very important. What did you say, a while back, you said something about..." He strained memory; memory submitted, yielded up. "Something about needing something. You said," he clenched his fists behind his back in the face of her massive incomprehension, the two moles near her mouth, one with a hair in it, never longer, never shorter – "You said, 'We need to get some more –' Now. Goodwoman. You need to get some more of what?"

But still she stood frozen. A figure bobbed behind her. A figure in a greasy apron. Probably the scullery maid. "If you please, Frow Widow Orgats," the kitchenwoman murmured, "you had been saying, a minute or so back, how we was needing to get more disinfectant. For the – please to pardon the word – for the servants' privy. In the yard."

Something was out of the ordinary at the Royal and Imperial Penitentiary Fortress, where his card was always sufficient to bring Smits, the Sub-Governor, bowing respectfully, and saluting, as well, when he had done bowing. Smits was a career screw, up through the ranks of the Administration of Guards. It was, of course, the Governor, Baron Von Grubhorn, who interviewed journalists and discussed with them the theories of Lombroso on The Criminal Type. It was the Governor of the prison who made the weekly address to the prisoners as they stood in chains, exhorting them on their duties as Christians and loyal subjects of the Triune Monarchy. But it was the Sub-Governor who checked the bread ration, saw to the cell assignments, and even tasted the prison stew – or, as it was unaffectionately called, "the scum" – and, had the Sub-Governor not done so, the bread ration would have diminished, more murders been committed in the cells, and the stew been even scummier.

Now, however, the Sub-Governor was neither bowing nor saluting. He stood in the mud at the entrance to the Fortress directing the emplacement of what seemed to be a Gatling gun. All about him were guards with rifles at the ready; they poured in and out of the entrance, moiling like ants. Eszterhazy stopped the steam runabout (whose bronze handbell no one here seemed to have heard) about two hundred feet away and proceeded on foot.

"What's wrong, Smits?"

The look Smits flung him was bleak as a rock. "Can't come here now. Away with you!" Peering, he recognized the approaching visitor. "Can't *come* here now, Doctor! Governor's orders! The prisoners are about to riot, sir, they think their bread ration is about to be reduced – a damned lie, but try to tell *them* that – Back, sir! I says, away with you! Don't you *hear* –" He gestured, said some words in a lower voice. Two captains and a number of ordinary guards began to trot forward, holding the rifles at the oblique, to bar his way.

Eszterhazy reached into his pocket, and holding his forearm up at the traditional forty-five-degree angle, thrust out the *Provot*.

Sub-Governor, captains, and guards alike, sweeping off their caps, fell on their knees in the mud, the Sub-Governor, who alone was unencumbered with a rifle, crossing himself repeatedly.

The Governor himself stood on the inner parapet, shouting at the prisoners below. All along the platform were guards, rifles pointing down into the yard. But no one could hear a word the Baron was saying over the noise of the shouting and the ringing chains of the convicts. He turned his head as Eszterhazy approached, and his mouth fell silent. That is, presumably it fell silent. At any rate, his mouth ceased to move. Eszterhazy stepped next to him and held up the *Provot*.

With one great and simultaneous crash of chains, the convicts fell on their knees.

A ringing, echoing silence followed.

"I have received this from the Emperori' Eszterhazy said. "I bring you assurance that the bread ration is not to be reduced."

They did not, after all, give three cheers for the Emperor. Perhaps it was shock. One man, however, in a loud hoarse voice, half-growled, half-shouted: "*Good old Bobbo!*"

"No punitive measures will be taken... this time... but you are to return to your cells, *at once*." The words were Eszterhazy's. The Governor, speechless, gestured to the Sub-Governor. The Sub-Governor barked an order. All the rifles went up – straight up. And stayed so. Down in the yard, someone (a trusty, by his red patch) cried, "*Hump, tump, thrump, fump!*" The convicts fell into ranks, turned about, and, line by line, in lockstep, began to file out of the yard.

Clash-**clash-clash-clash.**

Clash-**clash-clash-clash...**

The riot was over.

This time.

The Sub-Governor gave a long look at the sketch which Eszterhazy showed him. (The Governor was drinking brandy, and looking at nothing.)

"Why, yes, Sir Doctor," said Sub-Governor Smits. "Yes, I **do** remember him. You says to me, 'This one's got a bad lung, so keep him out of the damp if you possibly can.' Which I done, Sir Doctor, which I done, inasmuch as we of the Administration of Guards are human beings after all, and not animals like some would have it said." Even up here, in the middle story of the old tower, far above the cell blocks, the smell of sweat and urine and disinfectant seemed very strong. "Consequently is why he left here alive and in better health than he come in."

Eszterhazy stared. "It has been a fatiguing week, Sub-Governor. A fatiguing week." On the mottled wall, Ignats Louis, bifurcated beard and all, looked down benignly. "Assist my memory, please. When did I say this?"

Smits raised a rough, red hand to his rough, red chin. "Why ... Strange that I should remember, sir – his face, not his name – and you not, with your great mind. But, then, I never was one much for writing and for reading. But I knew by sight, as a boy, every beast in our township. Well. When. Why, when you examine his noggin, sir. Excuse me, Sir Doctor – we are rough men here – when you give the first of them free no-Logical examinations. Is when."

And so, after much digging up of old records and after much checking and cross-checking of the prison files, it was found:

NUMBER 8727-6. NAME Gogor, Teodro. AGE 25.
OFFENSE Forgery, 2nd class. STATE Confused.
REMARKS Perhaps Dement. Prae.

And so on.
And so on.
And so on.

"Well, well... I am much obliged. And now I must get back to Bella and think about this."

The Sub-Governor rose along with him, saying casually, "And so you think, Sir Doctor, that this old Lag, Gogor, he might be the one that's tooken the Holy Jewels?"

Eszterhazy once again looked at his sovereign's face. After a moment, he turned back to Smits. "Why do you think that?"

Smits shrugged and began to hold up Eszterhazy's overcoat for him. "Well, I dunno for sure, of course. But they were cracked from old St. Sophie's Crypt, it's been in all the papers. They say, the papers, that it was an amateurish job. Which it succeeded because the crib they were in, it was so old, the mortar was crumbly and so on. 'Amateurish,' but at the same time they say, 'Professional tools may have been employed,' yes."

Eszterhazy buttoned his coat. "Thank you, Smits. Yes – and so?"

"Well, Sir Doctor. It come into my mind as we were talking, this Gogor, he was in old cell 36-E-2. And who was in there with him? Szemowits, another fancy-writer (forger, that is). Plus a chap I can't recall his name, up for Rape, Second. And Old Bleiweisz. Do you recollect Old Bleiweisz? Well, he was a cracksman. One of the best, they tell me. Anyways, *he* said he was. Always talking about how to do it, and how *he* done it. And so, well, just perhaps, now, the thought come to me, maybe that is how this Gogor – if it *was* him – how he got the idea of how to do it. You see..."

Eszterhazy, nodding, buttoned his gloves. "I see. An interesting thought. Would it be possible to speak to this Bleiweisz?"

But the Sub-Governor said it would not be possible. "He's drawn the Big Pardon, as the lags say. He's under the flagstone now. What was it, now, as done for him? *Ah* yes."

He opened the door and gestured the Eszterhazy to pass ahead of him. "It was lungs, that was it. Dunno why. He was healthy when he come in."

Lobats did not seem to have gotten enough sleep lately. He looked at the paper Eszterhazy had given him, blinked, and shook his head. "What is this? Something about somebody sent up for a forgery, Second, seven years ago? – Better take this downstairs to Records, Doctor. I've got something... well... a lot bigger to worry about."

Eszterhazy said that he was sure of that, that he had suspected as much ever since he had seen Commissioner of the Detective Police Karrol-Francos Lobats so deep in conversation in the Pearl Market. Conversation with Jewelers' Association President De Hooft. So deep that Lobats had not even had time for a word with his old acquaintance and so-often companion, Dr. Engelbert Eszterhazy...

Was it unfair for him to be rubbing it in like this? Maybe. Maybe not. Eszterhazy did not want it thought that he, and everything that his immense knowledge and capacity had to offer, could be regarded as the toy of an idle moment, to be picked up, and to be set aside or ignored when someone else might want to...

"This Forgery Second, fellow may be the fellow you are so worried about. We will both need all the information on him you can find... in Records... or out of Records. Do you take my word for it? Or shall I show, shall we say, authority?" He had begun to have a superstitious notion that he ought to be chary about displaying the *Provot*, lest overexposure might... somehow... dissipate its power.

Lobats said heavily "I take your word for just about anything. But I am not so worried about a forger. I'm worried about – "

"A jewel theft. Yes."

For all his heaviness, Lobats got up quickly from his chair. "Well, it has been known for crooks to change styles. I sure hope you are right."

Records, however, had only records. Old records. Seven years old.

If Gogor, Teodro, had committed any more recent offenses against His Royal and Imperial Majesty His Realm, His Crown and Staff, he had not been apprehended for the crimes.

Those other and perhaps equally important sources of information upon which the police of the world's great cities (and, perhaps, its small ones, too) depend – to wit, informers – had nothing to say upon the subject, either. His former employers, against whom the forgery had been committed (and, interestingly enough, they did deal in job lots of oilcloth!), had heard nothing of him since. And wanted to hear nothing of him now. His family consisting of an exceedingly respectable brother and sister in the provincial city of Praz (and no city is more respectable than Praz) knew nothing of his present or recent or post-prison career, either. They did offer the suggestion that he might have gone to America. Or to Australia.

"He was in Gross-Kroplets this same year," Eszterhazy insisted. "Well. You keep onto that. I have some loose ends of my own which I must try to tie together. I shall see you tomorrow."

On the third floor of the house at 33 Turkling Street, Herra Hugo Van Sltski was (after Dr. Eszterhazy himself) supreme. Here was Dr. Eszterhazy's library. And Herra Van Sltski was Dr. Eszterhazy's librarian. This scholar had a bad complexion, a bad breath, and a worse temper, but he was familiar with all the dialects and languages of the Triune Monarchy – plus French, English, Latin, Greek, and Sanscrit – and he was absolutely indefatigable. His employer had only to send him, via the pneumatic tube, a message to this effect: *Gogor, Teo, in the Criminal Phrenological Examinations, First Series*, for the envelope to reach him, via the same tube, in less than five minutes.

He opened it and drew out the yellow-paper chart. Down the lefthand margin were listed the Proclivities, Propensities, and Faculties. Across the top were the ratings, ranging from Overdeveloped through Underdeveloped to Absent, with graduations between. At the bottom, in a series of small boxes, were the cranial measurements, taken by Eszterhazy himself, with calipers and other instruments (one of them, of his own invention). But he was not greatly interested in the measurements, a glance at them showing that Gogor had an average head as far as size and shape went. It had been his intention, after taking the readings of each quarter, to assess each reading, and to make a summary on the inner leaf of the chart. However, that year – the year he had first taken such readings of a large number of criminals – that year had also been an epidemic year. He had not had time to make the assessments. He had made them each quarter-year afterwards. Somehow, he had never gone back to the First Series.

Ah, well. So, then, now to it.

PHRENOLOGICAL ASSESSMENT OF TEODRO GOGOR,
AGED 25, NATIONAL SUBJECT.

The Region of the lower back of the Head:
> SOCIAL PROCLIVITIES. Amativeness: Very large. Conjugality: Underdeveloped. Philoprogenitiveness: Absent. Adhesiveness: Deficient. Inhabitiveness: Oddly developed. Continuity: Overdeveloped.

The Regions behind and above the Ears:
> SELFISH PROPENSITIES. Vitativeness: Average. Combatativeness: Uncertain. Destructiveness: Weak. Alimentiveness: Deficient. Acquisitiveness: Strongly but oddly developed. Cautiousness: Deficient.

The Regions approaching and reaching the Crown of the Head:
> THE ASPIRING FACULTIES, or, LOWER SENTIMENTS. Approbativeness: Strongly developed. Self-esteem: Overdeveloped. Firmness: Overdeveloped.

The Coronal Region:
> THE MORAL SENTIMENTS. Conscientiousness: Deficient. Hope: Excessive development. Spirituality: Excessive. Veneration: Excessive. Benevolence: Deficient.

The Region of the Temples:
> THE SEMI-INTELLECTUAL or PERCEPTIVE FACULTIES. Constructiveness: Slightly underdeveloped. Mirthfulness: Absent. Ideality: Strong. Sublimity: Overdeveloped. Imitation: Overdeveloped.

The Region of the Upper Forehead:
> THE REASONING FACULTIES. Causality: Excessive. Comparison: Weak. Human Nature: Deficient. Agreeableness: Average.

The Region of the Center of the Forehead:
> THE LITERARY FACULTIES. Eventuality: Well-developed. Time: Average. Tune: Defective. Language: Average.

The Region of the Brows:
> THE PERCEPTIVE FACULTIES. Individuality: Slightly underdeveloped. Form: Average. Size: Average. Color: Average. Order: Developed. Calculation: Odd. Locality: Average.

Eszterhazy considered a segar but decided to let the pleasure await him at the end of the task. He did allow himself the pleasure of addressing an observation to himself. "I foresee," he said aloud, "that great possibility, amounting almost to probability, that phrenology must give way to newer and younger sciences, which even now stand waiting at the door to accept, and without acknowledgment, the hard-won discoveries of their elder sister. The intangible aspects, the immaterial ones, will be taken over by psychology. The material and tangible ones, by physical anthropology. Calculations based upon the cephalic index and other cranial measurements have already taught us much about primitive man, and will try to teach us even more about his modern descendants." He bent to his work, then, lifting his head once more, said slowly "And it may be that these younger sisters of the sciences will find others, younger yet, waiting to supplant them...."

Long he pondered over the yellow-paper chart, and much he pondered. Overhead, in the great gasoliers wrought in red bronze in the shapes of mermaids with naked bosoms, the gas flames (each one cupped in the hands of one mermaid) cast their golden light all about.

One man may look at a mountain and see only rock. Most men, looking at a mountain, would see only rock. That one man in hundreds of thousands, trained in observation by geology, looking at the selfsame mountain, will see half a hundred different kinds of rock, will see indications of ores buried in mine and matrix deep below the surface (though not so deep as to be beyond delving and discovering), will know what ancient writhings of the Earth – ancientmost of mothers – sent which stratum buckling up or down and which stratum lying level as a rule-yard.

So it was in this case of Teodro Gogor.

And Eszterhazy, having been the first man, now proceeded to be the other.

The faculty of location was merely averagely developed. The fugitive (if such were the proper term) was thus not greatly attached to his native place, which now knew him not. He might indeed have gone to Australia (or to America), but nothing in his innate nature compelled him to be a rolling stone. The Faculties of Form, Size, Weight, and Color were also average. His sense of order was developed, naturally, or he could neither have planned nor carried out the audacious theft, however "amateurishly." His Faculty of Calculation, now. It had been marked "odd." His was no common covetousness, obviously; no desire for mere gold coin had moved him. He had been able to calculate how to commit the crime and how – for the present, anyway – to get away with it. Individuality, slightly underdeveloped. That fitted. He had a conception of himself as an individual – but as the wrong individual. For, whoever might (or might not) be the true King of Jerusalem, it was surely not he.

Dovetailing with this was the fact that both Approbativeness, comprising "the Desire for Fame and Acclaim," and Self-esteem were both overdeveloped – indeed, excessively so. And so was Firmness. No collywobbler could have set out to steal a national treasure... and done so. He was deficient in the Quality of Conscientiousness, but in that of Hope, he had far too much. When the Faculty of Spirituality is excessive, as here, there is an inevitable tendency toward the fanatic.

All true, all – now – obvious. And all, so far, just so much locking the stable door after the horse was gone. What did it avail, here and now, to realize that Gogor's Sentiment of Veneration was excessive? He might indeed be venerating the antique treasures. The point was, now, where?

"Deficient in Benevolence," very well, he would not fence the jewels in order to give the money to the poor. Indeed!

"Sublimity excessive, tending toward exaggeration." Obviously. "Imitation, overdeveloped." As true as anything could be true. Mirthfulness, entirely absent. Hmmmm. No use to look for him enjoying a comedy turn in a music hall, then.

Well. Now for the Reasoning Faculties.

Excessive in Causality: his talents lay more toward the theoretical. He had little analytic ability, for his Faculty of Comparison was weak. Deficient in Human Nature, he would have no discrimination - Eszterhazy sighed and shifted in his seat. So far, all of *this* seemed theoretical. "Merely average in the qualities of Time and Language, deficient in that of Tone." So it was no use expecting to find him at a concert, either. And surely a mere yawn and a nod of the head to see that, owing to a well-developed Faculty of Eventuality, he, Gogor, would probably possess a great interest in history.

"Deficient in Cautiousness." This might be to the good. He might very well tip his hand. "Acquisitiveness strongly but oddly developed." This was but a double confirmation of what had been disclosed in connection with Calculation. "Alimentiveness deficient," eh? Merely eats to live. Not likely to haunt the better restaurants, nor send out for caviar, gooseliver, or champagne. Likely to drink little alcohol or none. "Combatativeness uncertain." Would he fight for his "cause"? – or not? In the propensity toward "Destructiveness, weak." This was somewhat favorable; it seemed to add up to "Not Dangerous."

And in Vitativeness, Gogor was merely average. He had had a bad lung, but he had recovered from it. Mmm, well, so, nothing here, no point in posting watches before the apothecaries'.

And thus, so much for the Selfish Propensities. Now for the Social Ones. And now for a quick prayer that something, at least *some*thing would turn up which would be of help –

"Continuity, overdeveloped." Again, an indication of a possible fanatical devotion to some one thing. Inhabitiveness, or attachment to a place or cause, oddly developed. In other words – now that we have all the *other* evidence – a tendency to form strong attachment to an odd cause. Bully. How often to plow this same furrow?

And now, O God, only four left!

Adhesiveness (that is, friendship or affection): Deficient.
Philoprogenitiveness (love of offspring): Absent.
Conjugality: Undeveloped.
Amativeness: Very large.

And there it was. There it all was. And he might almost as well have skipped all the rest of it.

Eszterhazy clapped his hands in pleasure.

If one rules out Conjugality and Philoprogenitiveness, one rules out desire for home and wife, for children. If even Adhesiveness is ruled out, a mistress is also ruled out. And so, what is left? Amativeness is left. In fact: "*Amativeness is very large...*" Here we have a man with strong sexual passions, who has neither wife nor mistress. And so –

"Lord."

Eszterhazy, slightly startled, looked up. "Ah, Herrekk, what – ? Ah, yes, I clapped, didn't I. Ah... no... I had not meant – Wait! Herrekk!"

"Lord."

Eszterhazy thought for a moment. Then, "Herrekk. In the attic. The old pigskin traveling bag. The one with the Paris stickers on it. Bring it, please. But, first – take the stickers off..."

"Lord."

As the evening express from Praz was drawing into the Great Central Terminal, a man dressed in the height of the fashions of fifteen years earlier, and carrying a pigskin traveling bag of even earlier style, went up the side steps to the central platform. He walked slowly across, mingling with the crowds getting off the express, and went down the main steps and out the main gates – and drew back, nervously, from what wits called "the artillery attack."

"*Fiacre*, sir? *Fiacre?*"

"High-born Sir! This way! This way!"

"Fiacre, High-born Sir! Anywhere for a half-a-ducat!"

It seemed that half of the hackney coaches in Bella had assembled in the wide street outside the station. And as though, now, half of their drivers had flung down their leathers, and, leaping to the pavement, were intent on rushing the newly arrived passengers into their hacks by main force and what was called "grabbage."

And now see a tall and stalwart figure, an ex-hussar by the height and carriage of him, and resplendent in the uniform of a railroad terminal commissionaire, approach the newly arrived provincial. "All right, sir. Just please to tell me where it is as you'd like to go, and I'll take care of everything."

And he seems to interpose himself between the newcomer and the mob of coachmen, who seeing this, go bawling off and howling for other customers. Of which, after all, there seems no lack.

"Uh, I want, uh, I want to go... uh, go to... uh," and he gropes in his pockets for an address which is not there. Of course not. It never is when wanted. The commissionaire looks at this familiar scene indulgently. And he glances, with the barest trace of a smile, hid before it begins to show, almost, at the faded dandy.

"Did you want to go to a hotel, sir? I'm afraid one hears that the Grand Beatrix is full-up just now." Oh, what a relief for the visitor! Not to have to explain that he does not really *want* the famous (and justly so) Hotel Grand Beatrix, which would bankrupt him in one day, besides being, really, much, much, much too, well, *grand*. And yet, how flattering to hear that he is obviously thought to be a Grand Beatrix type! "There is the Austerlitz and the Vienna, of course, sir. Nice quiet places." The commissionaire knows full well that the visitor does not want a nice quiet place. "And there's the Hotel de France, very reasonable rates, the gentry tells me, sir. Of course," her he gives a very slightly roguish look, "of course, some say it's rather a bit too gay and fast there. But I daresay that the gentleman might not find it so."

Hotel de France! Gay and fast! Almost before he knows it, the commissionaire's whistle has blown, and there the gentleman is, and his luggage, too, luggage with not a single sticker to mar or mark its sturdy old sides, in a fiacre rattling over the stone-paved streets. But not rattling so very loudly. The stone paving-blocks are such smooth stone paving-blocks – quite unlike the streets of Praz, where ghastly primordial cobblestones, shaped like eggs, constitute the paving of the central plaza and adjacent streets, and everywhere else the natural soil and earth allow the streets to be as dusty, or muddy, as it pleases the dear God to ordain.

The sides of the Hotel de France are painted with enormous letters, three stories in height, which inform the world that **EVERY ROOM IS FURNISHED WITH THE GASLIGHT**.

"A room for *Monsieur*? But certainly! Delighted!" The clerk slaps his hand on the desk bell. "Garcon! Take *Monsieur*'s bags up to Room 30-D!"

Monsieur! And *garcon*!

Sure enough, 30-D, at least, is furnished with gaslight. Sure enough, they rode up in a hydraulic elevator, started and stopped (and, for all the visitor knows to the contrary Praz not even having a grain elevator, propelled) by a cable running through the center from floor to roof.

And, in an alcove in the hallway, only a few doors from 30-D, *there is even running water*, should one's pitcher run dry!

The French know how to live.

Lobats, meanwhile, had started at the bottom. Not, to be sure, at the very bottom. He did not bother with the two-penny drabs, poor wretched things, who plied their trade under the land arches of the Italian Bridge, or in the doorways of the alley round the Rag Market. He had engravings made of a series of sketches by Eszterhazy, and he was now out directing their distribution – not in broadside quantities or by broadside methods, he did not want them on lampposts, it was not intended to take such fairly desperate methods... yet. He was having them distributed where he thought they might do the most good.

In a dirty coffeehouse by the Old Fish Wharf, for instance.

"Hallo, Rosa."

"Oh, God, I'm not even awake yet" – it was two in the afternoon – "and he wants to take me to jail. *I haven't done nothing!*"

"Oh, we know that, Rosa. Look here. Ever see this mug? No? Sure? Well, if you do... or think you do... well, you know how to pass the word along. Somebody might do herself a very good turn. Particularly if she needed one done. "Bye, Rosa."

In a disreputable tavern behind the Freight Yards, for instance.

"Halo, Genau."

A greasy, shriveled little man in a torn jacket of the same description seems about to dive beneath the counter. But he only dives deep enough to come up with a piece of paper. Also greasy and shriveled.

"Oh, I don't want to see your tax receipt, Genau. Look here. Ever see this mug? No? Sure? Well, if you do... Somebody might be able to make a very good deal for himself, if you know what I mean."

Genau seems to know what he means.

In front of a cheap bakery in the South Ward.

"Hey, you, Tobacco. Come here."

Tobacco comes here, eyes bulging with honesty "I'm clean, Your Worship. Search me, 'few like. Haven't picked a tip since – "

" – since last night. Never mind. Take a look here. Eh?"

Tobacco takes a look. Shakes his head. "Not a regular."

"We'd like to see him, just the same. Twig? Secret fund. Twig?"

Tobacco Twigs. "I'll be sure and letcha know. We don't like irregulars, anyway. Mucking things up and making things difficult for the trained hands. *Sure. I'll* letcha know."

"Hallo, Lou..."

"Hallo, Frou..."

"Hallo, Gretchen..."

"Halo, Marishka..."

Marishka blinks her painted eyes. Gives a nod. A very tired nod. Genteelly smothers a yawn. "Sure. He's a bit dotty ain't he? But not *dangerous.*"

Lobats: "You *have* seen him, then? When?"

Marishka sips, licks whipped cream off her painted lip. "Last night," she says, indifferently. "All night. Nothing special." She means, first, that her last night's guest had no very *odd* habits, and second, that he had paid only a standard fee.

"Where? Know where he might be?"

Marishka no longer even bothers to shrug. "He came in from the street," she says. "And he went back out into the street." She returns to her cup of coffee. It is all so very dull, life and its demands. They come in from the street. And they go back out into the street.

Over and over. However. Others can do that work. There is one thing more, which Doctor Eszterhazy had advised not be neglected. And Lobats, who has a little list (written, this time – he has many little lists, and quite a few long ones, in his head). One by one he checks them off, shop after shop, and fitting-room after fitting-room. Then, scratching his head, he goes farther afield.

Frow Widow Higgins, Theatrical Costumiere, was not from England, as the rich accents of her native South Ward testified. But the late Higgins had been born there. The late Higgins, however, was very late indeed, and his widow made little mention of him. She looked up from her sewing machine, through which she was running a tunic of 16th-century design... one which much needed the restorative attentions of the machine, and which, in fact, might indeed have been in semi-continual use since that century. She looked up from her sewing machine, and for a moment rested her foot at the treadle.

"Yeah," she said.

"When?"

"Oh... Maybe last month..."

Lobats wants her to tell him all about it. And, politely, for Frow Widow Higgins is of an entirely respectable and, God knows, hard-working character, he asks that she understand that he means *all* about it. Frow Widow Higgins runs her fingers over her tired eyes. Then she sums it up.

"He paid in cash," she says.

Many are the brightly dressed ladies who pass in and out of the saloon bar of the Hotel de France, rich in lace, with very rich color in their cheeks, and with very Large hats that many egrets have died to adorn. They are agreeable to letting the gentleman from Praz buy them a richly colored drink. They listen with arch interest to his story. After all, every gentleman has a story. They make remarks indicating interest. "And you can't settle the estate without him?" they repeat. "*Oh*-what-a-*shame!*" Well, any excuse will serve when a dandyish gent from the provinces wants to come up and have his bit of fun. There are few nicer pigeons to pluck than these dandyish gents from the provinces, after all. But the gentleman from Praz can't seem to take a hint. And so, one after another, hints as to dinner... the theater... supper... champagne... the opera... not only not being forthcoming, all such hints even on the ladies' parts meeting with no more response than, "Yes, but surely *some*one must know my brother; *he has lived in Bela for years!*"... well, sooner or later, the richly dressed ladies sigh and excuse themselves and move on.

Even if only to another table.

It is late.

Mlle. Toscanelli.

Mlle. Toscanelli is from Corsica. And if that is not French enough to suit any of the customers of the saloon bar of the Hotel de France, well, *oh-la-la!* Mlle. Toscanelli has no intention of wasting the evening over a peppermint shnops. She looks at the tintype of the brother of the gentleman from Praz. "This has been retouched," says Mlle. Toscanelli.

"It is my brother Georg. We cannot settle the estate, you see, without him."

Mlle. Toscaneili has a question, one which seems to indicate that emotions other than the purely sentimental sometimes animate the bosom of the daughters of the warm south.

"How much is it worth to you to find him?"

A faint change seems to come over the gentleman from Praz, in his obsolete finery and with his funny-fancy manners. He meets the hard, bright, black little eyes of Mlle. Toscaneili.

"Fifty ducats," he says. *But no tricks!*"

Mlle. Toscanelli says, "*In advance.*"

She counts the five notes of ten ducats each, snaps the tiny beaded and be-bijou'd reticule, starts to rise. "One moment, I wish to send a note," says the gentleman from Praz. "He is – where?"

He is in Hunyadi Street, Lower Hunyadi Street; Mlle. Toscanelli does not recollect the number, but there was an apothecary on the corner and a bicycle shop next door to it.

It was as she said. However, the entire block had been erected by a builder who had used one set of house plans. All the houses look alike, and Mlle. Toscanelli could not remember which one it was. Not even the sight of the police, while she was still gazing up and down the block, aided her memory. And, when even the offer of another fifty ducats failed, it had to be assumed that she was telling the truth.

Ah, how may police, and so suddenly, in Lower Hunyadi Street! And in the streets behind. And all around – The apothecary's lips trembled. "But there was nothing illegal about it," he protested. "I have a *license* to sell opium. Fifty pillules of the anhydrous, here, all properly noted in my Record Book. See? See? Well, if I am shouted at, I cannot *think* what house!"

By the time he had gotten his nerves and his memory together, the police were being reinforced by soldiery. The residents of Lower Hunyadi Street seemed divided between a desire to utilize the best seats, those by their windows, and view the show – whatever its purpose might be – and a desire to barricade their windows with bedding, china closets, and clothes cabinets.

"Open up, Number Forty-four! Open up! Concierge! Porter!"

Fifty years of almost unbroken peace under the Triune Monarchy had not fully persuaded the inhabitants out of the habits formed during fifty previous decades of almost unbroken war. The gates of the houses in Bella tend to be thick.

"Well, may as well send for the firemen," said Lobats.

Axes, ladders, a full siege. Eszterhazy was sure that the porter – or someone – was watching. Someone who could open the doors without a violent assault – if he – or she – wished to.

"Hold up," he said. The police drew back. Then the soldiers. Eszterhazy walked across the street toward Number 44. Halfway across he stopped, drew his hand from his pocket, and, arm at the traditional forty-five-degree angle, held up the *provot*. A great sigh seemed to go up all around him. A moment later the gates swung open. He gestured to Lobats.

They walked in.

A woman, not so old as concierges are generally assumed to be, stood to one side, sobbing. "The poor man!" she cried. "The poor man! So suppose he is cracked. What if he does think he is King? Does that hurt the real King?" The two men went on through the empty courtyard and started up the stairs. "Don't be hurting him!" the woman screamed. "Don't you be hurting him... the poor man."

He sat facing them, as they went in – and it had not taken them long to get in – but in a moment they realized that he was not really facing *them* at all. He was facing a full-length mirror. Somehow he had made shift to fix up a dais, and he had draped the chair all in crimson. It made do for a throne. He sat in his sleazy "robes" of state, cape and gown and collar of cotton-wool spotted with black tufts to resemble ermine. It was all false; even across footlights it would have looked almost false. His head was slumped to one side.

But the crown was on his head, his telltale head; the crown with its glittering jeweled pendants was on his head, so tightly that it had not fallen off, and the orb and sceptre, though his hands had slid into his lap, still his hands clenched them tightly.

For most of his life he had been no one and nobody. For now, however, he was as much King of Jerusalem as the Crown Jewels could make him – or anyone – King of Jerusalem.

The crown and orb and sceptre of the ancient and mysterious Regalia. They, and the fully fatal dose of the fifty pillules of anhydrous opium.

Introduction to
FROM A LETTER TO THE KLEINS

PEOPLE WHO KNEW AVRAM PERSONALLY, know that some of his best writing was in his letters. He was writing letters to his friends on the day that he died. A letter from Avram was a special treat among the junk and bills in the mailbox, and his friends still miss receiving them. We are lucky that many friends treasured his letters, and saved them, and were kind enough to send us copies.

This untitled, undated, playful little "play" was sent to his dear friends in New York, Simmy and Nancy Klein. We owe them heartfelt thanks.

Grania Davidson Davis

FROM A LETTER
TO THE KLEINS

The scene is the Stock Room of a Ritual Fringe Factory in the quaint Old World Village of Dishrag-on-Sinke, Yorkshire. As curtain goes UP, the shop steward, a scrofulous Magyar named Egon Hagyvad is seen talking to Pinprick, a peripatic colporteur of Union Prayerbooks.

Egon: ...like I was saying, gaffer, us Union men gotta stick together.

Pinprick: (quoting) "Let us now read responsively."

Egon: Amen. Verily, verily.

Pinprick: To business, enough of sacred conversation.

Egon: Yus. Now, as I see it, the plan is to disrupt the manufacture of *tzitzis*...

Pinprick: (blushing) Please! That *word* –

Egon: *Darft mir enshuldigen, guvner*; the manufacture of ritual fringes in East Yorkshire. Driven to despair by the shortage of this ecclesiastical commodity, the yokels will pay anything for a koosherra bindle: And how will they be able to get one?

Pinprick: Only by buying the Complete, one-volume-including-notes, neo-Morocco plasticene-bound, edition of the Union Prayerbook. (rubs hands) Yuk yuk. (chuckles). With each volume they get one bindle of our smuggled fringes. Godolphin Klein, the ace contrabandist of the East Riding of Yorkshire

Egon: Ah, there's a clever cove, if you like, Godolphin Klein is. Fancy that latest trick of his, smuggling the fringes in marked as diamonds. Well, like I was asaying, gaffer Pinprick, tomorrow at four o' the clock, I throws a spanner into the number 3 engine, as works the treadle on the knottier.

Pinprick: That will bring them to their knees.

Egon: Hark, someone's coming...

(Enter FitzMendel Klein, a sprig of the local aristocracy.)

FitzMendel: I say, d'you like my new get-up? Zippers on the knee-breeches, the vewy latest thing in Williamsburg... Tell me, is it weally twue that my blacksheep cousin, Godolphin is now a diamond bwoker?

Egon: So they say, Master FitzMendel.

Pinprick: A respectable calling.

FitzMendel: But what of the family business? The Kleins have always made tzitzis.

Egon: Well, you are still young, Master FitzMendel. We may yet hope to see a bride & bairns at Dishrag Manor House.

FitzMendel: Ah, the old faithful family wetainer...how long have you been with us?

Egon: Forty-three years, come next Tu Beshvat, Master Egon.

FitzMendel: Well, well, all of that? Wemind me, when it comes to the fiftieth – to double your wages, Egon. That will make them tuppence-ha'penny.

Egon: Gaw bless, you, Master FitzMendel. Ah, how I do recall your dear old Zaidey, Sir Sroolic DeVere Klein, him as was here when I first came as prentice boy in the looping-shed.

FitzMendel: Yes, yes, but, please, no emotion. I must be off to the cock-fights, else I shall be late for tachunin again afterwards: must keep up the family name. (leaves)

Pinprick: Well, he's out of the way, young wastrel...have you the spanner prepared?

Egon: I can't do it, gaffer, and that's a fact.

Pinprick: What! Why, I'll have you broken for this. Our whole plan depends on your compliance.

(enter an old fish-wife)

Fish-wife: Herrings, herrings, who'll buy my frisher herrings?

Pinprick: Get out, get out.

(Fish-wife throws off shawl and reveals self as –) Godolphin Klein!

What's the meaning of this?

Godolphin: Them customs agents is on to me, lads. Someone split, and if I gets my maulers onto him as done it, why (growls).

Pinprick: All is lost. Melancthon Pinprick is a doomed man.

(Sinks onto a bale of wool, mechanically opens his Union Prayerbook.) "Let us now read responsively".

Godolphin: Hark! What's that? The sound of orse oofs! They're here. My musket, lads, where's my musket? We'll make a game end of it, we will. Godolphin Klein will never swing on the old black tree. My musket! (shrieks, as a troop of Customs Agents rush into the stock-room)

First Customs Agent: In the King's name!

Godolphin: Have mercy! Think of my family name!

Custom Agent: You should've thought of that when you was a-smuggling in of them traditional appurtenances, me lad.

Egon: Excuse me, but aren't you the grandson of Old Dame Cicely Klein?

Agent: Well, and what of it? Say a word against the old bezzom and I'll –

Godolphin: What, have we the same paternal bubba? Cousin!

Agent: Hear, let me have a closer look. (looks) As I live and hope to eschew shaatness –

Second Agent: Allow me to introduce ourselves. This is Revenue Officer Athelstan Klein –

Godolphin: OOm Beroofen.

Athelstan: Likewise.

Second Agent: – and this is Revenue Officer Donalbaine Klein –

Godalphin: Tip us your mauler, lad.

Second Agent: Ethelred Klein – Trevelyan Klein – Pendennis Klein – Colquohon Klein – (Godolphin shakes each by the hand) – and me umble self, Bournemouthe Klein.

Athelstan: Well, this do put a different light on the matter, and that's for true. Seeins it's all in the family, like, I don't think we'll be too hard on you.

Trevelyan: Not on old Tanta Cicely's aynickle, we wouldn't.

Penndenis: Say, a golden guinea each and a split in the swag.

Colquohon: And a tot of prime Jamaica all around, for the hoost.

Godolphin: Me lads, you're true chips off the old butcher block, all of you. Well, I must needs consult my mates here. Egon, Melancthon – ?

Egon: The family name is all that concerns me in mine ancient age, boytchicle.

Melancthon: Ah, wurra me. I must submit. But its hard, blokes, its cruel hard, to see the loss on a deal I've worked on so long. I've had a ard life, tykes; ard, it was, from the very day I was found abandoned in a basket on the steps of the Ethical Culture School, a wee bairn, and no identification except a non-sectarian tract clutched in me tiny fist, and on me right bosom a slivovits-colored birth-mark (there is a cry from the door).

FitzMendel: A slivovits-colored birth-mark? Egad, Egon, I am undone!

Egon: Master FitzMendel, sir, I don't understand.

FitzMendel: In the will of my late zaidey, Sir Sroolic DeVere Klein (all present remove their cocked hats at the mention of this name), all his property was left to his love child, Itzicle Enfant de l'Amour Klein, that he had of Maggie Katz the kitchen slut –

Godolphin: Aye, I've hearn tell summat o' that bubba-maaseh: the bye-blow was stolen by the charcoal burners one morning when Maggie had hung him out to dry.

Bournemouthe: And in default of finding him, the whole estate, house, & factory devolved upon the late FitzKlein Klein, Esquire, and then on his son –

FitzMendel Klein: FitzMendel Klein. But now that the true heir has been found, I can give up the whole gesheft, and brother! What a relief. I don't care if I ever look a lobtzedeckel in ponim erein. I'll run off to the gypsies and live a carefree life on the heath and heather, stealing pushkies and kissing all the Beth Jacob girls. Heigh-ho, Yoiks, Yidden!

Egon: I must call you Master Itzicle now, Master Itzicle (late Melancthon).

Master I: Scarce can I believe mine own earn...Egon! Godolphin! Call the peasants! Have the vicar shecht an ox! Give all the Revenooers a purse of gold apiece! Ring the bells in the shteeble! (A scene of wild joy ensues, people rush to and fro, a merry blaze is soon kindled in the ox-pit, of Union Prayerbooks, & then the whole lot of quaintly garbed East Anglians are dancing morrisdances to the tune of "*In haz der rebbe gait* " as

    the

      curtain

        falls.

Introduction to
THE METAPHYSICAL FORCE

THIS STORY WAS ONE OF THE "discovered" manuscripts that were found among Avram's papers after he passed on. It had never been published, and we aren't sure when it was written. There was no date on the manuscript. The story was published posthumously in 1995 in *Century*, a fine magazine of imaginative fiction. It concerns the power of prayer in the life of a young boy named Jay Kay.

Grania Davidson Davis

THE METAPHYSICAL FORCE

FANNY KAY WAS AN AMBERSTEIN before she married Sam Kay: Not the Ambersteins who used to have the quilt store on Beech Street, the other ones. Old Mrs. Kay, Sam's mother, was the sister of the late Dr. Mortimer Steinmetz. He had his office in the Bijou Building; it's still there, but the son-in-law, Dr. Murray Potasnik, has it now. Jay Marshall, Fanny and Sam's little boy, had some idea of this relationship, but to him the main thing about the Bijou Building was that he attended a dancing class at Miss Suzanne's studio there. Unwillingly.

It was the same thing every single time. When he came home from lunch his mother would give him a clean hanky and car fare and the bag with the dancing pumps in them and comb his hair with lanolin cream and he would pout and mumble until finally she had to say, always, "Shah! Not another word! You – are – going!"

On this particular afternoon and in this particular class, not counting the girls, there were only four boys: Dale Cowen, Jeffrey Fineburg, Sheldon Stein, and Jay Marshall Kay. He was hiding under the piano. Some of the children were laughing and some were chanting the alphabet and Dale Cowen-very tall for his age – was yelling, "Let him alone! Go away and let him alone!" One of the girls, Janey Reizell, a big clumsy thing, as graceful as the bird they called the elephant (a lot of good dancing lessons were going to do her); Janey was bent way over and was yelling under the piano that if she weren't afraid of getting her dress filthy she would go right after him (Jay) and that would fix him. So finally Miss Suzanne had to see.

"He *hit* me, Miss Suzanne," said Janey, very angry. "Jay *hit* me. That little sissy. Can't even take a joke."

"*Good* for you!" Jeffrey yelled. "I hit girls lots of times. I don't let girls get away with anything. I hate girls."

"Well, they were teasing him," Dale said. "They know he doesn't like to be teased about his name. It hurts his feelings."

And Sheldon kept saying, "Should I climb under and get him, Miss Suzanne? I can get him out. I'll climb under and get him out, huh, Miss

Suzanne?"

Miss Suzanne was tall and still had the same figure she had had in *Scandals* of 1927, and red hair which Sadie Einhorn in the beauty shop never had to touch up even a little. Finally she got the kids almost quiet. But then Janey had to lose her temper all over again.

"*Jay Kay!*" she screamed. "*Aitch-Eye-JAYKAY-Ell-Em-En-Oh-Pee!*"

There was a scream of rage from under the piano.

"All right, Janey, that's enough!" Miss Suzanne said briskly. "Your mother isn't paying for you to waste your time. I want you to go over to the far corner and I want you to practice your steps: *Now!*"

A tear-choked voice from under the piano said, "I'm not afraid of her. Big old fat thing," it snuffled.

"She's gone away. Everyone else has gone away. You come out now, too. Jay? I can't stand here talking to you, I have *work* to do." She walked away to the cluster of children. "Everybody take their positions, now," she said. "Are we all ready? *One*, two..."

Jay was a stocky little boy with a blunt nose and what they call dirty-blond hair. How did he get that name, which was so easy to make fun of? (Although if he wasn't in a tantrum about that, it was something else.) Well, his grandfather, Old Mr. Kay, who had that tiny grocery store on Frog Hill in the Slovak section, *his* name at one time used to be Kaminsky or Kalmonovitz or *something* long and complicated. Well, maybe not complicated for Slovaks. And there was a salesman, an American man, a Gentile, who used to call him "Mr. K." So when the children got after the old man to change the name, he changed it to "Kay"

All right. Well, the old man died, shortly before Sam and Fanny had the boy, and naturally they wanted to name it after him so he could have a name in this world, but his name was Jacob Moses. Now, you can't name a child Jacob Moses in this day and age, that goes without saying. Sam's sister Ethel suggested Jeffrey Martin, and she insists till this very day that if *she* had suggested Jay Marshall, Fanny would have named the boy Jeffrey Martin. But how is it that Fanny didn't foresee that Jay Kay is a funny-sounding sort of name? After all, she's not a stupid woman. Well, it never entered her mind. She always thought of the boy as Jay Marshall and nothing else and she always called him that and nothing else and she never for a *moment* thought of anyone calling him simply Jay Kay In short, a mother's heart. And when Louie Axelrod, a brother of Sam's aunt Ida, he's always joking, and when he said, "Jay Kay? Is that a name or an anagram?" Fanny got very angry and never had a good word for him afterwards.

When Jay got home from the dancing class, after a ride on the trolley during which he daydreamed that he captured Janey Reizel and took off all her clothes and cut her into pieces with a saw-edged knife; just as he was going in the house, he heard a voice calling, "Yoo-Hoo! Jay Marshall! Over here in the car!"

Leaning over from the driver's seat of the car was his mother's friend Anna Goldman, who was a career woman, never had married, but built up a very good business in her office – mimeographing, addressographing, things like that. From time to time Fanny used to say to her, "Why don't you meet somebody? Leave it to me. Why shouldn't you get married?" But Anna always said, "What do I need it for?"

She lived upstairs over Mrs. Ida Steinmetz and her daughter Caroline, and Caroline's husband Dr. Potasnik. He used to pour out his heart to her. He had a good location for his office, one would think, on the same floor with Miss Suzanne's studio and the Estelle-May Beauty Parlor which Sadie Einhorn had taken over. But did he benefit from all the parents and customers who must have seen his name every time they passed? No, because they all had their own dentists, and as for their children, they sent them to this Dr. Edgar Krann, who had a wonderfully modern office with the toys and with Mickey Mouse movies actually playing on the walls and with special nondecay-causing candy for the children, and who knows what else?

"But Mother Steinmetz makes a face like a bad taste in her mouth if I so much as mention that," Dr. Potasnik complained. "She says, 'And where did Dr. Krann's money come from?' she asks. 'I know whose father speculated with hoarded sugar in 1918 when my brother Louie Axelrod was freezing half to death in Camp Yaphank.' And she looks at me as if it were my fault. I told her, 'Mother Steinmetz, it would be an investment just like any other one you would make,' but she just says, 'Don't tell *me*, I know.' And yet there are some people who would call me lucky."

Anyway, Anna leaned over and spoke to Jay "Well, well, the busy businessman," she said, grinning to him has he walked over. She was always saying silly things like that, and after he answered her questions he prepared to go in the house.

"Oh, no, my fine-feathered friend," she said. "You are going to come with me. I am taking you to *my* house. What will people think? 'Robbing the cradle' is what they call it," she giggled.

"Who said I'm going to your house?" Jay asked, suspicious.

"Your mother is who; she had to go away. And here, as proof, are your pajamas – your toothbrush – your slippers – the book you were reading – *and* – what is this?" She rummaged in the brown paper bag. "It is... no, it can't be... can it be licorice?"

Ignoring her nonsense, Jay asked, what about his father?

"He had to go away, too. No. No. I'm very sorry. No more questions till you get in the car. Are you trying to freeze me to death?" she snickered. So Jay got in and they drove to her house, which was, of course, Mrs. Steinmetz's house.

Now, although the late Dr. Steinmetz's sister, also deceased, had been Sam Kay's Aunt Hennie, and although Aunt Ida Steinmetz had never once in her life come near Fanny and Sam's house, Anna Goldberg always took Jay in to say hello to her in his occasional visits. Fanny was invariably annoyed by this, but Anna told her not to be silly.

"Listen, Fanny, she could do a lot for the boy if she ever took the notion," Anna said. "She has only that one daughter who it looks like will never have any children if she and her nebbich husband live to be a hundred and twenty."

Fanny would shrug and raise her eyebrows.

And Ida always gave him a cookie from a grocery-store box (Fanny would comment, "American lady, she's too good to bake like her sister-in-law did") and look down on him and ask him questions which he would answer in an embarrassed mumble, or say he didn't know; while Anna Goldman watched them with the tip of her tongue between her teeth and a little bit of a smile on her face as she watched and listened, her eyes flickering from one to the other.

Aunt Ida Steinmetz got her money's worth out of the cookie. "How is your daddy's business coming along?" she'd ask. "Where did his partner's wife go for the summer? What's your Cousin Hershie doing, the one who married the daughter of Genzleman-the-butcher?" And if Jay mumbled that he didn't know, the blue-gray-haired old lady would frown her eyes at him through the glasses which pinched the bridge of her sharp nose, and ask, "What do you mean, you don't know? Your parents never talk about it? They must talk about it. Or does your mother tell you not to tell me? What's the matter, I'm not your father's aunt?"

Of course, she was correct. How often did Fanny warn the boy, "Don't tell her a thing. If she wants to find out, let her come and ask. Who was there? What did *they* have to say? You don't remember? Why, you're not an infant, you must remember. Go on. Eat my heart out. Just like your father. I can stay in the house the whole day long, I don't have to go anywhere, I don't have to know anything."

This was a sore point with her. Sam Kay and his sister Ethel and the partner Morty Jacobson, had a cash-and-carry wholesale business way out in the country. Sam got up with the roosters, before Jay did, and by the time he got back at night the boy was in bed. He used to leave breakfast for him – a glass of orange juice, three pieces of toast, a glass of milk left out for the chill to be taken off, and the butter so it would be soft enough to spread, and jelly, and maybe a piece of cake. Fanny slept late in the morning because she couldn't sleep at night. Whose fault was that? *Her* fault? If she could help it, things would be different. That's what she used to tell Jay.

"What kind of life do I lead?" she would ask. "You call this living? I don't go to the movies with my husband like other women. I go with Anna Goldman. And when was the last time I went to New York and saw a play? Your memory doesn't go back that far. Shooshy Ganzler was still on Broadway the last time I saw a play."

Shooshy Ganzler was Miss Suzanne. Suzanne Ganne was her professional name, and she had been in Ziegfeld's Follies.

"How is it that your father's partner, Morty Jacobson, comes into town during the day and your father can't? Hmmm?"

Jay would mumble that he didn't know.

"You don't know. Neither do I know," Fanny would say, picking at her chin. "If you listen to your father, *he'll* tell you that it's because Morty does the buying. But I notice his car was parked in front of his house yesterday for two hours. *Two hours.*"

And she told Jay how hard his father worked at the Place, the terrible hours, and how little he got from it. She used to tell Sam the same things, but you might just as well talk to the wall. Sam Kay had a big, blank face, and a long chin, and he just looked straight ahead and chewed his food. Often, at night, Jay could hear his mother talking when he got up for a glass of water.

"You're *killing* yourself," he used to hear her saying. "You're wearing yourself *out*. Take a job with decent hours. Make them buy you out." If she looked and saw Jay, she would be annoyed and say, "What are you doing up? Get back to bed."

Sam was so tired he used to fall asleep in his chair. On Sundays he slept late, too. Then he went for a walk with Jay. The boy talked and talked, but his father seldom said a word, he was so worn out.

Jay was sorry to realize that his father worked so hard and he wondered if there was some way he could assist him. So finally one day he asked I him, "Daddy, could I help you at the Place?"

Sam said, "Hmmm?... No, how could you help me?"

"I could take the bus after school," the boy said. That way, he wouldn't have to go to Miss Suzanne's; but, really, he *did* want to help his father. Sam just went on walking, but Jay kept after him for a long time, pestering him, so finally he said, "Maybe at some future date you can help me."

And that was all he said. So Jay spent most of his time, when he wasn't in school, with his mother; and he was so often in one tantrum or another until she said she didn't know *who* he took after. But it's a funny thing, when you come to think of it, what she said about Morty Jacobson spending so much time at his home. Because in the middle of the afternoon of the day that Jay came home and found Anna Goldman waiting, about two o'clock, while Morty Jacobson *was* at home, Sam Kay was bringing something heavy up from the cellar at the Place, and he must have tripped. He fell down the stairs. There was only one customer at the Place at the time, he heard some noise, and he found Sam unconscious.

So that was where Fanny was when Jay came home, she was in the hospital with Sam.

Sometime during the night, in the stuffy bedroom where Anna Jacobson's father used to sleep while he was still alive, Jay was awakened by a telephone ringing; but he went right back to sleep again. In the morning he lay in bed a while, waiting for someone to call him. At home his father always used to set the alarm clock and leave it in his room. But as no one came, he got up, and found Anna Goldman drinking coffee in her kitchen.

"'*Lazy Mary, will you get up, will you get up; Lazy Mary will you get up, so early in the morning?*'" she sang at him, in a funny voice, making faces, as if he were two years old. Jay looked at the clock; it was 8:15.

"I'll be late for school!" he cried.

"And what if I told you that you don't have to go to school today? Special arrangement with the Board of Education."

"I'll be late for school!" Jay repeated.

"You don't have to go today, I said. Listen." She paused, wet her lips. "Your mother may want to take you some place today. *May*, I said. So she arranged with Miss Wheatley – "

"*When* did she arrange it?" Jay demanded. "Miss Wheatley wouldn't be in school yet."

"Well, so she arranged it yesterday."

"Where is my mother?"

"She'll tell you when she sees you. Curiosity killed a cat. Ask me no questions and I'll tell you no lies."

Jay was disgusted with her nonsense and went and got dressed. He knew that she was probably not telling the whole truth; he was aware that grown-ups lied all the time, not only to children but to one another; but what he didn't know was that since three o'clock in the morning his father had been in a better world. After he was dressed, Anna took him downstairs to Mrs. Steinmetz's house, and went off (she said) to work, after some more silly talk.

Aunt Ida Steinmetz made him a breakfast such as he had never seen before: waffles and maple syrup, jello with whipped cream and nuts, poached eggs. In short, he didn't find his visit unpleasant, as he had expected. He was even allowed to examine some huge plaster models of teeth which had once belonged to his late Uncle Mortimer. During the afternoon she went out, on what sad mission we know, leaving Jay with her daughter Caroline, Dr. Potasnik's wife, a thin lady with pink skin all around her eyes. By this time Jay felt sure that something very much out of the ordinary was happening, but the idea he had in mind was that his mother was in the hospital having a baby, and having decided that his cousin Caroline wasn't so bad, he asked her.

Caroline said, "Oh, dear," and put her hand to her head.

Not having any children of her own and living with a rich mother who never even let her daughter so much as touch cold water (they had a woman in every day to clean), Caroline had lots of time on her hands. This explains why she was so interested in religion, because, naturally, a woman who's busy around the house and raising children has no time for that. For a while she used to go to Christian Science meetings; then a college friend of hers, a Mrs. Harriet Dolber, not a local person, got her to go to Jewish Science meetings in New York. Some Rabbi founded this movement, he died, and his wife took it over. Then Caroline began going to the regular Temple in town every Friday night with her husband, and she seemed to get a lot of comfort out of it. Religion, that is. And she was always reading these books on the subject.

So she told Jay that his father had gone to Heaven.

"How do you know?" is what he said.

And she said, "Well, dear, the greatest teachers and philosophers in all ages have told us so, and we have to believe them."

Well, even though the Kays lived on Warren Street, which is just around the corner from the Hollis Avenue synagogue, they had called up old Rabbi Stein to be at the funeral, instead of Rabbi Camler from Hollis Ave. On the High Holy Days, the Kays went to Rabbi Camler's *shul* since it was right around the corner, but Sam and his sister Ethel had come originally from Frog Hill and they knew old Rabbi Stein from when they were children. He buried their mother, he buried their father, and now he was burying Sam; and he preached a wonderful eulogy in Yiddish that had everybody crying but at the same time it gave them all a lot of comfort.

They sat *shiva* at Sam and Fanny's house – that is, Fanny sat the whole seven days, but Ethel said she had to go to work, there was so much work and only her and Morty Jacobson to do it, so after three days she went out to the Place every morning, but when she came back at night she kept sitting shiva till the week was out. You're allowed to do it that way if you have to. And, of course, on *Shabbas* you don't sit shiva because you're not allowed to mourn on the Sabbath. And the people brought baskets of fruit and boxes of candy and cake and cheese, and so on. And they had a *minyan* of men who came in every morning and evening – you only need ten, but there were more – and they said the regular prayers and then they were going to say *kaddish* for poor Sam.

But when they first got back to the house from the cemetery the only thing Fanny could think of to say was, "How will I ever tell Jay? How will I tell him?" And then Anna Goldman had come in and she chased all the old women from the apartment house out of the kitchen and she made the supper. When she heard Fanny moaning and crying, how could she tell the boy? She came in and let her know that the boy was already told, and in a very beautiful way. At a time like that, with so much on her mind, this was a big load taken off Fanny's shoulders.

One of the old women in the apartment house was a Mrs. Weintraub, her husband used to be a tailor for a big men's clothing store, but he retired a few years ago. He's a very religious man, he never went to the store on *Shabbas*, and since he was such a good workman he was able to get away with it. With all those people the apartment was crowded. Mr. Weintraub lit the candles and he put a glass of water and a napkin there, like the custom is, and he led the prayers. When they were almost finished he turned and he said, "Where is the son? He has to say *kaddish*."

Fanny said, "Oh, no, he's too young. Mr. Weintraub said, "He isn't too young. And Fanny said, "But he doesn't know how to read Hebrew." So the old man asked him if he could read English. Of course he could. And the old man showed him in the back of the prayerbook were the *kaddish* was written in English letters. And Jay read it and his mother cried, but at the same time she stopped moaning.

This went on for a week and Jay read the thing very well. He asked Mr. Weintraub, "Why do we say *kaddish*?"

The old man told him that every prayer is a metaphysical force – imagine telling such a thing to a child – and every time the congregation says amen to his prayers, so this metaphysical force is elevating his father's soul. His father's soul gets the credit for it, so to speak: for eleven months the soul is being judged and every time he says *kaddish* it helps his father. So after the week was over, the *minyan* didn't come to the house anymore, and Jay started going to the synagogue with old Mr. Weintraub. It was right around the corner, after all.

And it was the funniest thing. Jay had never lifted a finger to do a thing for himself. His father used to make his breakfast for him. Now he began to make it for himself, and he even started to make it for his mother. So, lo and behold, for the first time in years, Fanny began getting up early

"If my son can get up in the darkness" – because by this time it was almost winter – If my son can get up in the darkness, then the least I can do is get up and make his breakfast." Which she did; the eighth wonder of the world.

She also told Anna Goldman that Jay had told *her* that he was glad he could do something for his father now because he was sorry he had never been able to before when he was working so hard. He told her how his father had once said to him, "Maybe at some future date you will be able to help me." And of course Fanny cried while she was telling this, and telling her other troubles.

"I'll never get over it," she said.

"You'll get over it," Anna said.

The synagogue doesn't go by the clock, it goes by the sun. When it gets dark earlier, they hold the services earlier. Which meant no dancing lessons for Master Jay Marshall. There wasn't time between when school was over and when they started in shul. Miss Suzanne said she understood, and no doubt if the truth were told and known, she was just as relieved not to have him, with his temper and tantrums.

And speaking of these tantrums, one afternoon who should knock on the door but Miss Wheatley, Jay's teacher. Fanny welcomed her with a smile, but her heart was in her mouth, because the last time she had seen this Miss Wheatley was at a PTA meeting, and after the meeting and after beating around the bush, the teacher told her that Jay was always crying in the classroom and on the playground. Always some scene. Fanny had said, well, it was because he almost never saw his father. She thought to herself, though, what does this old maid know about what it means to raise a child?

Miss Wheatley came in and they had a cup of tea and she paid her condolences. And then Fanny asked, with her heart in her mouth, "How is Jay Marshall doing in school?"

Miss Wheatley said, "He is doing very well. He is a fine boy"

Fanny didn't know if she was coming or going. What, no complaints that the boy was this and he was that?

"I think that his unfortunate loss has made him face up to his responsibilities," the teacher said. *What* responsibilities? You'd think he had to go out selling newspapers or something! "He seems so much more adjusted" she said. "He isn't as sensitive as he used to be. He gets along better with the other children."

"It was the shock of losing his father so suddenly," Fanny said. "It made him grow up quicker." She had to say *something*.

Miss Wheatley nodded. "I *had* thought – before this happened – of putting him in the class play. But I realize that it's not possible. And of course, Jay doesn't need it now as he did before. I thought it might have given him confidence. But he seems to be doing so well that it really doesn't matter."

And she explained to Fanny that she asked Jay if he would like to be in the class play and he told her he couldn't be in an entertainment because he was in mourning for his father. And he said, furthermore, that he wouldn't be able to attend the rehearsals after school anyway because he had to go to the synagogue before it got dark, to say the prayers for his father. And after a while she left and Fanny began to think, and the more she thought, the less she liked. And one or two things, other things, came into focus that she hadn't thought about.

She was still thinking about it the next afternoon when the bell rang and who was it but Anna Goldman. "What are you doing away from your place of business in the middle of the day?" Fanny asked.

"I'm taking a late lunch hour," Anna said. There was a kind of funny look in her eyes. "And I brought you some visitors," Anna said. Up the stairs came Mrs. Mortimer Steinmetz and right behind her, Rabbi Camler. Bringing up the rear was Mrs. Steinmetz's daughter, Caroline Potasnik.

"Aunt Ida! Caroline!" said Fanny, giving them a hug and a kiss. This was the first time either of them, to say nothing of the Rabbi, had ever been to her house.

"Oh, my dear child," said Aunt Ida. "If anybody knows what you are going through, it is I. You think you'll never get over it. I thought the same. But I survived my grief. And so will you. So will you." And she sighed and sat down, opening her Persian lambskin coat and patting her blue-gray hair. "Rabbi Camler, of course," said she, waving her hand, "needs no introduction from me.

"Of course she'll survive," the Rabbi said. He was a big burly man with a mustache and eyeglasses and a little dab of hair under his lower lip. "A Jewish mother always finds the strength to bear the heavy burdens which

Life so often thrusts upon her."

Fanny said, 'Thank you. Thank you." She wanted to go into the kitchen to get some refreshments, but Anna Goldman pushed her down in the chair.

"*I* know what's in your mind. *Oh*, no. You just sit right there and receive your guests. And when Fanny still tried to get up Anna shook her fist and made a face. So she let Anna go into the kitchen, and they all had a sad conversation together about the unexpected death of Mr. Sam Kay, a young man in the prime of life with never an unkind word to say about anybody, the circumstances of his accident and death, and so on. And Fanny explained why they had happened to have old Rabbi Stein at the funeral.

"Of course, of course," Rabbi Camler said. He had very hairy hands and the funny thing was that his hair, even his mustache and eyebrows, didn't seem to have any color – not light or anything, just colorless. "I understand. You were quite right. Perfectly." He cleared his throat and made a noise like *huh-huh*.

Out popped Anna Goldman from the kitchen, where she had put the kettle on, and she sat down, her eyes flickering from face to face.

Caroline spoke for the first time. "And how is dear little Jay?" she asked.

Fanny gave a deep sigh. "I don't know what to tell you.... How should I put it?" She explained how poor Sam, may he rest in peace, had been away most of the time at work. Jay almost never saw him. And now, of course, he never would. "He seems to be with*drawing*, if you know what I mean. He won't participate in any extracurricular activities. Simply refuses." Aunt Ida clicked her tongue and shook her head. "Now don't think for one minute that I have anything against religion. Heaven forbid. I think it's a wonderful thing. But for a boy his age. I mean, he isn't ten yet. To get up so early in the morning to go to *shul*. And every evening, too. He was always a very sensitive child. That's why I put him in the dancing classes, to let him mingle with the other children. But now he won't go. He won't even participate in the little play his class in school is putting on. I don't know what to do."

Anna Goldman got up. "Excuse me. I'm just going in the kitchen. I'll be right hack." For a moment nobody spoke. Then Caroline said, "Well – " and Anna sang out, "I'll be right back. Just one moment." So they had to wait for her. She brought in tea and cookies.

Fanny said, "Oh, Anna, what would I ever do without you?" and Anna said, "Don't be silly."

"Not for me, thank you. I just had lunch. *Huh-huh*," the Rabbi said.

Aunt Ida raised her heavy eyebrows. "I hope you're not worrying about *kashruth*, Rabbi," she said. "I can assure you that my nephew's wife keeps a kosher home." How she had the nerve to assure anybody of anything about her nephew's wife's home, seeing that she had never set foot in it before, is indeed a question. And anyway, it wasn't even true; Fanny didn't keep a kosher home, and in fact this was one of the things Jay had begun to ask questions about, and she didn't care for *that* one bit. But she kept her mouth shut, and so did Anna Goldman, who knew the true state of affairs. And the Rabbi took the tea and cookies. After all, what he doesn't know won't hurt him. He must have had a light lunch; he ate everything, and had three cups of tea.

"I remember when dear Daddy passed away," Caroline said. "I don't know what I could have done if it weren't for my Faith."

Fanny pointed out that Caroline, however, was a grown woman at the time.

"Well, it's a very good thing nonetheless that someone is saying *kaddish* for the late *nifter*," the Rabbi said, meaning Sam.

"But does the Jewish religion insist that a child of that age say *kaddish*? I mean, can't another person say it, even though not related?" Aunt Ida asked.

"Well, as a matter of fact, yes," the Rabbi admitted, with a *huh-huh.*

Mrs. Steinmetz was triumphant. "You see!" she exclaimed. "*I* knew that. I remember my late father telling me that. What a religious man he was!" And she began telling what a religious man her father was, and this and that. "So you see that I *know* all these things," she said.

"Oh I'm sure of that," the Rabbi agreed. Then he said, "Listen. The *shammes* is in the *shul* for three daily services. And he says *kaddish* for various business and professional men whose schedule doesn't allow them to come in person. So you'll give him a few dollars," he said, not looking at any person in particular, "and the *shammes* will say the *kaddish* for the late Mr. Kay, may he rest in peace.

"The *shammes*." Aunt Ida said, indignantly "Why should the *shammes*? Aren't you there for every service?" You could see that the *shammes* wasn't going to get anything from *her*.

The Rabbi coughed into his hand. "Well, yes, I am," he admitted. *Huh-huh.* Aunt Ida opened her purse and took three twenty-dollar bills from it.

"I want you to say it, Rabbi," she said.

Anna Goldman said, "Well, *isn't-that-nice!*"

And Fanny said, "Oh, Aunt Ida, *please –* "

Rabbi Gamier said, "Mrs. Steinmetz, it isn't necessary to – I'll be glad – money isn't – *huh-huh.*"

But Mrs. Steinmetz quelled them all with one look from her eyes. "Why, what are you talking about? What, my own husband's nephew? Are you – all trying to hurt my feelings?" So they had to assure her that they weren't trying to hurt her feelings. The Rabbi had to accept the money and Fanny had to comment. "Well, all right, then," Aunt Ida said, looking everyone in the eye in turn. "You'll give me a receipt later," she said to the Rabbi.

Then Anna Goldman had to go back to work and so did the Rabbi. So Fanny and Aunt Ida had a long talk about the condition in which Sam Kay's affairs were left, and what Morty Jacobson wanted to do about Sam's interest in the Place, and what Ethel had to say, and what Fanny thought about it all and what Aunt Ida thought about it all. And so we see that Death does draw people together, because they became very close from that time on. Aunt Ida never had thought much of Morty Jacobson, either.

After everyone had gone, Fanny called up Miss Wheatley at home. She apologized for this. Then she informed her that Jay Marshall's period of mourning was over. "I quite agree with you about his being in your class play," she said. Miss Wheatley began to sound doubtful and she said "We-e-lll," but Fanny went right on. "I have every confidence in your good judgment," she said. "And I want you to insist upon his being in the play. Don't take no for an answer." And she impressed her and she agreed.

Because, when you come down to it, what good did it do Fanny, what good did it do *her* – all this religion and synagogue-going? Not that *she* would have been the one to stop the boy from saying *kaddish* for his father – what would people say? How would it look? But since Aunt Ida Steinmetz, after her dramatic reappearance on the family scene, since Aunt Ida had liberated her by the generous gift to the Rabbi, the whole picture was different. As long as the boy didn't have to go to the synagogue anymore – and these old rules and religious customs, as well we know, were made for a bygone day and age – why *shouldn't* he be in the class play and, for that matter, in the annual Spectacular of Miss Suzanne's students? Why shouldn't she, his mother, get some *nachas*, some pleasure, from her only son? Didn't she have enough heartache as it was?

So that's the way it happened. Jay Marshall began to lead a normal life once more. It had been quite a struggle, quite a strain, on his mother while it lasted, getting up so early. Now that there was no need for it, she took a much-needed rest and remained in bed each morning. She set out things for Jay's breakfast before going to sleep at night.

How did Jay react? Does a child that age know what's good for him? Did he appreciate being able to participate once more in games with other boys instead of spending so much time in the company of adult men? He didn't show a bit of gratitude for Aunt Ida's liberality. He made one scene after another at home. But his mother was determined he should lead a normal life, and he had to give in.

Miss Wheatley was true to her word and put Jay Marshall in the class play. It was a small part, much to his mother's disappointment. How did Miss Wheatley expect to give him "confidence" by just letting him speak one single line and the rest of the time he just stood around like a dummy? How could Fanny invite people to go and see her son, as she had planned, in a play where all he had to say was, "General Washington, here is an important message"? Why, they would laugh at her, and say things about it when she wasn't there. Miss Wheatley's action was a great disappointment to Fanny and she pinned her hopes thereafter on his taking what she hoped would be a prominent part in the Annual Spectacular of Miss Suzanne's studio.

When Jay went back to Miss Suzanne's she did her best to make him feel welcome. She said, "Well, I'm sure we are all glad to have Jay Marshall back with us again." And all the children said, Hello, How are you, Hi.

Janey Reizell said, "I'm sorry about your father, Jay."

He looked at her and his eyes got big and his lower lip started going out, and he turned away and started changing into his pumps. Then Dale Gowen had to pick that moment to go where the coats were hanging, to get his handkerchief out of his pocket.

Jay yelled, "Leave my coat alone!" And, mind you, Dale was a good friend of his. Dale was so shocked, he just stood there. Then Jay threw a pump at him.

"That will be just about enough of that, young man," Miss Suzanne said. "You pick up that pump and you tell Dale you're sorry." Instead, Jay began to cry, and then he ran over and hid under the piano. Miss Suzanne just threw up her hands. "Well, boys and girls," she started to say. Then she stopped. "Never mind. Let's take our regular places. Dale. Dale? Over here. Janey, Sheri, Lynn, Gail, Jeffrey, Sheldon... *in* line."

And they left Jay all by himself.

INTRODUCTION TO
TANTA SORA RIFKA AND
EVERYBODY HAS SOMEBODY IN HEAVEN

THIS MANUSCRIPT WAS FOUND among Avram Davidson's papers after his death. On the cover page he had scribbled a note, "Novel fragment, later 1960s." These two chapters were all we found. There were no notes, outlines or other materials, which might have allowed me (or another author) to complete the novel as a "posthumous collaboration."

Yet each chapter stands alone as a wonderful story, worthy of publication. We can only imagine what a magical novel this might have been, about a mysterious Jewish woman who is a spiritual leader named Tanta Sora Rifka.

Grania Davidson Davis

TANTA SORA RIFKA

MRS. LEOPOLD REGENSBURG SAT in the chair, hair white and dressed in a becomingly old-fashioned mode, eyeglasses on her somewhat large nose, hands folded neatly in her lap. A sealskin coat of somewhat antique cut was draped partly over the chair. Big Sadie and Little Sadie and Sadie Stern were there, so was Birdy Becker and a lot of others; Bryna peeped in from the kitchen. And once again Mrs. R. was prevailed upon to tell her story, because some of them hadn't heard it and everybody who had, wanted to hear it again anyway.

"Well, if it will interest you, of course, my dear friends," Mrs. R. said. "It was the night of November the 6th, the anniversary of my beloved mother's passing way. I had lit the electric memorial light, I had taken my medicine and said, as I always do, of course, the Shema and a short prayer from the heart; and I turned out the light and composed myself for sleep – "

In what was meant for a whisper, Birdy said, admiringly, "She looks so Jewish, but she talks so refined."

"Shhh!" the others said, clicking their tongues and frowning before they remembered to show love, then they smiled and patted Birdy and nodded and smiled at Mrs. R., she should go on with the story.

"Sleep," said Mrs. R., "must have come almost at once, because when I awoke I saw that the hands of the clock had scarcely moved. But I am ahead of my story. I had fallen asleep and in my dream I awoke, if you follow me, I woke up but I was still in my dream. And there was my dear mother, so to speak, standing beside my bed, as it were. 'Oh – Mother!' I exclaimed, filled with joy at seeing her dear face once more. She looked down at me and she said, 'Get up, daughter...why are you lying there asleep when there is a mitzvah waiting for you to do?' Well! You may all conceive of my astonishment! *Nothing* like this had ever happened to me before in my life! Oh, of course, I had occasionally dreamed of my dear mother, but such scenes had always been of the past, when I seemed to be a child once more, such as, for example, taking the steamboat to Long Branch – but this, I knew, was in the present. I was struck dumb with amazement. And my dear mother said, not precisely annoyed, for she never lost her temper, I only remember the single occasion when she saw a man kicking a horse which had fallen on the ice on Amsterdam Avenue near 70th Street and when he failed to heed her remonstrance, she did actually strike him with her umbrella – but now she said, oh, gently, but very, very firmly, 'Amelia, don't you hear me? Get up, there is a mitzvah for you to do.' And then I found my tongue...

"I said, 'Why, mother dear, what is the *nature* of this mitzvah, this meritorious deed, which you say is waiting for me?' And she merely shook her head at me, as though in surprise that I continued to dally, and she vanished from my sight. And then I did wake up, that is, all the way up, and I turned on my bed-light and looked at the clock, and I saw, as I say, that the hands had scarcely moved. It had all taken place in less than a moment...

"Well, of course, then I did get up, and, really not knowing what else to do, I dressed and I went all through the apartment, but everything was just as I had left it, everything was in place, and so I sat down and tried to compose my thoughts. Now, of course, not all dreams are of immediate importance or of equal importance, some are mere recollections of the past or of hopes – sometimes, I am afraid, of vain hopes – for the future... Once, for instance, I dreamed of attending the wedding of my second son, Leonard, and I was overjoyed, for the bride, as I recall to this very day, was a *lovely* Jewish girl – but it was not to be, for he passed away in 1935 without ever having married at all...but we dare not say that dreams are never of important consequence, we have the lesson of the Bible for that, haven't we? – And it just seemed, well, it seemed so *significant* that this dream of all dreams had come on the anniversary of my beloved mother's having passed away herself. I *knew*, I just *knew*, that *this* dream meant something. I may have sat there for hours, trying to calculate. But no answer came to my troubled mind. And so, finally, I dressed up and I went down into the streets, thinking I must find the answer somewhere. It was bitterly cold and I was thankful I had thought to dress up warmly. No one was about on the streets but me, it seemed, and I could hear my footsteps echoing. Now, as you know, it was a long, *long* time since I had ever ventured out that late, and alone, but I felt no fear. I remembered what my dear Grandmother Sousa had once said, that no harm comes to one who is engaged in the performance of a mitzvah. Well, I had *still* to *find* my mitzvah," Mrs. R. said, smiling and chuckling as she spoke, "but I was confident. I had faith. And so I walked on, and I walked on, not knowing precisely *where* to direct my footsteps. I passed through neighborhoods where I had not been in so *many* years and I passed through neighborhoods where I had *never* been, and then, although as I say there was *no* one about, it was so late, so cold, and many of the houses were boarded shut, and then a person came out of one of the houses; I saw a light burning dimly in an upstairs window; it was a woman, she did not see me at first for she was looking the other way and I saw her throw up her arms as though in despair, and then she looked in my direction and she did see me."

"Little Sadie," said Birdy Becker, nodding and smiling.

"Yes, I was later to learn that it was our dear little Sister Sadie Weinbaum, but at the time, of course – well, I continued walking, but I quickened my steps and my heart began to beat a bit faster and then we were face to face and I stopped. And this very fine person looked at me and I said not a word and at length she said, 'Are you Jewish?' And I said that I was, and she said, and *never* will I forget her words and I will always continue to give thanks to Our Father in Heaven that I was privileged to hear them; she said, 'Then please come upstairs with me, don't be afraid, but there is a mitzvah we have to do.' And I burst into tears and Sister Sadie said, 'Don't be *afraid*, don't be *afraid*!' – not understanding, of course, that these were tears of *joy*, for then I *knew*, you see, I *knew* that my dearly beloved mother had actually come down from Heaven and spoken to me in my dream," she said, wiping her eyes with a little handkerchief, "and this was so to speak the fulfillment of her prophecy – that I should be *privileged*, that *I* should be so privileged!" Composing herself, she continued the story, telling how she and Little Sadie had climbed the stairs to the top floor and of what they had found there. Poor Sister Reichman had just gone to a better world, the little girls were crying and sobbing, the husband was like a dead man himself, of no use at all; how the two women had cut the straws out of the broom and spread them on the floor, there being no other straw in the house, and had taken Sister Reichman off the bed and laid her on the straw and covered her up, tenderly –

"What-she-didn't-do!" burst out Bryna, at the kitchen door, no longer able to contain herself. "What-she-didn't-*do*! – I heard, I heard, who didn't hear? There wasn't a penny in the house, the house was like ice, that *mamzer* landlord – "

"Show love! Show love!" they all chorused.

Bryna's face fell, turned all colors, she swallowed. "So I'm sorry, we should all love him, he should feel our love, if more people loved him he would be a better man – cold as *ice*! The apartment – So what did she do, this one, Sister Regensberg? She called up this one, she called up that one, the undertaker, the doctor, the police, this nephew and that cousin, she called up lawyers and she called up Rabbis, down from Harlem in a taxicab – in a *taxicab*! – who paid for it? She paid for it! – comes two Schwartzes, husband and wife, right away she tells him, break open the lock on the cellar and put *coal* on the furnace – the wife starts to get the place clean, poor Sister Reichman, three weeks she was in bed, couldn't lift a finger. – Comes *food*, who knows from where comes food, that hour of the night!

Comes clean blankets, she wraps up the children in the blankets puts money in the husband's hands, sends them off to a hotel with one of her nephews, they shouldn't have to stay there all night with the toyter in the same room," Bryna paused for breath, her face deep red. "What-she-didn't-do!"

But Mrs. R. shook and continued to shake her head. "I was nothing," she insisted. "I was only the instrument. I understood that clearly. I was only the *kayly*, the instrument or vessel, as our dear Tanta Sora Rifka has taught us to think of it."

"– the *Neshomas*, of the Neshomas," said Big Sadie, nodding vigorously.

"Certainly. The vessel of the dear Souls in Heaven...my mother, my beloved grandmother, and all the other worthy Souls passed on into that Better World. Their instrument. At first it was my dear mother alone, but then, after the funeral, when there was more time to talk of such things, it was explained to me. And under*stood*. I understood that it was not her alone, but that Tanta was a latterday prophetess, though she herself modestly pretends not to understand the term, that she is *the* vessel, the chief instrument, through which all the beloved Souls make their wishes known to us down here below. I have been a Seeker for many, many years," said Mrs. R., raising her hands and clasping them. "I have sought in the Conservative tradition in which I was raised and in the Reform tradition into which I married and in the Orthodox tradition, which, difficult as I always found it – the language, for one thing, you know – but, still, the venerable Mother-faith of us all, we must admit that. I have sought in Ethical Culture and in *Coue* and in Unity and I at one time sedulously perused the works and teachings of Mrs. Eddy, for I believe that there are many roads to truth; and I have investigated Bahai, and Buber with his wonderful Chassidic parables, and lately Clement – my great-nephew, Clement Cahn – has lent me some very interesting things about something new called Zen.

"Jewish Science, Mrs. Lichtenstein, a wonderful woman – but now I feel I know: my search is over. When I was taken at long last to meet that truly marvelous person, that living saint, so simple, so humble, eschewing and avoiding any title, even Founder, even Leader, merely preferring that she continue to be known as Tanta, as Auntie..."

EVERYBODY HAS SOMEBODY IN HEAVEN

HOW NICE THE BAKERY SMELLED when they were bringing out the fresh rolls, tumbling them from the heavy wire trays into the bins in the showcase and at the back behind the counter and in the window. The rolls were round and brown and so crisp and they had poppy seeds all over the top. They came off, the poppy seeds, while the rolls were tumbling out, and they came off in the brown paper bags the customers took them home in, and they came off on the tablecloth while the rolls were being spread with sweet butter. But there were always enough left on, the crisp brown crust broken open to the sweet white insides, up to the last bite. And even afterwards with a little bit moistened finger, the moon seeds were picked up and crunched. Nothing wasted.

Mendel Luft was the name of the man who owned the bakery, and he was small and brown himself and he had little black dots here and there on his face. Were they moon seeds too? Probably not. Waiting to swoop was his mortal enemy, an old man by the name of Stuhlman, who came in every day even before the rolls were ready, and never spoke, just looked at the walls. A word about those walls.

This was not one of those new bakeries, imitation white tiles from floor to ceiling, fancy signs with pictures of fancy modern women smiling over cream cakes, and the cream cakes in a cooler across from the counter. This was one of those old bakeries, it was painted brown the day it was first painted God knows how many years ago, brown walls, brown ceilings, and every time it had been painted since it was still painted brown, as though it painted itself brown. If the customers had come down the two steps and saw another color they would have stopped dead, sure that Mendel Luft had died and the place was taken over by some new owner. Max Weiss in his speckled overalls painted it every year during the inside days of Passover when Mendel Luft took his vacation at Lightman's Hotel in the mountains.

"Whaddaya want?" he asked Old Man Stuhlman.

The old man lifted his long nose and turned his back. Then he went over to the rolls in the window and picked up one of them. "They're fresh, they're fresh! They just came out of the oven, they're so hot they could burn your fingers, and he's got to squeeze them! Don't squeeze the rolls!" he shouted. But the old man just pulled in his long, drooping lower lip, making the little goat's beard bob up. He carried his two rolls over to the counter and put them on the glass top. Then he put his hand in his pocket and took out his change purse. Then he counted up his pennies and put them on the wooden counter. Mendel Luft, muttering and scowling, put the rolls in a brown paper bag. And the old man Stuhlman left, his head down, his nose down, his lip once again down, his little goat's beard down. Tomorrow it would be the same all over again.

What was there besides poppy seed rolls? Rye rolls, like little tiny loaves of rye bread. Onion rolls, flat, with a big hollow in the middle, where the onions lay. Shiny brown bagels. Pumpernickel in three sizes. Corn bread, bread such as they used to bake in the days of old, and as in ancient years, huge vast loaves of corn bread, each round one an armful. Nobody ever got an entire loaf. It was sold by the pound. What else was there? Cake? There was cheese cake by the slice, honey cake and sponge cake, each with paper still sticking to it. There was eyerkichol, shaped like a wig, and kichelach, shaped like butterflies and sprinkled with sugar. There was no such thing as white bread or whole-wheat bread, such things you could buy in grocery stores. There was challa, braided and golden brown, with poppy seeds and without poppy seeds. Some people call it barchas or berchas.

And *some* people call it 'holly', but with such people, who live in places like Wisconsin or Oklahoma, Mendel Luft has nothing to do.

Most of all and best of all, there was bread. "Bread," without any other description, means rye bread. Mendel Luft's bakery sold the original rye bread, a loaf which tapered at either end, which had been painted with egg-white before baking so that it came out an even richer golden brown than the challa, the glaze having crackled like old oil paint, with kimmel seeds on top and sides; and on the bottom a thick white layer of flour, or meal. This was definitely not the bread of affliction which our Fathers ate in the land of Egypt. If they ate it in the old country, who knows and who can say. We weren't there. But they ate it in America in the first generation and in the second generation and even somewhat in the third generation. And now that we are already in the fourth generation and it is almost impossible to find the real, true, Jewish rye-bread (easy enough to find imitations of imitations), because the bakers' sons didn't become bakers, they became everything else but not bakers, and the results of all this we see on all sides, and is it a coincidence?

But in the time about which we are talking, bread was taken for granted. It was appreciated, and it was available. And right after old Stuhlman went out with his head down and his hand in the small of his back so that the little bakery bag bobbed up and down, the door opened and closed again and a woman came in and looked around and nodded her head at everything and nodded and smiled and then she nodded and smiled at Mendel Luft. And he stopped scowling and muttering and he looked at her, and he said, "Yes, Sadie?"

She said, "God wants all this bread to go to the poor people."

Mendel said, "All right. And God is going to pay for it, too?"

She had her pocket book on the wooden counter and she nodded and said, "Mmm-hmm" and opened the purse and asked, "How much is it?"

He rocked his head from side to side a little bit, as she wasn't looking at him, and he told her the amount. She said, "Mmm-hmm," and went on opening the inside of her purse and took out money and began to count out the amount.

"Sadie, this is a lot of bread," he said.

"The rolls, too," she said, looking up. "Oh. You didn't know. That's not my name."

"The rolls, too. – That's not your name? What is your name?"

"Sora," she said. "Sora Rifka. You'll help me carry it out, please?"

Mendel Luft looked to the right and to the left and waved his hand. But nobody else was there to help him. "Carry it out where? Sadie – all right, so Sora – What are you going to *do* with it all?"

She said, "I have a pushcart." She smiled and chuckled. She said, "What am I going to do with it? I'm going to give it to the poor. God wants it."

He made a little mound with his breath. She was already putting rolls into the wire baskets they had just come out of, still smiling, still chuckling, and now she began to sort of sing a little to herself. Mendel Luft put his hands to his head and pressed. Then he put his hands down, then he spread them out, then he gave a big sigh. She opened the door and went out, and he followed her. Sure enough, she had a pushcart. It was lined with newspapers. She dumped the basket of rolls and started back for more.

He followed her. "Listen...Sora Rifka...listen..."

She put the basket in his hands and gestured to the bread and rolls, and began to fill another, Breaking off her humming or singing, she said, "I'm listening. I'm listening."

"Listen." He put a hand to his face. "God told you He wants what?"

"The *Neshomas*," she said. She looked from him to the other – bread and rolls and made a humorously deprecating face that he hadn't begun to fill his basket; and so, slowly, he began to do it.

"The – the Neshomas –?"

She had filled the basket. "The souls," she said. "God tells them, and *theyyyy*...." she strung out the last word in a sing-song tone, "tell *me*." And she went out and he, slowly, followed.

Somebody else followed in after them. A woman. "A half-dozen seeded rolls," she said. A heavy woman, with a big, red face.

Mendel Luft said, "Sorry. Sold out." He faced her and put his hands on his hips. Sora Rifka began to fill another basket.

"Whaddaya mean, sold out?"

"Sold out means sold out."

The woman looked as though she didn't know whether to be bewildered or angry. She half-turned. Sora Rifka met her eye and smiled and nodded and began to sing under breath. "*You're* buying them all? So I suppose you have a store somewhere. All right." She put down her bundles, fumbled in her purse. "You'll sell me a half-dozen seeded rolls..." The baker looked from one to the other.

Sora Rifka said, "These are God's rolls and outside is God's pushcart and I'm giving it all to the poor and if *youuu*...are a *poor* person... so take what you need..."

The woman's mouth went open and didn't close. She looked at Mendel Luft and she looked at Sora Rifka. Then she muttered, "A poor... I'm not rich, I work for my living... Poor? I don't need charity... Just sell me six rolls?"

"God's rolls are not for sale," Sora Rifka told her, cheerfully.

"Well, I believe in God, too," the woman said. "I live alone and I don't have nobody –"

Sora Rifka paused, balancing the basket. Still smiling, she shook her head. "Everybody has somebody in Heaven," she said.

The woman nodded a slow, heavy nod. She said: "Yeh. Sure." She looked to Mendel Luft. He shrugged. Suddenly the woman became angry, she made a quick movement, her bundles slipped, she grabbed for them, gathered them up again, and, her lips pressed together, jumped up the two steps. At the door, she turned around. "You're crazy," she said. Mendel Luft just looked. She stuck out her tongue at him, then, her head up and her mouth in an angry pout, away she marched.

The last roll dumped in the pushcart, the last huge loaf of corn bread cut in quarters, Sora Rifka put her hands to the wood and hunched her shoulders – "Something I forgot," she said, straightening up. – "What, Sadie, what?" – She shook her head at him, smiling: "*Dos iz nisht myne nomen.*" – "*Nu.* Sora. Sora Rifka. What?" – "Sell me some bags."

He drew in his breath in self-reproach, in deprecation of even the possibility that he might sell them, trotted back into the store and returned in a second with a hastily snatched-up armful, brown paper bags of all sizes and thrust them in between the loaves. He told her that if a hundred people had bought, he would have given out a hundred bags.

"And listen –" he called after her, as she toiled away, stooing over the bar of the cart. "Listen – Be careful."

She smiled, nodded, her mouth moved, making sounds, if not words. He saw her stop, reach out and beckon to a woman passing by with a child. Saw her pack a large bag. Saw her bend and push on. Watched her till she was out of sight.

Ho, ye who are thirsty, come ye to the water. Yea, buy wine and milk without money.

EILEEN GUNN'S stories and articles have appeared in *Isaac Asimov's Science Fiction Magazine, Science Fiction Eye, The New York Review of Science Fiction*, and other magazines and anthologies. Her work has been nominated twice for the Hugo Award, included in the *Norton Book of Science Fiction* and other anthologies, and translated into French, Italian, German, Japanese, and other languages.

Her personal web site, *Imaginary Friends* (www.sff.net/people/gunn), features snippets of fiction, interviews done for *Omni Online*, and the hypertext version of *The Difference Dictionary*, a concordance to William Gibson and Bruce Sterling's novel *The Difference Engine*. The site was chosen a Project Cool Site of the Day in 1997.

Gunn currently lives in San Francisco with her partner John D. Berry. Since 1988, she has served on the Board of Directors of the Clarion West Writers Workshop.

A Biography Of
Avram Davidson:
Water From A Deep Well

By Eileen Gunn

AVRAM DAVIDSON was a fascinating puzzle: an irascible and difficult man who inspired widespread love and loyalty; a brilliant, prolific writer who was unable to make even a modest living from his writing; a self-taught scholar of languages and cultures, who in his youth failed to graduate from three colleges. His work – nineteen published novels (with perhaps another half dozen as yet unpublished) and over two hundred stories – celebrates the variety of the human imagination, and vividly delineates the peculiarities of individual men and women.

The question that arises most often about a startlingly creative person is, where did it come from? Where is the well that is the source of this individual's creative energy and style? In the case of Avram Davidson, that is a particularly compelling question: the well is a deep one, and its waters are intoxicating. The essays in this collection, coupled with letters from Avram's youth, strongly suggest that the well at which Avram first slaked his intellectual thirst was Judaism, and that the encouragement he received within his religious community convinced him that he had a duty to write.

That this should be the case is a triumph of nature over nurture. Avram was not born into a particularly observant household. His family was socially and culturally Jewish – they attended services during the high holy days and shared in the rich trove of Ashkenazi Jewish culture – but they did not keep a kosher kitchen or attend synagogue frequently. In his teens, in the late 1930s or early '40s, he became interested in Orthodox Judaism and became involved with a group in Yonkers who identified with the Agudat Israel movement, an Orthodox organization that aimed to reestablish the authority of the prominent Rabbis as the supreme institution of

Jewry. It opposed secularist elements in Jewish culture, especially in the settlement of Eretz Israel, which it felt should unite the people of Israel under the rule of the Torah. Thus began a spiritual journey that lasted Avram the whole of his life; it led him first to Israel and ultimately to Japan.

Avram Davidson was born in 1923 in Yonkers, New York, a respectable working/middle-class city on the Hudson River, just north of the Bronx. Yonkers was then, and for the most part still is, a community of small, distinct neighborhoods, divided by hilly north-south glacial ridges and several major parallel parkways. The northern end of town, which borders on the village of Hastings, displays majestic Colonial and Gothic-revival houses, museums, leafy parks and bikepaths. The eastern side, close to Bronxville and Scarsdale, is more densely populated than the north, but still has a suburban flavor. The southwestern section, along the Hudson River, is the least fashionable part of town; Avram's family lived there in a large apartment building on Hawthorne Avenue, in a neighborhood of 19th century brick workers' row-houses, a buffer zone between failing factories of crenelated brick and tree-lined streets of large woodframe houses.

Avram attended the public schools, Number Three elementary school and Hawthorne middle school, and did not learn much Hebrew or Yiddish. He grew up during the Depression, but knew little of its deprivation. Members of the Davidson family were partners in the New System Laundry, and Avram's father, whose own father had been a farmer, worked there as a deliveryman. The Davidsons struggled during the Depression, but his father held onto his job, and they never went hungry – though Avram recalled mending holes in his shoes with cardboard and wrote that he realized, in retrospect, that he had never since that time eaten potatoes so frequently and in so many different forms.

His father, Harry Davidson, though like Avram short of stature, was a former prize fighter – he had taken the 1912 New York State Amateur Boxing Championship in the flyweight division. Harry's family had come from the Baltic ports of Riga and Memel, and had been in the United States for a generation. Avram's mother Lilly (nee Lillian Adler), came from a large family of Hungarian Jews. Avram and his younger sister Rhoda grew up in an extended family of Yonkers aunts and uncles and cousins, almost entirely on his mother's side – the Adlers, Kleins, Schlossers, Greenwalds, and others. "I had aunts," he wrote. "Boy, did I have aunts."

Avram read science fiction magazines – he was not the first future writer to be hooked by *Thrilling Wonder Stories* – and he wrote his own versions of the stories he read, tales of time travel and slave ships from space. He listened as well – does a kid have a choice? – to his relatives' stories of family and the old country, and the tradition of Jewish tales was part of his childhood.

Harry and Lillian Davidson's marriage was not a happy one. In 1943, while Avram was in the Navy, his parents separated permanently. His father left the laundry business and returned to the land, moving to rural New Jersey, where he worked on a chicken farm. His mother remained in Yonkers, and despite Harry's entreaties over the course of several years, Lillian, raised in the city and avowedly middle-class, refused to join him. Avram remained very close to his mother, and although he kept in touch with his father, their relations were friendly but a bit distant.

After high school, Avram lived at home and attended New York University in Manhattan for two years. In December, 1942, at the age of 19, he went into the Navy, specifically with the hope of seeing action in Europe against Germany. Although he objected to being trained as a soldier for reasons of conscience, he volunteered as a medical corpsman.

Avram's given names had been Adolph Abram, and at about the same time that he entered the Navy, he changed his name, at least informally, to Avram: the transition can be seen in letters he received during his earliest days in naval training. To his military buddies, he was known as Dave; to his friends and family, as Avram. In 1974 or '75, he changed his legal name to James Abram Davidson, and he continued to use the names in different contexts: he was Avram to his family and to everyone he knew in his writing career, and he was Dave (or occasionally James) to those whom he knew through his study of the Tenrikyo religion.

During his teenage years, Avram had become passionately interested in Orthodox Judaism. In a letter to his cousin Herbie, written during his Naval training, he sketches a quick portrait of himself at 18 or 19. "Did Sylvia tell you how, while schmoozing after supper one nite in her sister's home, and discussing observant Jews who couldn't speak Yiddish, the brother-in-law was reminded of seeing at the succah in a little Bleecker St. restaurant, a bearded bloke ('obviously,' he said, 'a yeshiva Bochur'...) who couldn't speak the Mamma-loschen, and whom he was obliged to defend when the fellow left, as 'all the old beards thought it was simply awful.' Of course, it was none other than yours truly...." In a foretaste of his later multi-layered writing style, he gives not his picture of himself, or his friend Sylvia's picture of himself, but Sylvia's recounting of her brother-in-law's description of the reaction of a group of elders in Avram's presence. And yet, through those layers of perspective and the haze of 60 years, we get a cheerful portrait of a very young man searching for his religion, in an environment that does not necessarily welcome him.

After training in Florida at the Banana River Naval Air Station and in San Diego with the Marine Corps, he shipped out to the Pacific front with the First Marine Division. He wrote frequently and affectionately to his mother, whom he encouraged to become more observant in her religious life. He also corresponded with various cousins and aunts, with several Rabbis, and with his friend Sylvia, a young woman who, like Avram, was associated with Agudat and who encouraged him in his religious observances. She sent him copies of the *Orthodox Times* and clippings about Army Air Force pilots who successfully kept kosher.

In the Navy at that time, even in Florida, keeping kosher was very difficult, and Avram experienced a good bit of hostility for his religious commitment. He wrote to Sylvia: "I am still dubious about overseas kashrus. I know your A.A.F. Agudists did keep k., but they were at settled bases, with regular arrival of mail, & could take food on their planes with them. I will be with some Marine outfit, flitting from island to island, possibly weeks without mail or packages. I need not say that I will do my best, but I am not too hopeful." For more on the difficulties of remaining observant in the military during World War II, see "Dan Cohen," in this collection.

One of his Rabbinical correspondents, Rabbi Leimon, not only encouraged Avram to write, but urged him to write novels. Avram wrote to Sylvia that Rabbi Leimon "suggested that I utilize the form of the Religious novel as a means of reaching the Jewish masses. As an essayist, he says I could not do this. Well, as I told him, one cannot sit down & grind out a novel like a pound of hamburger, & expect it to be good. But I will undertake it (this is confidential, & I mean it!) & bit by bit try to get it done. I plan to use some of my own experiences, but I don't intend it to be an autobiographical novel. Emotionally, spiritually, it will be my story, but not factually...." Many of the short essays that Avram wrote for *Orthodox Jewish Life* (some of which are reprinted in this volume) seem to be rehearsals for such a novel. The earliest ones carry the weight of an obvious moral, but in the later stories that burden is lighter: without losing the moral edge, the writing becomes more subtle. Avram's first novel, *The Corpsman*, fits the description he gave Sylvia Klein; it utilizes some anecdotes of his life in the Navy, and yet is not really an autobiographical novel: it does not tell the story of Avram's experiences in the war. Avram never finished it; an excerpt, "Blunt," was published in *The Magazine of Fantasy and Science Fiction* in 1998.

The only combat Avram saw was in Okinawa, with the First Marine Division, 5th Regiment. The battle for Okinawa, the largest amphibious assault of the Pacific Theater, took three months and resulted in the deaths of 12,000 Americans and over 100,000 Japanese. Avram was there only at the very end of this bloody and horrific battle, but he saw more than enough suffering. Many years later, in correspondence with a friend who was a Viet Nam veteran, Avram had this to say about his battle experiences: "I also saw mortars, but just for a few days, wobblin and whistlin... but although I dunno for sure which way they were aimed, say, none of them landed near me. My personal war was very very brief." And yet, even during that short period, he witnessed ghastly injuries, maggot-ridden corpses, and other horrors of war. By Avram's own account, he never thought about his experiences in battle until forty years later, watching a TV documentary in 1982, when he suddenly began to cry. "Then I dried up until, about two and a half years later, reading about the First Marine Division (5th Reg.) on Okinawa, I recognized something familiar, and began to cry again, and did so for two days. Now I don't watch or read. It all had to be, and is gone; let it stay so." While on Okinawa, he contracted what seemed to be a minor infection, swabbed some antiseptic on it, and got on with his job. For the rest of his life, the infection returned intermittently to plague him.

In October, 1945, after the Japanese surrender, Avram landed with HQ Company, Third Battalion, the Fifth Marines, at an outpost of Tientsin, probably Ta-ku, about 70 miles southeast of Beijing, their task being to oversee the repatriation of the Japanese population of North China. From the port, they moved to Beijing, a relatively comfortable post, where they stayed until the end of the year. Avram's description of his first whiff of the North China mainland evokes the impact this short stay in China had on him: "...the smells of 'night-soil' (human excrement), garlic, soft-coal smoke, sweat, piss – blind me, bind me in blindfolds for a thousand years, and of a sudden demand me answer 'Say what smells and stinks and reeks there out the pitch-black night, and what odor and what strong thick 'nose'?' would I need make answer, make murmur, 'Tis the deep thick indescribable stenk and odor of The Great Coast of Great, Great China, sans incense and sans mask.'"

In Beijing, Avram followed the scent of China. He studied Mandarin. He explored the city and talked to its people. He had tea with one of the last of the Imperial eunuchs. After only a few months, the Marines' mission was done in China, and Avram left in early 1946. China left its mark on Avram, however, and he later regretted that he hadn't stayed. In two stories written in the 1950s, "The Dragon-Skin Drum" and the superb "Dagon," he writes evocatively of his time in Beijing. His earliest story about China, "The Land of Sinim," which deals with the historical Jews of Kai-Feng, is included in the present collection.

Avram went back to America because he was planning to get married – not to Sylvia, as one might expect from their affectionate letters, but to a woman named Edith, an officer in the WAVES, whom he apparently met in the service. Their families were introduced to one another, but at some point soon after Avram returned to the U.S., Edith told him that she had decided to marry someone else. Although Edith was in New York during Avram's time in China, and they presumably corresponded, none of their letters survive.

In the years immediately after the war, Avram lived with his mother in Yonkers and pursued a writing career. He took a class in short-story writing at Yeshiva University in Washington Heights from Professor Irving Linn (the celebrated Chaim Potok was one of the other students), and contributed weighty essays to the school's yearbook, signing them A.A. Davidson. A classmate later described him as "a young man with a short black beard, sitting very quietly in class." He also wrote stories and poems for *Jewish Life*, and presumably worked on his novel. He was, in a sense, studying to be the writer he later became.

But Avram's interests did not revolve completely around writing. Starting in 1947, he tried secretly to volunteer as a medical corpsman in the Israeli military. In the autumn of 1948, after waiting a year and a half, having given up hope that he would be accepted, he received a phone call: "Can you leave tomorrow?" At the time, U.S. law provided that service in a foreign military (or even voting in a foreign election) resulted in immediate loss of U.S. citizenship, and Avram's presence and activities in Israel would continue to be a loosely held secret until he returned to the U.S.

Arriving in Israel, he found a new-born country rich in history, a scattering of people he had known in New York, and a world in which his assumptions were constantly being undercut – a source of amusement to him throughout his life.

From his letters:

...The ship's doctor speaks a purely original English and is hopelessly convinced that "anything" means "nothing" ("Why you put him this? This is anything!"). He makes up the sick list in what I, confused no end, took to be a peculiar form of medical Latin, and only recently discovered to be Portuguese....

...I got a three day pass to visit Tiberias & the Sea of Galilee, also called Lake Tiberias, and Yam Kinneret. It is one of the oldest Jewish settle-

*ments and the inhabitants patronize newcomers whose families have been
there a mere century. The old part of town was ruined in the fighting, but
the Tiberians still daven in those of their synagogues which are merely
semi-ruined. The Chassidim speak Yiddish with an Arabic accent. One old
graybeard in a striped robe asked me from whence I came.*

> *"From the Lands of the Covenant (the United States)," I answered.*
> *"And what city?"*
> *"Oh," says I, "You never heard of it. Called Yonkers."*
> *"Ah, yes," says he, "the N.Y. Central passes through it on the way*
to Albany..."

Avram enjoyed Tiberias so much that he considered settling there
permanently, and examined a number of business possibilities, from opening an exporting business (an idea quickly dismissed) to starting a co-op-
erative dairy farm/ice-cream factory with the help of a grant from the Israeli government. Eventually, he would turn his hand to sheep farming.

In the spring of 1949, Avram applied for a discharge from the
Israeli military, and when released took a job in a hospital in Jerusalem. He
sought work in Aden, but the job fell through, and he went to Tel Aviv to
make plans to return for a visit to the U.S. "The only part of Tel Aviv I like
is the view of the Mediterranean.... Jerusalem was wonderful – no place
like it in the world." "A Song of Degrees," included here, is a delightful
account of the novelties Jerusalem presented to a New Yorker at that time.

In another letter, he wrote his first genuine (although light-hearted)
financial lament, "Do we ever change, my child, any of us? I hope I've
changed in some ways at least; I'd like to make some money for a change."
This theme would continue in his letters for the next 45 years, its mood
becoming progressively darker. At the time, however, he was merely concerned that writing about Israel would not pay the bills. Fortunately for us,
he didn't let that stop him, and his articles about life in Israel, published in
Jewish Life and *Commentary*, are included in this volume.

He returned to the U.S. slowly, via Cyprus, Paris, and London. He
used his European experiences, though they were of short duration, evocatively in later writing. For a lively snapshot of Cyprus, see "Caphtor and
Other Places."

Back in the U.S. for an extended visit, he searched for a college
that specialized in sheep husbandry or offered individual courses in sheep
management for non-matriculated students. It was obvious that he did not
want a general degree in agriculture: he wanted to find out as much about
sheep as he could in a relatively short time, and then take that information

back to Israel. He ended up studying animal husbandry for a few semesters at Pierce College of Agriculture in Canoga Park, California, near Los Angeles. Avram was particularly interested in the possibilities of a strain of hardy sheep for breeding and pasturage in the Israeli desert. He returned to Israel in the summer of 1951, and pursued sheepherding there, while continuing to work on a novel, probably *The Corpsman*.

Israeli shepherds were not as enthusiastic as Avram was about fat-tailed sheep, and to make matters worse, he "hit a snag" in his novel. He returned to the U.S. in the summer or fall of 1952, and resumed living with his mother in Yonkers while aggressively pursuing a writing career.

Avram's interests and writing style had changed since his earlier stories for *Jewish Life*: his range had become more sophisticated and his tone less didactic. Although the stories still made strong moral points, these were no longer spelled out for the reader; they had to be inferred. He used more dialogue in his stories, and had developed a great ear for patterns of speech, the turns of phrase that mark a region or a particular speaker. This would be a hallmark of Avram's writing for the rest of his life. The editor of *Jewish Life*, Saul Bernstein, was not completely sure he approved of the way Avram's writing was changing; he continued to buy Avram's stories, but his editing suggestions now sometimes included major cuts.

When one door closes, another opens. *Commentary* was a better-paying market than *Jewish Life*, as Bernstein himself admitted, and Avram was selling there more frequently. In addition, Avram was trying to sell into the high end of the science fiction and fantasy market, a genre he'd enjoyed since childhood. He received a lot of encouragement from new acquaintances in that field, notably from editor Anthony Boucher and the writer Ward Moore. In 1954, he sold his first story into that market, "My Boyfriend's Name is Jello," to Boucher for "The Magazine of Fantasy & Science Fiction." This was not actually his first published fantasy story: that honor goes to "The Fisherman," a sophisticated little tale that is included here. "Jello" was an immense hit and was reprinted in the magazine's annual hard-cover collection of its top stories. Avram's next story in *F&SF*, as the magazine is known, was "The Golem," a story that has been widely anthologized and is also part of the present volume. *F&SF* remained an enthusiastic publisher of Avram's stories over the course of his long career.

Avram's productivity increased with success, though he admitted that he wrote mostly as the spirit moved him. He didn't make much money, but he made enough to live on. He wrote more short stories – fantasies, mysteries, science fiction – and the more he wrote, the more he was recognized as a writer of humor and of moral depth. He started receiving awards. In 1957, "The Necessity of His Condition" won the Queen's Award from Ellery Queen's Mystery Magazine. In 1958, Avram received the Hugo Award of the World Science Fiction Association for his short story "Or All the Seas with Oysters....," still his best-known work. The science-fictional conceit behind this story gives a biological explanation for the fact that you can never find a safety pin when you need one, no matter how many packets of pins you buy, but your closet regularly fills up with coat hangers, though you never purchase any at all. It has entered the popular imagination, and most people who have heard of it may never have read a word of Avram's writing. In 1962, he was given the Edgar Award by the Mystery Writers of America for his story "The Affair at Lahore Cantonment," a tour de force of nested tales-within-tales that spins off of Rudyard Kipling's poem "Danny Deever."

With his enthusiastic reception into the world of popular fiction, Avram wrote less that was intended specifically for a Jewish audience. After the end of the Fifties, he sold his stories to secular publications, with the exception of the excellent "Who Is Ethel Schnurr?" which appeared in *Jewish Life* in 1970. His fine ear caught the rhythms of speech not only of Jews, but of the other immigrant and native players in the New York comedy, and in the wider world in which he traveled.

Avram was still not bringing in very much money, despite his awards, so in 1962 he accepted the position of executive editor of *The Magazine of Fantasy and Science Fiction*. During his two-year tenure, he bought stories by such legends as J.G. Ballard, Roger Zelazny, and Philip K. Dick, and encouraged many new writers who are now well-known, including Stephen King and Gregory Benford. In 1963, under Avram's editorship, *F&SF* won the Hugo Award as the Best Professional Magazine.

In addition to launching his editorial career, 1962 was a banner year for Avram's writing and a notable one in his life. His first collection of science-fiction stories came out in 1962, as did his first novel, *Joyleg* (a collaboration with Ward Moore), and a collection of true-crime histories, *Crimes and Chaos*. He also published a substantial number of short stories in the pulp mystery magazines. In February, Avram, then 39, married Grania Kaiman, now Grania Davis and (of course) the co-editor of this volume, at the home of writer Damon Knight in Milford, Pennsylvania, a small town in the Pocono Mountains. The ceremony was a traditional one, and the celebration was highlighted by Chassidic dancing, and by writer Theodore Sturgeon singing folksongs and playing the guitar.

The Davidsons lived in New York City, just above Central Park, until after the birth of their son Ethan in November, 1962. They then moved to Milford, where they rented a small house on the Delaware River. It looked like a good place to raise children, and was home to a growing community of writers and editors of science fiction and fantasy.

After only a few months, a dispute with their landlady ("the Witch of Milford," a friend of Avram's termed her) about digging a garden forced them to find somewhere else to live. Avram and Grania wanted somewhere that they could live comfortably on a part-time editor's income, giving Avram adequate time to write. Grania also had hopes of a writing career, but was for the time-being fully occupied with the baby.

In the spring of 1963, Avram and Grania, with baby Ethan, two cats, and a dog named Herman Mudgett, left the U.S. for Mexico, where they planned to stay for a couple of years – just until he started making good money from writing. They found a cold-water hacienda in Amecameca, a town that sits 8000 feet high on the slope of the volcano Popocatepetl. Avram continued to edit *F&SF* by mail.

In his novel *Clash of Star-Kings* (whose intended title was the less lurid *Tlaloc*), he described Amecameca: "...a narrow-gauge steam railroad whistles its way through burro-iferous streets which may, conceivably, have been paved during the Juarez Administration or the reign of Maximilian which interrupted it; and over choo-choo train, donkeys, muddy lanes, sixteenth-century church, serape'd *Indios* and all, broods the great blue bulk of Popocatepetl." Avram was still a conscientiously observant Jew: although Amecameca was well known for the quality of its beef, he preferred, to the puzzlement of his Gentile friends, to go to the nearest kosher butcher, several hours away in Mexico City.

While in Mexico, Avram resigned the editorship of *F&SF* in order to have more time to write. He wrote productively, but reported considerable trouble selling his work, which he attributed to his remoteness from the New York publishing industry and to some neglect by his agent. Nevertheless, in the next few years Avram published a remarkable number of novels. In 1964, his first solo novel, *Mutiny in Space*, was published, as well as *And On The Eighth Day,* the first of two novels published under the house name "Ellery Queen." (The promotional copy rightly terms *And On The Eighth Day* "one of the most curious adventures that has ever befallen Ellery Queen.")

A nuisance suit instituted by the Milford landlady required Avram to make an expensive trip to New York, contributing to the couple's financial strain. In the spring of 1964, Avram and Grania reluctantly concluded that their marriage was not a compatible one. In the early summer, Grania moved to Oakland in the San Francisco Bay Area, where she and Avram each had many friends, primarily writers and readers of science fiction. Avram followed a few months later with Ethan. He found a place nearby in Berkeley, and he and Grania remained friends, sharing childcare responsibilities, and later collaborating on stories and novels.

In 1965, three new Davidson novels appeared: *Masters of the Maze*, *Rork!*, and *Rogue Dragon*, as well as the second Ellery Queen book, *The Fourth Side of the Triangle*, and a second collection of stories. In 1966, *The Kar-Chee Reign*, *The Enemy of My Enemy*, and *Clash of Star-Kings* were published. With all these books coming out, how could Avram have failed to be prosperous? The answer is simple: they didn't pay very much, sometimes as little as $750 per book. Even in 1966, an income of three or four thousand dollars a year would not go very far.

In December of 1965, Avram traveled via Mexico to British Honduras (now Belize), with the immediate thought of traveling about and writing a book on the area, and a longer-term plan of investigating the possibility of living and working there. Belize is a land of many cultures and races, where a Creole dialect of English, rich in colorful phrases and archaic usages, is the predominant language, with Spanish and Mayan also widely used. A center of Jewish culture it isn't. In trying to determine whether a food animal called a gibnut was kosher, Avram asked if it had hooves. "Of course it have hooves," his informant snapped. "How do you think he get around? He have hooves like a cat or dog."

Avram found Belize a congenial and inexpensive place, and stayed through January. Later in the spring of 1966, he returned and rented a house in Stann Creek (now Dangriga), a seaside town in an important citrus-growing agricultural area. Grania and Ethan followed from San Francisco, so that the boy could be near his father. Ethan, then four, was sent by plane, to avoid the rigors of a land journey, and his mother followed overland via Mexico with a woman friend and the friend's son. The two women and their sons lived at Gale's Point, a village on a sandbar surrounded by bush and lagoon, accessible only by water, and many hours distant from Stann Creek.

Avram investigated business opportunities there and bought an interest in a piece of land called Moho Bul, fifty acres on the Moho River, ten acres of which were already cleared and planted with fruit trees. It included a thatched-roof house and a dory, and a quantity of old-growth mahogany trees. Moho Bul, however, was extremely isolated, surrounded by roadless jungle, and a long charterboat ride away from the remote southern town of Punta Gorda, itself reachable only by ferry. And the jungle offered, as jungles do, an especially favorable habitat for mosquitoes. Avram found that he really couldn't bring himself to settle in the area. Grania returned to California in December, 1966, and Avram and Ethan followed a bit later. Avram retained his rights to the land, and hired a local resident to tend it and harvest the fruit. He wrote a charming account of his first trip, but was never able to sell it, and later used British Honduras (renamed by Avram "British Hidalgo") as the setting for a series of fantasy stories featuring the adventurous Jack Limekiller.

In June of 1968, Avram returned to Belize with Ethan, to pursue running a business there in partnership with his friend Alan Nourse. Avram, after all, had experience on kibbutzes in Israel and had studied animal husbandry, and was still looking for a money-making career to support him while he wrote. Dr. Nourse, a medical doctor and a writer of popular science-fiction juveniles, had money he wanted to invest, and felt he could do so and help a friend at the same time. They purchased a small fleet of well boats, suitable for the shallow coastal waters inside Belize's boundary reef, outfitted them with gasoline engines, and set up a business in Belize City hauling sand for local cement makers. But the business experienced a series of reversals and quickly failed. Avram sent Ethan back after two months, and returned himself not long after.

To say that Avram was peripatetic is to understate the reality of the situation. During much of the celebrated Sixties, when he was not traveling to Mexico and Belize, Avram lived in a variety of apartments, mostly shared with others, in Berkeley and San Francisco, including one on Ashbury Street that was just up the block from the home of the Grateful Dead. In the Seventies, to escape rising rents, he moved to Marin County. He had long been in the habit of giving an amusing sobriquet to each residence, and including it in his address, in the British manner. In Milford, he and Grania lived at "The Mare's Nest." The place in Novato was "Far Fetch," the house in Mill Valley "The Flea Circus." It lent a prosperous air of the landed gentry that was totally at odds with his financial state.

During all this time, Avram wrote and published novels and stories. Series books (especially trilogies) were regarded by genre publishers as the key to commercial success, and Avram tried three times to produce a successful series. *The Phoenix and the Mirror*, begun in the early 1960s and published in 1969, proved to be the beginning of what Avram came to regard as his lifework. It took the form of a historical fantasy novel set in an imaginary time: the first century BCE, as imagined by late-medieval Europeans. The story of the sorcerer Vergil captured Avram's imagination; he spent the next twenty years researching and trying to write a multivolume work that did justice to his idea. The two other books that started as series beginnings, *The Island Under the Earth* (1969) and *Peregrine: Primus* (1971), are also charmingly erudite fantasies, but he never published the final volumes he planned. *Peregrine: Secundus*, intended as the second of three volumes, appeared in 1981.

During the 1970s, Avram supported himself, just barely, with his writing, and with writer-in-residence posts at various universities, including the University of California, Irvine, the College of William and Mary in Virginia, and the University of Texas at El Paso. He also taught at several of the Clarion Writers Workshops. While living in Mill Valley, researching the Vergil Magus series, he started a series of stories for the express purpose, he said, of making some money without having to do any research. The results of this experiment are the Eszterhazy stories, which draw only upon his imagination and, as he put it, 58 years of reading omnivorously. (With perhaps just a nod to his Hungarian forebears.) A collection, *The Enquiries of Doctor Eszterhazy*, won the World Fantasy Award in 1976 for Best Collection, and two subsequent stories in the series were nominated for the Nebula Award of the Science Fiction Writers of America. The Crown Jewels of Jerusalem, included in the book you're now holding, is one of these stories, a dark little tale wrapped in layers as light as a Viennese pastry. In 1979, his strange and evocative story Naples was given the World Fantasy Award for Short Story.

In 1980, he moved to Washington state, first living near the town of North Bend, in the foothills of the Cascade Mountains, then in Bellingham, a port and college town up near the Canadian border. In 1985, plagued by poor health and continued financial problems, he moved into the Washington Veterans Home at Retsil, on Puget Sound near Bremerton. Avram could not adjust to the lack of personal freedom that life at Retsil entailed, and when he could afford to, he left Retsil and found a place to live in Bremerton. That city, though it offered few of the cultural amenities of Seattle, on the other side of the Sound, had a large naval base, good public transportation, and significantly lower rents than Seattle.

In 1986, he was awarded the World Fantasy Award for Life Achievement, and traveled to Seattle to accept it at the World Fantasy Convention. Too frail to walk any distance, he used a wheelchair at the convention, and was unable to get up on the stage to accept his award. He continued, despite his physical setbacks, to work on the Vergil epic, and a second volume, *Vergil in Averno*, was published in 1987. He managed the information in a set of cross-referenced notebooks and card files, a sort of two-dimensional hypertext that enabled him to locate detailed quotes and sources on a large number of subjects. A number of Vergil-related short stories have appeared in *Isaac Asimov's Science Fiction Magazine*. The third novel, *The Scarlet Fig*, and a book of "fascicles" or pamphlets, *The*

Notebooks of Vergil Magus, have yet to be published.

In the mid-Sixties, Avram was still religiously observant and was attentive to his son's education as a Jew, but he had become spiritually restless. He had become interested, in the 1950s, in the New Thought movement, started in the 19th Century, which emphasized a connection between a mystical awareness of God and the health of the body. Avram was especially interested in finding a New Thought practitioner with a Jewish approach. A decade later, the infection he had contracted on Okinawa still bothered him, and other health problems had arisen: conventional medicine had not helped. In the San Francisco Public Library in 1962, he came across a book on Tenrikyo, a Japanese religion based on Buddhism and Shinto. Tenrikyo holds that selfish thoughts cast a shadow over our lives, and that illness results from this self-centeredness; by correcting mistaken, self-centered use of their minds, people can receive the blessings of good health. He wrote to the church's world headquarters in Japan for more information and, over the course of the next decade, became very interested in its tenets.

When he was in the hospital for surgery in 1970, he said, the Tenrikyo practitioner made him feel better, but the Rabbi made him feel worse. This could have been due, he admitted, to the Rabbi's cigar. Avram saw that Tenrikyo's emphasis on living a joyous life, "sweeping away the mental dust that accumulates from daily living," offered an antidote to the depression from which he suffered, and he felt that he needed help in controlling his fierce outbursts of temper. He became a Tenrikyo practitioner, and studied in Japan at the religion's headquarters. In accordance with the practice of Tenrikyo, he set up an altar in his home for the spirits of his mother and of a deceased woman friend. He assisted in the translation of songs and documents about Tenrikyo and introduced his family and some close friends to the religion. Tenrikyo was an important part of Avram's spirituality until the end of his life, but it did not supplant his identity as a Jew. He did not discuss his religious beliefs casually, and he had many close friends who had no idea that he was not still a conventionally observant Orthodox Jew.

The shadow of the Holocaust haunted Avram throughout his life. He changed his name because of it. He would not ride in a German-made car, nor would he allow his writing to be printed in German. "I will not dip my bread in my brothers' blood," he said, when other writers tried to persuade him to sell to lucrative German markets. In the 1980s and 1990s, more and more American publishers were bought by German-owned conglomerates, and Avram would write to the editors, telling them regretfully that he could no longer submit his stories to them. This included some of the top markets for science fiction and some of the editors who were most enthusiastic about his writing. "It was not my choice to think about the Holocaust every day of my life," he said.

Avram died in Bremerton, Washington, on May 8, 1993, not long after his seventieth birthday. His collection of essays *Adventures in Unhistory* was newly published, and a short story had recently appeared in *Issac Asimov's Science Fiction Magazine*. After his death, his son Ethan found the following note in Avram's apartment, pinned prominently to the wall: "In the event of my death: What a foolish phrase. Of course I am going to die. When I die, I want to be cremated, and I want the ashes to be buried at sea by the United Sates Navy, with whom I had the honor to serve. And I want a marker to be placed in a military cemetery with my name on it and a star of David." He was proud of his service as a medical corpsman, and he was proud of his identity as a Jew.

Avram was not a financial success, he was not a commercial success. He was a wonderful and original writer who dedicated pretty much his whole life to writing and to trying to establish and maintain a meaningful relationship with God. Avram's religious exploration may be the only activity – including writing – that rewarded him consistently throughout his life.

I would like to acknowledge and thank the many friends of Avram who have told me stories and sent me copies of letters. Special thanks are due to Jim Allen of the Virginia Kidd Agency, Poul and Karen Anderson, Rabbi Jacob Beck, Gregory Benford, Charles Brown, Mike and Sue Ellwell, John A. Favareau of the Yonkers Public Library, Gregory Feeley, Dick Gibbons, William Gibson, Gary Glasser, Richard Grant, Simcha and Nancy Klein, Damon Knight, Neil Kvern, Olav Martin Kvern, Ursula Le Guin, Hugh Leddy, Vonda McIntyre, the Rev. Mr. Hisao Niwa, R. W. Odlin, Dean Wesley Smith, Michael Swanwick, Leslie What, Kate Wilhelm, Ted White, Paul Williams, and of course Grania and Stephen Davis and Ethan Davidson. Very special thanks are due to Henry Wessells, who has been tireless in locating documents and verifying details of Avram's life, to Rhonda Boothe, Jerry Kaufman, Paul Novitski, and Tamara Vining, who typed many interviews and letters, and to John D. Berry, who provided emotional support and dinner.

I am preparing a book-length biography of Avram Davidson, and welcome corrections, additional information, copies of letters and photographs, and anecdotes about Avram. Please send email to gunn@radarangels.com.

Eileen Gunn

ALSO AVAILABLE FROM
PITSPOPANY PRESS

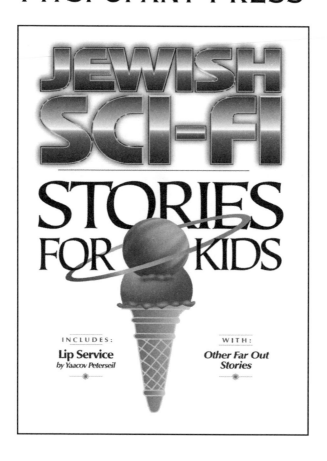

ISBN: 0-943706-73-4 (hardcover)
       0-943706-74-2 (softcover)

Toll Free: 1-800-232-2931
Email: pop@netvision.net.il
Website: www.pitspopany.com